Fundamentals
of Economics
for Business

Second Edition

Fundamentals of Economics for Business

Second Edition

David Barrows
and John Smithin
York University, Canada

Captus Press

 **World Scientific**

Co-Published by
Captus Press Inc.
Units 14 & 15, 1600 Steeles Avenue West,
Concord, Ontario, Canada   L4K 4M2
Telephone: (416) 736–5537
Fax: (416) 736–5793
Email: info@captus.com
Internet: www.captus.com

and

World Scientific Publishing Co. Pte. Ltd.
5 Toh Tuck Link, Singapore 596224
USA Office: 27 Warren Street, Suite 401–402, Hackensack, NJ 07601
UK Office: 57 Shelton Street, Covent Garden, London WC2H 9HE

British Library Cataloguing-in-Publication Data
A catalogue record for this book is available from the British Library.

FUNDAMENTALS OF ECONOMICS FOR BUSINESS, SECOND EDITION

ISBN-13 978-981-279-737-7
ISBN-10 981-279-737-8

For Marlene, Sheila,
Arthur, Frances and George

To Allison, Nicholas and Emily

Contents

Preface

This book is offered as a flexible resource for instructors teaching economics courses in business education programs. The project was originally designed around the typical one-semester MBA core course, covering both microeconomic and macroeconomic topics. However, it has evolved to the point where, with an appropriate choice of material among the different chapters and appendices, we feel it will be suitable for a wide variety of other offerings including, for example, one-semester macroeconomics courses at the undergraduate or graduate level, one-semester microeconomics courses, executive development programs, and a number of different six-week "mini-courses". We make some suggestions about different potential course structures below.

Traditionally, one of the main problems with textbook selection for courses in business programs is that although prospective business decision-makers clearly do need a sophisticated understanding of economic principles and problems to manage effectively, most are not intending to become professional economists, and certainly not academic economists. Yet most of the textbooks on the market are written in an encyclopedic fashion, as if the audience consisted entirely of future professors. We have tried hard to avoid this trap (though it must be admitted that the second edition has "grown" quite a bit in response to "market demand"). A second problem, we feel, is the tone of many of the existing textbooks. The typical business student is *already* a savvy professional in her or his own field, or very soon will be. They require an approach that is more in the nature of a manual or a guidebook than a pedagogical exercise, and this is what we have tried to provide. The book is specifically designed for use in business programs, to provide balanced coverage of topics in microeconomics, macroeconomics, and international economics. The end-of-chapter summaries provide a series of "practical take-aways" from the point of view of the businessperson.

An important feature of this book is that it is a "global book", not only in terms of topic coverage, as we take an international perspective throughout, but also in that we do not focus on the institutional specifics of any one political jurisdiction. Rather we intend the book to be equally useful to decision-makers in a variety of international contexts around the world. One of the byproducts of globalization is that, in the modern world, similar issues and topics tend to arise, and close analogies in terms of policy-making institutions will be in place, to some extent regardless of geographical location. One way in which the individual instructor can add value and customize the course offering is by discussing specific local institutions and how they correspond to the generic examples discussed in the text.

We have added 23 case studies (numbered 1–23) in the form of mock newspaper articles or press releases, usually set in some future time period and with fictional companies and individuals. Obviously, we have no way of knowing whether or not the scenarios depicted will come to pass, nor do we necessarily agree or disagree with the imaginary viewpoints presented.

There are three or four points made in each case that are relevant to the course material, and in class discussion the objective is simply to identify each of the points being made. In our own teaching, we supplement this material with similar articles from current newspapers or websites that are relevant to our own students, and carry out the same exercise. We imagine that other instructors will wish to do the same.

In this second edition we have also added two new "real world" case studies:

A. The Baranti Group case study: added as an Appendix to Chapter 6.
B. The Caterpillar case study. This case is presented at the end of the book but can be used, if the instructor wishes, in most chapters. For students/instructors using this case, we have provided study questions and hints at the end of each relevant chapter.

As with the cases, we have also "constructed" the various data sets that are presented. These refer to a fictitious economy and, again, are set in a future time period (as of the time of writing). As instructors in this day and age of the internet, we think there is little point in a textbook struggling to maintain a facade of being "up to date" by presenting numbers relating to (say) a year or two years before the time of publication (and perhaps several years prior to the time the student is actually using the book). This is a waste of time in a world in which the very latest numbers are always available at a keystroke. The focus in this book is on preparing the manager to process and analyze similar data when encountered in the real world, rather than to record any specific historical time period. Instructors will find that an important valued-added exercise in class is to access the current data relevant to their own group of students, and show how this compares to the material in the text.

When new or unfamiliar concepts are introduced for the first time, they appear in boldface. They are usually explained close by in the text. We have not provided a formal glossary, but students can search the internet for further information.

Answers to the end-of-chapter problems and a resource package for instructors containing useful teaching aids, such as PowerPoint presentations for class lectures, are available for download.

Alternative Course Structures

In what follows we propose some *suggested* course structures for a variety of different purposes for which the book might be used. No doubt instructors will customize according to their own syllabus, and will find the material sufficiently flexible to be able to do this.

A one-semester micro/macro course (e.g., the MBA core course)
> chs.:   1, 2, 3, 5, 6, 7, 8, 9, 10, 11, 12, 14

A one-semester course (macro-based)
> chs.:   1, 8, 9, 10, 11, 12, 13, 14
> appendices: 3, 8, 9, 11, 12

A one-semester course (micro-based)
> chs.:   1, 2, 3, 4, 5, 6, 7, 14
> appendices: 3, 8

Executive development
> chs: 2, 6, 7, 8, 14, 10 (part), 12 (part)

Mini course (macro)
> chs.:   8, 9, 10, 11, 12, 14

Mini course (micro)
> chs.:   2, 3, 4, 5, 6, 7

Some Useful Websites

Below there are some web addresses that students and instructors might find useful for accessing data, etc. We have focused on some former G7 countries plus China and India (two rapidly developing nations with very large populations), and on international organizations. The latter have data for most other countries, and it is a simple matter to search for comparable sites in each national jurisdiction.

Central Banks

Bank of Canada	http://www.bankofcanada.ca
Bank of England	http://www.bankofengland.co.uk
Bank of Japan	http://www.boj.or.jp
European Central Bank	http://www.ecb.int
Federal Reserve Board	http://federalreserve.gov
People's Bank of China	http://pbc.gov.cn
Reserve Bank of India	http://www.rbi.org.in/

International Organizations

International Monetary Fund	http://imf.org

OECD   http://www.oecd.org
The World Bank   http://www.worldbank.org
World Trade Organization   http://www.wto.org
UN Economic and   http://www.un.org/docs/ecoso
     Social Council (ECOSOC)

Ministries of Finance

Canada   http://www.fin.gc.ca
China   http://www.mof.gov.cn
France   http://www.finances.gouv.fr
Germany   http://www.bundesfinanzministerium.de
Italy   http://www.tresoro.it
India   http://www.finmin.nic.in
Japan   http://www.mof.go.jp
UK   http://www.hm-treasury.gov.uk
USA   http://www.treas.gov

Statistical Agencies

Bureau of Economic Analysis (USA)   http://www.bea.gov
Eurostat   http://epp.eurostat.cec.eu.int
Statistics Canada   http://www.statcan.ca
UK Official Statistics   http://www.statistics.gov.uk

We wish to thank all of our colleagues in the Economics Area at the Schulich School of Business for their invaluable assistance in the preparation of this second edition.

We want to acknowledge the special contribution of Farrokh Zandi for providing material for the Appendices to Chapters 4 and 5.

1

Business and Economics

Introduction

As the titles of both the book and this introductory chapter already indicate, the target reader for this text is a person involved in a business education program of some kind, whether an MBA program, an undergraduate commerce degree, or an executive education program: in other words, a current or future business decision-maker. We hope, however, that it may also be interesting to members of the general public as a sort of "user's guide" to contemporary market-orientated capitalism. There are, of course, many excellent textbooks in economics already on the market, but as long-time business educators, there are none we (the authors) have found to date that quite meet the needs of this target audience. Hence the need for the present volume.

Learning Objectives

The learning objectives of this text can be briefly stated. They are for the reader:

- To understand the basic principles of economics, at least as they apply in a system of "market capitalism"

- To be able to use these principles to interpret current events and trends, both in the domestic economy and the global economy

- To understand the implications of what is happening in the economic environment for business decision-making and business strategy

Experience in teaching and discussing these ideas over many years suggests that our readers will be starting out with widely varying backgrounds in formal economics. We have tried to present the material in such a way that these differences will not really matter. We hope not only that the basic principles can readily be grasped by someone who has had essentially no previous exposure to economics, but also that those who have already spent many years on the indifference maps, differential calculus, and matrix algebra of standard university economics courses will be able to find something new, primarily in the angle of approach. The guiding principle is always to present those elements of economics that will be useful for business executives and the general public in their day-to-day activities. To put it another way, what does the business executive "need to know" about the way in which the market economy/capitalism actually works?

In a popular TV show (some decades ago now), there was a joke about the "Five Minute University", the point of which was that the key ideas that students spend so many years laboriously acquiring in university could actually be understood in five minutes. Here is what Five Minute U. would have to say about the two subjects in this book:

BUSINESS: Buy *low*, sell *high* (i.e., make a profit)
ECONOMICS: *Demand* and *supply*

Obviously, as educators we cannot agree with the premise of this joke. However, perhaps we can turn it around and at least make some use of it for our own purposes. We can say that the main reason for the business executive to understand the principles of demand and supply, of economics generally, and to anticipate likely changes, is precisely to be able to run a successful (i.e., profitable) business, and to be able to know what the above phrases might actually mean in specific situations and over specific periods of time.

Microeconomics, Macroeconomics and International Economics

Academic textbooks on economics typically divide the subject into two main branches: **microeconomics** and **macroeconomics**. Microeconomics is supposed to deal with the behavior of individual firms and markets, and the detailed workings of the price mechanism. Macroeconomics, on the other hand, studies the behavior of the economy as a whole, encompassing such things as economic growth and development, and inflation and unemployment. In this book, we must deal with both branches. In the contemporary global economy, moreover, *both* microeconomics and macroeconomics should have a strong international flavor. In microeconomics, for example, an "individual firm or market" might mean a multinational firm, or a global market. In macroeconomics, when we speak of the "economy as a whole", do we mean a national economy only, or the entire global economy? With this in mind, here are the main issues that we think decision-makers should be aware of in each field:

MICROECONOMICS
Decision-makers should understand:
- the basics of demand and supply and the workings of the price mechanism
- how to analyze production costs
- the importance of market structure
- the relevance of market structure to business strategy
- trade and competitiveness in the global economy

MACROECONOMICS
Decision-makers should understand:
- the relevance of economic indicators and the basic data of the macroeconomy

3

- the debates over fiscal policy, budget deficits and surpluses, and the national debt
- the relationship between money and inflation
- the debate over stabilization policy: is there a trade-off between economic growth and inflation?
- the role of interest rates in the conduct of monetary policy
- the balance of payments, international capital flows and the implications of alternative exchange rate regimes
- the key concepts of international finance

One feature of the current process of globalization, and the apparent absence of any viable alternative economic order to market capitalism after the collapse of communism in the 1990s, is the extent to which similar issues and problems, and even similar institutional frameworks and modes of economic policy-making, now face the business executive in many countries around the world. Therefore, this text takes an essentially international perspective on most of the topics discussed. We do not focus on the institutional specifics of any one jurisdiction, such as the USA, Canada, or China. Rather, we intend the text to be equally useful to decision-makers in a variety of national contexts around the world. In the modern world similar issues and topics will arise, and close analogies in terms of policy-making institutions will be in place, to a large extent regardless of geographical location. This is certainly true with respect to the large number of international institutions.

Optimal Resource Allocation versus Dynamic Economic Growth?

In considering economics as an academic discipline or as a body of knowledge about economic affairs, the astute prospective consumer of economic research should be aware that there have always been certain tensions among practitioners as to the scope and method of the science. In effect, to quote from a recent textbook on economic sociology, there are "two (competing) definitions of the economy".[1] These tensions are somewhat related to the micro/macro distinction made above, but not in any very precise or clear-cut manner.

The first definition of the economy revolves around the very meaning of the term "economizing". From this point of view, economics is simply the science of rational choice. It is essentially about scarcity, and the need

---

[1] Carlo Triglia, *Economic Sociology: State, Market and Society in Modern Capitalism* (Oxford: Blackwell Publishers, 2002).

for individuals, firms, and societies to "optimally" allocate scarce resources among competing ends. So conceived, the principles of economics apply very broadly indeed, across a wide spectrum of social systems and historical periods. Nonetheless, it tends to be taken for granted that a market-orientated system is, or would be, the most efficient in achieving this goal. It would be fair to say that this conception of economics as the study of optimal resource allocation has often been the main focus among academic economists and in textbooks. This approach is often characterized as **"neo-classical economics"**. At the most basic level, it can be illustrated by the venerable "guns and butter" diagram, also known as the **production possibility frontier**, an example of which appears in Figure 1.1. For the contemporary reader, we make the choice the more general one: between "industrial products" and "agricultural products".

The basic idea here is that, in the economy depicted in the diagram, if all the existing (and scarce) resources are fully employed and efficiently used, it would be possible to produce and consume any combination of the two classes of products depicted along the bow-shaped frontier. At one extreme, if all resources are devoted to agricultural products, the economy would be at point A. At the other, producing only industrial products,

Figure 1.1:   The Production Possibility Frontier

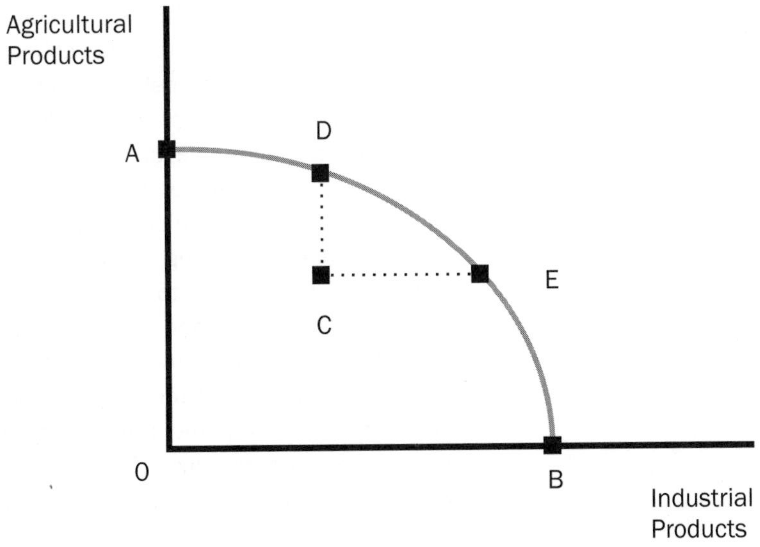

it would be at point B. The bow shape is a result of the reasonable assumption that some of the resources are more suitable in one use than the other, and hence the trade-off becomes progressively more difficult the closer the economy gets to either extreme. Apart from the two extremes, any other combination of industrial products and agricultural products along the frontier is also technically possible. If, however, the economy is actually at a point such as C, the resources are being used inefficiently. This is because, with some improvement in economic organization, it would be possible to have more of both types of products without having to give up anything at all. That can be achieved by a move to the frontier at some point between D and E. This is a question of **economic efficiency**. As mentioned, much economic research, particularly in academia, tends to be preoccupied with this issue and how to achieve it. Most frequently it is argued

Case Study 1

"Public Utilities are Back"
New York; May 2, 2030

The experiment with privatization of key public infrastructure services, such as transportation, energy, and water supply, appears to be a failure. A recent OECD study argues: "It was never logical to try to create competitive markets in situations of natural monopoly. It seems to be impossible to create competition in, for example, the provision of water supply. The efficient supply of water requires a strong public sector presence, in particular to ensure short and long-term safety and security. With its fixation on short-term stock market valuation and rates of return it has become apparent that the private sector is not an economically efficient deliverer of these types of public infrastructure services."

that a greater reliance on market mechanisms in the conduct of economic affairs is the best (and perhaps the only) means of attaining this goal. Note that points above the production possibility frontier are not attainable in the present state of technical knowledge.

Another important concept well illustrated by our graphical framework is the central economic idea of **opportunity cost**. Once the economy is operating on the production possibility frontier, for example, at D, the only way to acquire more industrial products (say, by moving to E) is to give up some agricultural products. This is achieved by reallocating some resources from the production of the latter to the production of the former. The opportunity cost of the extra industrial products is the quantity of agricultural products foregone. This is a lesson economists never tire of pointing out, sometimes expressed by the phrase, "There's no such thing as a free lunch."

Clearly, a focus on economic efficiency, in the sense just described, does not say much about which particular combination of goods actually will be chosen, and still less does it prescribe which goods *should* be chosen. In a market system the general idea is that consumer preferences, acting via market forces, will decide the matter. Nor is the question of the distribution of the goods and services very high on the agenda in this type of discussion (meaning exactly who gets what). The latter issue is referred to as the question of **equity** (as opposed to efficiency). In fact, there is often discussion of a trade-off between economic efficiency and equity. A frequent argument by proponents of market solutions to economic problems is, in fact, that any attempt to change the distribution of income by other than market means (such as by economic regulation of various kinds) will be "inefficient". By damaging incentive mechanisms, such efforts may cause the actual level of production to fall back below the frontier of what is technologically attainable — that is, to drop back to a position like point C.

In any event, this focus on the question of the optimal allocation of resources and economic efficiency is one view of what economics is all about. The second definition of the subject matter of economics, however, comes closer to the study of what Adam Smith originally called *The Wealth of Nations*.[2] That is, it would be more of an inquiry into the underlying causes of **economic growth** and **development**. This may be not so much a question of making the best use of existing resources, but of identifying the characteristics of the social system that are conducive to the creation of *more* resources — that is, the creation of new wealth. Such a study would tend to have a dynamic rather than a static perspective, and be more

---

[2] Adam Smith, *An Inquiry into the Nature and Causes of the Wealth of Nations*, edited by R.H. Campbell and A.S. Skinner (Indianopolis: Liberty Fund, 1981 [1776]).

in the nature of a genuine social science or political economy than an abstract theory of rational choice. The sort of questions involved here would be about such things as the social, legal, and institutional factors leading to economic development. What, for example, is the significance of technological change, of entrepreneurship, of investment, and of capital accumulation? Similarly, what is the role of population growth, education, the acquisition of new skills by the work force, different forms of corporate governance, and so on?

One method of incorporating the growth perspective into the framework of the production possibility frontier is to interpret growth and technological changes as shifting that frontier over time, as is illustrated in Figure 1.2. In other words, with growth the society can consume more of everything, as additional productive resources can provide more output during the growth process. There may still be something essential that is missing from this picture, however, as economic development is arguably as much a process of transformation or qualitative change as it is simply a quantitative change, or "more of the same". There will typically be new products and services, new technology, new methods of production, new forms of social organization, and so forth.

Which of these two competing perspectives should the student of business economics adopt? We do not hesitate to say that the short answer

Figure 1.2: **The Production Possibility Frontier Shifts Out with Growth**

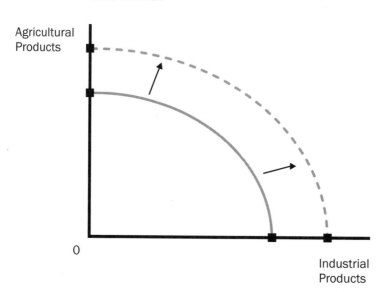

Case Study 2

"World Migration at an All-Time Low"
United Nations; August 15, 2050

The UN today reported the lowest level of net migration since data have been collected. The report suggests that there no longer seems to be any need for major emigration or immigration for economic purposes. With a growing and more integrated world economy, production and consumption have become decentralized, and population growth has actually diminished in Africa, Latin America, and Asia. Manufacturing and service activities have been decentralized and are located closer to the major markets and population centers. This process is creating job opportunities as well as markets for consumer goods in these areas. As a result, the need for economic migration, in search of employment and income-generating opportunities, is at an all-time low.

must be, at least to some extent, both. After all, the optimal or efficient use of resources in production is obviously very significant from the point of view of the bottom line. Nonetheless, we suspect the alternative perspective, emphasizing growth and change, will often be the more congenial to entrepreneurs and strategic managers who naturally look at the economic process from the perspective of innovation, development, and the creation of new wealth. We cannot pursue these issues any further in the context of these introductory remarks, but note that they will emerge again at many points in the book. In particular, the existence of these tensions will be able to explain why there are occasions on which the managerial perspective may actually differ from the conventional economic wisdom on certain issues.

Chapter Summary

- While perhaps far from the ideal of "perfect competition" (see Chapters 5 and 6), market capitalism and globalization are the dominant economic order.

- Economists examine economic issues from both a micro and macro perspective.

- Micro and macro are interrelated. For example, macroeconomic growth depends on competitive micro structures in the financial, labor, and productive sectors of the economy.

- Economists tend to be concerned with the best allocation of existing resources. While this is obviously an important issue, it may be that businesspeople are more concerned with issues of economic growth, competitiveness, innovation, etc.

- The notion of opportunity cost captures the trade-offs businesspeople make every day. If I expand my operations, for example in India, I will have fewer resources for the Chinese market.

Problems

1. What are the key microeconomic issues and why are they important?

2. What are the key macroeconomic issues and why are they important?

3. In the long run, what might be the trade-off between "efficiency" and "equity"?

4. What is opportunity cost and why is it important?

5. What is meant by the "neoclassical" approach to economic analysis?

6. What is assumed when constructing a production possibilities frontier model?

7. How is unemployment of any resource shown on a production possibilities frontier model and what is the economic implication?

| # The Comeback of Caterpillar

Productivity

1. How does the heavy equipment industry improve a country's productivity?

Hint: *Capital investment plays an important role in shifting the production possibility frontier.*

2. Discuss the factors that have improved productivity at Caterpillar:
   - Outsourcing
   - Employee involvement
   - Plant modernization
   - Information technology
   - Joint ventures
   - The movement from batch to cell production

Hint: Productivity measures output relative to factor inputs. Business must determine the optimal allocation of resource inputs. Caterpillar used each of these factors to improve productivity.

Appendix 1.1

Leading Economic Thinkers

This appendix describes the views of some of the leading economic thinkers of the past, whose names frequently come up in economic discussion and whose ideas are still influential in various quarters today. Anyone participating in the economic debate should have a least some familiarity with these ideas.

Adam Smith (1723–1790)

Adam Smith, the author of the *Wealth of Nations*,[1] was the original defender and expositor of the operation of the **free market** and the price mechanism, which he took to be the most salient characteristic of the developing industrial capitalism of his time. He demonstrated the power of market forces with the famous metaphor of the "**invisible hand**", whereby price signals guide the economy in the allocation of resources, and advocated a "**system of natural liberty**" rather than the detailed regulation of industry. According to Smith, price and profit incentives ensure that goods and services are provided, that living standards rise, that people do not starve, and so on. Further, the competitive pressures generated by markets are what keeps the system on the rails, and prevents the exploitation of either consumers or workers. The actual growth of wealth is attributed to the "**division of labor**" — that is, to the improvement in productivity generated by the specialization of functions within the production process, as the volume of output increases. The famous example of the "Scottish pin factory" was the main illustration of this idea.

Although Smith was certainly an advocate of the free market, he was perhaps not as naive on questions of governance as some later advocates of economic liberalism and "neo-liberalism" in the 19th, 20th, and 21st centuries. Government remained an integral part of the overall vision of the

---

[1] Adam Smith, *An Inquiry into the Nature and Causes of the Wealth of Nations* (Indianapolis: Liberty Fund, 1981 [1776]).

functioning of society. Specifically, there was a clear role for government in providing the legal framework of property rights, for the maintenance of national defense, and to undertake those **public works** that are necessary to support the infrastructure of the economy, but would not be profitable in the private sector. The system of natural liberty was, therefore, not one in which government or governance was absent, but simply one in which the authorities refrained from the detailed regulation of the marketplace, so as not to interfere in its operation. Politically, the overall message that Smith conveys about the burgeoning capitalist economy is an optimistic one. The basic message is one of social harmony. As long as market forces are left to operate unhindered, there will be a continual increase in prosperity. Moreover, economic growth will tend to benefit all the social classes as living standards generally rise, with no serious conflict between them.

There was however one major omission from Smith's overall vision of capitalism that would probably seem glaringly obvious to someone encountering such a social system for the first time, but has nevertheless seemed quite natural to most of the succeeding generations of classical and neoclassical economists. Smith was one of the originators of the tradition, followed thereafter by almost all orthodox economic theory down to the present day, to downplay the importance of "monetary" factors — money itself, credit, and finance — in determining economic outcomes. Every economist is familiar with the slogans that express this point of view, such as "**money is neutral**" or "**money is a veil**". Underlying this stance is the view that economics deal fundamentally with the barter exchange of goods and services, as opposed to the accumulation of financial resources, a view still predominant in the textbooks and journals of mainstream economic analysis. For Smith, in his day, a major preoccupation was his indignation at the perceived errors of his "mercantilist" predecessors, including the idea that "wealth consists in ... gold and silver", or the money of the time. Smith's point is the familiar one that "real" wealth does not consist in money, but in the valuable goods and services that money can buy. From the point of view of the social scientist, however, such an attitude does seem to ignore one of the most crucial elements of the "social technology" of the capitalist system. It is true, after all, that "money is power" in any given social setting where that money is accepted. Smith's lead on the role of money in the system was nonetheless followed by the vast majority of later economists, and the idea that "fundamentally" the economy can be thought of as an extended system of barter exchange remains a crucially important element of the vision of the economy to which like-minded thinkers have adhered ever since.

Smith was the first modern economist to understand the importance of scale, specialization and productivity improvement as key elements in the process of economic growth and development.

Karl Marx (1818–1883)

In place of Smith's prediction of gradual and harmonious progress, Karl Marx, writing 90 years later, sent out just the opposite message about the likely development of the capitalist system. In *Das Kapital*,[2] Marx predicted only continual **class conflict**, the increasing immiseration of the workers, and ultimately the inevitable collapse of the system. Marx was clearly animated by a hatred of capitalism and of "bourgeois values" in general, and was only too happy to predict its demise. He developed a theory of **exploitation** and "**surplus value**", based on the **labor theory of value**, with labor itself being kept in its place by unemployment, the creation of the so-called "**reserve army of the unemployed**". However, according to Marx the system must inevitably break down. As capital accumulation proceeds, and ever larger capitalist concerns squeeze out the smaller ones in a "dog eat dog" struggle, the rate of profit falls. There is a series of ever-widening crises and eventually the system collapses, to replaced by a supposedly more humane and rational system of **socialism**. Ironically, however, socialism itself remains largely unexamined by Marx as an alternative social system. As to how it will come about, how it will function, how it will improve matters in society, and so on, Marx says nothing.

On the question on which Adam Smith was criticized above, that of integrating a coherent vision of money into the overall system, it can be argued that Marx (like Smith and most later neoclassical economists) also did not have an adequate theory of money and finance, or of their role in capitalism. Profits emerge simply as a result of exploitation, rather than entrepreneurship financed by credit creation.

In effect, Marx could see the winners and the losers that emerged as a result of the Industrial Revolution that was then taking place. Today, countries continue to search for policy approaches that allow for the benefits of economic growth while mitigating the negative impacts on the more vulnerable members of society.

Joseph Schumpeter (1883–1950)

The work of Joseph Schumpeter, the author of *The Theory of Economic Development*,[3] and *Capitalism, Socialism and Democracy*,[4] is often compared in method, analytical style, and scope, to that of Marx. There is a crucial dif-

---

[2] Karl Marx, *Capital*, Volume I (London: Pelican, 1976 [1867]).

[3] Joseph Schumpeter, *The Theory of Economic Development*, (Transactions Publishers: New Brunswick, NJ, 1983 [1934]).

[4] Joseph Schumpeter, *Capitalism, Socialism and Democracy* (London: Routledge, 1992 [1942]).

ference, though, in that whereas Marx hated capitalism and was its would-be nemesis, Schumpeter was an equally ardent admirer and supporter of the system. The reputation of Schumpeter has undergone a major revival in recent decades, mainly because the issues raised in his discussion of the development of capitalism — for example, the role of the entrepreneur and the importance of innovation — are once again popular themes in the 21st century. This is illustrated, for example, by the relatively recent emergence of the new academic field of "entrepreneurship" or "entrepreneurial studies" in business schools. It was Schumpeter, in fact, who originally made the **entrepreneur** the hero of the economic drama. This figure is to be distinguished from *both* the financial capitalist and the business manager as the driving force responsible for innovation in capitalism. Innovation and entrepreneurship lead to the emergence of profit opportunities within what would otherwise be a static environment, and thus provide the conditions for growth, development, and change. Entrepreneurs are not so much a class as a group — a small elite within the society blessed with unusual qualities of drive, courage, leadership, etc. In a different type of society they might be military leaders or feudal lords, but in a commercial environment they content themselves with innovation in business. So long as this spirit of entrepreneurship remains strong, the capitalist system will have no difficulty in "delivering the goods" economically, with rising prosperity and continually higher living standards. Indeed, Schumpeter is not at all worried about the tendency to monopoly and industrial concentration that were of such concern to the neoclassical economists and Marx. If there is a monopoly in railroads, for instance, to use an example relevant to Schumpeter's own time, some entrepreneur or another has the incentive to get around this by inventing the automobile. It is also obviously easy to think of far more recent examples, such as in the field of computer technology. Schumpeter refers to this process as creative destruction — new industries and technologies are continually being created and the old ones destroyed. The "**perennial gale of creative destruction**" is, in fact, the essence of the system. In the modern business literature, this process is often referred to as "disruptive innovation". The concept is consistent with the notion of social evolution.

On the contentious issue of money and credit, some writers have given Schumpeter high praise for recognition of the role of bank financing and endogenous credit creation in providing the wherewithal for entrepreneurial innovation to take place. At one point, Schumpeter even went so far as to argue that this was the "*differentia specifica*" (most obvious differentiating characteristic) of the system.[5] This is a far cry from the continuing neglect of this point in modern mainstream economic theories of barter exchange.

---

[5] John E. Elliot, "Introduction" to *The Theory of Economic Development* by Joseph Schumpeter (Transactions Publishers: New Brunswick, NJ, 1983 [1934]).

There is a caveat, however, in that credit financing appears to Schumpeter only to be relevant during the actual period of innovative change. He does not seem to appreciate that the need to obtain financing also applies to routine business activity.

Although Schumpeter was known as the great champion of capitalism, he actually finally agrees with Marx that the capitalist system is "doomed". However, this is not for economic reasons but mainly for sociological ones. Capitalism is successful economically, but becomes increasingly unpopular with disaffected intellectuals, who will bring it down "from within". This analysis must have seemed right on the money given the intellectual climate of the mid-twentieth century, at which time most intellectuals were critics of capitalism and adherents of the political left. However, 40 years later, around 1989–1991, it would have seemed too pessimistic. By that time there had been both a "conservative revolution" in economic ideas and policy-making in the West and, subsequently, the spectacular collapse of communism itself in Central and Eastern Europe. At this point, the capitalist economic system and the civilization dependent upon it must have seemed quite secure. But, of course, there are always further swings of the pendulum on these issues and, in the early twenty-first century, the reader will surely be able to think of a number of contemporary public policy debates that seem to fit Schumpeter's analysis once again.

John Maynard Keynes (1883–1946)

Keynes's *The General Theory of Employment Interest and Money*[6] was arguably the most famous book on economics of the twentieth century, and it put forward yet another vision of the essence of capitalism. Unlike the majority of other writers, before and since, his theory of "**effective demand**" focuses on the genuine difficulties that capitalist entrepreneurs face in the **marketing** of their output. As the term implies, this effective demand corresponds to actual purchasing power in monetary terms, and not some notional "wants" derived from the perceived value of output *before* it has been marketed (as in orthodox economic theory). Keynes, therefore, denied the presumed automatic self-adjusting mechanism that most other writers, except Marx, attributed to the market system. If aggregate effective demand was deficient there could be a state of permanent widespread unemployment — that is unemployment could persist in the "long run", not just in the "short run" during a temporary downturn or recession. This analysis was obviously highly relevant to the period when Keynes was writing in the 1930s, the years of the **great depression**. A corollary for our own time is

---

[6] John Maynard Keynes, *The General Theory of Employment Interest and Money* (London: Macmillan, 1936).

that if there is to be economic growth there must also be demand growth, but this recognition is something that now seems to have almost entirely disappeared from the economics mainstream. Keynes observed that, for the first time in history, it was possible for output/production to exceed demand. Business people today understand this concept all too well — hence the need for sophisticated marketing initiatives to stimulate the perceived need for the good or service.

Perhaps the most significant element of Keynes's new vision of the 1930s was the notion of a "**monetary theory of production**" that would indeed take money, credit, and finance seriously as a key part of the process. The "Keynesian revolution", however, was ultimately only a partial success in challenging accepted views on economic theory and policy. In the long term, it failed to win the "hearts and minds" of the majority of the economics profession — partially due to flaws in the technical aspects of the theory itself, and partially due simply to the depth of commitment to the alternative tradition in academia. Nonetheless, Keynes did introduce the important notions of the "**monetary economy**" or the "**entrepreneur economy**" (similar to Schumpeter) — and at least tried to explain how this would differ in its operations from those of the hypothetical "**barter economy**". The basic idea is that economic system labeled here as capitalism is pre-eminently a monetary system. Those responsible for production, whether they are entrepreneurs or corporations, must first acquire financial resources to do so. The ultimate proceeds from the sale of goods are also sums of money. Intuitively, therefore, in such an environment, and contrary to the view that "money does not matter", the monetary system takes on major significance. In particular, this applies to the rate of interest, "the terms on which" (Keynes 1936) financing is available and which constitutes the price of money.

Friedrich von Hayek (1899–1992)

Hayek, the author of *The Road to Serfdom*[7] and *The Fatal Conceit: the Errors of Socialism*,[8] was one of the main intellectual sponsors of the so-called "conservative revolution" in economic policy-making of the late twentieth century. This was a reaction against *both* socialism and Keynesianism, but in retrospect it was probably a mistake for Hayek to conflate these two enemies, the one being a definitely anti-capitalist doctrine, whereas the other was pro-capitalist but based on a different understanding of how the system works than that of Hayek and his followers.

---

[7] Friedrich von Hayek, *The Road to Serfdom* (Chicago: University of Chicago Press (1994 [1944]).
[8] Friedrich von Hayek, *The Fatal Conceit: The Errors of Socialism* (Chicago: University of Chicago Press, 1988).

Hayek's argument was an update of Adam Smith's "invisible hand", about how what Hayek now called the **"extended order"** (the market) functions, and how it will outperform any other form of social organization. The new twist on Smith, however, is that the market is now conceived of as an analogy to a self-organizing system in the biological or neurological sciences (with prices supposedly providing "information" to the actors in the network). It is, in fact, a model of social behavior (of which there have been many other examples) derived from outside of society itself, and based on processes in the physical or natural world. According to Hayek, it is this quasi-natural mechanism, rather than any human intentionality, that is the force responsible for the development of the system and for prosperity.

The crucial issue is that as the system is thought to be spontaneously generated, without conscious design, it is too complex for any one individual to comprehend. It follows that any attempt to interfere with its operation will likely be damaging, and that it is essentially not *possible* to devise any major policy measures to improve, modify, or ameliorate the system with killing the goose that lays the golden eggs. (There are caveats regarding the provision of some minimum level of social services, but this is the basic argument). This rules out the regulation of industry, and most of social policy, fiscal policy, activist monetary policy, environmental policy, etc., in a comprehensive return to **"laissez-faire"**. This is the essence of the modern neo-liberal program in both the national and international arenas — hence Hayek's staunch opposition to anything that might resemble socialism. Quite literally, the adoption of socialist measures will eventually cause the collapse of civilization and mass starvation. Hayek, in fact, lived long enough (he died in 1992) to witness the important historical events that seemed to triumphantly vindicate his theories.

Milton Friedman 1912–2006

Milton Friedman, the co-author (with Anna Schwartz) of *A Monetary History of the United States*,[9] and (with Rose Friedman) of *Capitalism and Freedom*[10] and *Free to Choose*,[11] was probably the economist whose name was best known to the general public in the mid-to-late twentieth century. With Hayek he was one of the most important intellectual leaders of the anti-

---

[9] Milton Friedman and Anna J. Schwartz, *A Monetary History of the United States, 1867–1960* (Princeton: Princeton University Press, 1963).

[10] Milton Friedman and Rose Friedman, *Capitalism and Freedom* (Chicago: University of Chicago Press, 1962).

[11] Milton Friedman and Rose Friedman, *Free to Choose* (New York: Harcourt Brace Jovanovich, 1980).

Keynesian and pro-market turn in economic thinking (the conservative revolution) during those decades. Friedman will always be associated, in particular, with the twentieth century revival of the **quantity theory of money** under its modern name of **monetarism.** In this view, inflation is "always and everywhere a monetary phenomenon" — that is, inflation is basically caused by a money supply that is growing too fast. Inflation is identified as a major social problem, perhaps *the* major social problem, and the blame for it is attached firmly to those responsible for the conduct of **monetary policy**, the officials at the **central bank**. Central bankers can be blamed also for the opposite fault, allowing too slow a rate of growth of the money supply, or even letting the money supply fall. It is believed that this can cause a recession and unemployment, at least in the short run. Friedman and Schwartz attributed the Great Depression in the USA in the 1930s precisely to this cause. In the microeconomic field, Friedman was, like Smith and Hayek before him, always a believer in the power of market forces, and an opponent of **government intervention**. The titles of his two main co-authored books on the subject are self-explanatory in their defense of the "free market".

2

Demand and Supply: The Basics

Introduction

The most basic, and in many ways the most lasting, lesson to be learnt from "Economics 101" relates to the fundamental concepts of demand and supply and their interaction. These are usually presented in a simple graphical format involving demand and supply "curves". The word is in quotes because in this chapter, for simplicity, we will actually assume only straight-line relationships between price and quantities demanded and supplied. The main issue that is important in reality is the *direction* of the relationship between prices and quantities. Will a reduction in price lead to an increase in the quantity demanded of any particular product or service? Will an increase in price lead to an increase in supply? And so on. The principal technical tools for analyzing demand and supply conditions in particular markets, then, are the demand and supply schedules or curves.

The **demand curve** shows an estimate or conjecture about the relationship between the price of any particular product or service and the quantity of that product that will be demanded by consumers. It is usually assumed to slope downward, in the general case, for most products and services. In other words, the lower the price of the item, the greater the quantity of it that will be demanded. Technically, this is because of a presumption of **diminishing marginal utility** (MU) for most individuals and most products. The more an individual has or consumes of any one item, the less valuable or desirable will any additional or "marginal" quantity seem to that individual. Therefore, the price to be paid for marginal quantities of the item will decline the greater the quantity already consumed. This underlying individualistic concept is also assumed to translate into a downward-sloping demand curve at the market level.

An additional fundamental assumption is that a price expressed in dollars (or yen, or Euros, or pounds) is indeed a meaningful concept in terms of what the dollars or yen will buy. Essentially, this means that when the price changes in the market we are analyzing, the prices of other goods and services, whether these are **complements** to, or **substitutes** for, the product under consideration, must be assumed to remain the same. Similarly, it means that over the relevant time horizon, the overall purchasing power of money remains predictable. Therefore, what the demand curve is supposed to illustrate is the conjectural relationship, as seen by the analyst or businessperson, between the price and the total quantity demanded of the given product, holding constant all the other factors that might be expected to affect demand. It represents a statement to the effect that if the price happens to be, say, "x dollars", then the analyst expects the quantity demanded to be "y units", assuming that all other relevant factors remain unchanged. Changes in any of the other factors that might affect demand, such as changes in total income, changes in the prices of other goods, or simply a change of taste or fashion, must then show up as horizontal shifts in the entire demand curve. This would be a shift to the right in the case of a change in a factor that tends to increase demand, or to the left, for a change that tends to reduce demand.

As mentioned, the consumption decision is derived from conjectures about the underlying needs, wants, and desires of the individual consumer. It is sometimes called "effective demand" because we assume that the individual has sufficient income to make the purchase: that is, it is not simply a wish. Individuals are faced with a wide variety of goods and services in the marketplace. Assuming that the individual's income is finite (limited) then choices must be made. Individuals attempt to maximize the benefits, or **utility**, of their purchases, subject to the limited budget at their disposal. Logic suggests that individuals will attempt to maximize the utility of all their purchases, subject to the budget constraint. This occurs when the prospective additional utility from each purchase is equivalent. At this point there would then be no basis to reallocate purchases among competing goods and services.

The **supply curve**, meanwhile, is supposed to illustrate the relationship between price and the quantity supplied to the market by firms or entrepreneurs. *If* it has an upward slope, this will be due to the **diminishing marginal productivity** (MP) of the variable inputs to the productive process. If, say, more labor is employed in the productive process, progressively fewer additional units of output are forthcoming, prices will have to rise to cover the increase in production costs. However, note that whether or not this assumption (that the supply curve slopes upward) is true in any particular marketplace must depend on the actual characteristics of the production process. In some large-scale industries, for example, it is often argued that the opposite is true: that is, costs fall, or at least remain constant, as output increases. As with the demand curve, other types of changes in supply conditions (other than those relating to the scale of output) must show up as shifts in the curve. Examples would be changes in the prices of productive factors, such as increases or decreases in wages, or a technological change in the production process.

Market Price

To illustrate the concept of **market price**, let us assume for concreteness that we have a demand curve and a supply curve, in a particular market, given by these numerical equations:

$$(2.1) \qquad P = 24 - Q \qquad \text{(demand)}$$

$$(2.2) \qquad P = 3 + 2Q \qquad \text{(supply)}$$

Here **P** stands for price (for example, in dollars), and **Q** for quantity (in whatever units are appropriate), over a given period of time. This "market" is then illustrated in Figure 2.1.

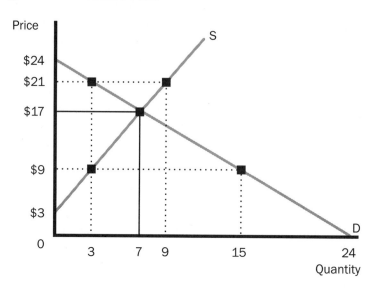

Figure 2.1:   Market Price

We can tell from equations (2.1) and (2.2) that when the price is as high as $24, no one is prepared to buy any units of this particular item. As the price falls, they are prepared to buy successively more units. However, the demand is not infinite. Even when the price falls to zero, the maximum quantity demand is only 24 units. On the supply side, apparently it is not worth the while of firms to supply any units at all to the market until the price reaches at least $3. However, as the price rises beyond that level, they are prepared to supply more. For example, if the price *did* rise as high as $25, firms would be willing to supply a total of 11 units (but would not, in fact, be able to find any buyers at that price).

Turning now to the diagram in Figure 2.1, suppose that the price is momentarily as high as $21. The quantity demanded at this price is 3 units, and the quantity supplied is 9 units. In this situation of supply greater than demand, the usual presumption is that market prices will tend to fall, and that production will be cut back. The falling prices in turn will stimulate more demand. The adjustment process will continue until the market is in **"equilibrium"**. At this point demand and supply will be equal, an **equilibrium price** will be established, and neither the demanders nor suppliers will have any further incentive to change their behavior. There is no reason the situation should not then remain the same, with the same price ruling and the same quantities produced and consumed, period after period, until there is some definite change in the prevailing market conditions. It can easily be seen that in our example the equilibrium price is $17, and the equilibrium quantity is 7 units. Now, suppose that the price in the market momentarily goes as low as $9. In this situation, there will be a larger quantity demanded (15 units) than is supplied (3 units). Now the argument is that prices will tend to be bid upward in the marketplace, and that consequently supply will increase. At the same time, the higher prices will tend to reduce demand. Again, the adjustment will be complete when the equilibrium market price and quantity are reached.

The basic conclusion suggested about the workings of demand and supply, therefore, is that if ever prices are "too high" or "too low", the tendency of market forces is to cause an adjustment in one direction or the other, and to re-establish a market equilibrium of price and quantities supplied and consumed. Of course, some markets "clear" faster than others. A sophisticated stock exchange will clear in seconds, while the market for a large recreational property could take months, or even years, to clear.

Once this tendency to market equilibrium is established, the other main purpose of demand and supply analysis is to provide some qualitative results about likely *changes* in market price and quantity when market conditions change. For example, what will happen if the incomes of buyers in the marketplace increase?

For these purposes it is sometimes useful to distinguish between changes in quantity demanded (or supplied) along the curve, due to changes in price, and "changes in demand" (or supply) shown by shifts of the curve, and due to other factors. See Figures 2.2 and 2.3.

Figure 2.2: **Movements Along a Demand Curve Due to Price Changes Versus Shifts of the Curve**

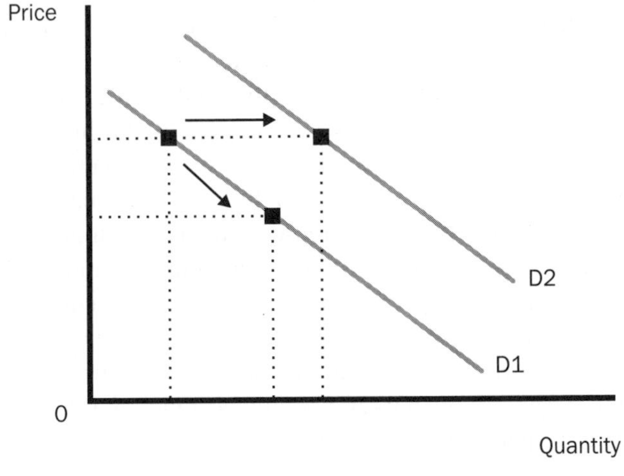

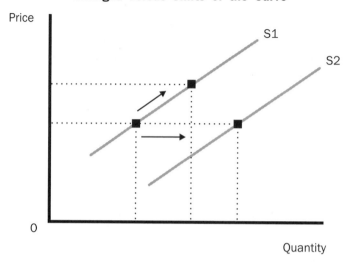

Figure 2.3:   **Movements Along a Supply Curve Due to Price Changes Versus Shifts of the Curve**

We illustrate these ideas below with three possible examples of demand or supply shifts, two of which are assumed to occur on the demand side and one on the supply side

Changes in Market Conditions

The first case to be looked at is the one originally mentioned above. Suppose that there is an increase in the incomes of the consumers in this market. If the product concerned is a so-called **normal good**, the presumption would be that the demand for this item at each price will increase. In other words, the demand curve will shift out and to the right. This is illustrated in Figure 2.4. As can be seen, the impact of the increase in demand is an increase in both the market price and in the quantity produced and sold. The price will increase from P1 to P2, and the quantity from Q1 to Q2. At the original price P1, the increase in demand initially sets up a situation of **excess demand** (demand greater than supply), and this will lead to an adjustment to the new equilibrium along the lines discussed above. Once the adjustment has been made, the presumption again is that the new higher equilibrium prices and quantities will prevail for some time, until there is another change in market conditions. One of the major purposes of marketing is actually to do just this, to shift the demand curve outward and to the right.

Figure 2.4:   The Effect of an Increase in Income

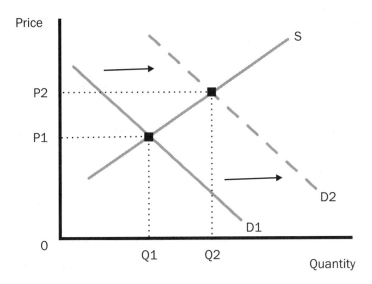

Now consider a change in conditions on the supply side of the market. For example, think of a technological change that improves productivity *at each level of output*. This will tend to shift the supply curve out and to the right, as illustrated in Figure 2.5. As the costs are lower at each level of output, the prices that must be charged to cover those costs can also be lower. The result of the technological innovation in production is to lower the market price of the product, and to increase the quantity produced and sold. The equilibrium price falls from P1 to P2, and the quantity increases from Q1 to Q2. The so-called "Moore's Law" of computing power is a good example of this process. Ever since microcomputers were introduced in the 1980s, and up to the time of writing, there has been a continual increase in computing power, and a continual decline in the real price of computers.

As a third example of a change in market conditions, suppose that the product we are dealing with has been around a long time, and comes to be perceived as old fashioned or out-of-date. This need not even be for any genuine reason of obsolescence, but just due to a change of tastes or fashion. This is shown in Figure 2.6. We imagine the demand curve shifting back and to the left as the product becomes less and less popular. The market price falls from P1 to P2, and the quantity also falls from Q2 to Q1. In this case, business strategy asks the question, "Can we revitalize the brand, or must we exit the business?"

Figure 2.5: **An Improvement in Technology**

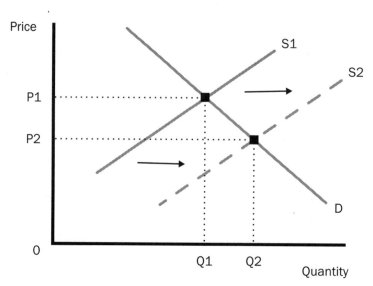

Figure 2.6: **A Change in "Fashion"**

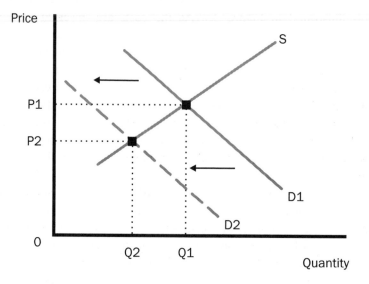

From the three examples above it is clear that the demand/supply apparatus can be used to predict at least the general direction of the likely change in prices and quantities when market conditions change. The reader will be able to think of many more examples. What happens, for instance, when the price of some other product, that is a close substitute for the item we are interested in, either falls or rises?

The Concept of Elasticity

Perhaps one of the most useful concepts in demand and supply analysis, certainly from the point of view of a person interested in business strategy, is that of **elasticity**. For example, the **price elasticity of demand** for a particular product predicts the percentage change in quantity demand for a given percentage change in price. This is a key empirical aspect of demand conditions from the strategic point of view. It makes an estimate of how much (and in what direction) revenue will change when prices are changed. Admittedly, this is not the be-all and end-all of business decision-making. In the first place, an increase in revenue does not necessarily mean an increase in profits (and vice versa), as costs may change as well. Second, the information is of more use to a firm that controls a large share of the market than one that has many competitors. (On both of these points, see the discussion in Chapter 4.) Nonetheless, it is an important starting point for such decision-making. There is also an analogous concept on the supply side, known as the **elasticity of supply**. This would predict the percentage change in quantity supplied for a given change in price. In fact, the concept of elasticity can be generalized still further. The **income elasticity of demand**, for example, would predict the percentage change in demand for a given percentage change in income, and the **cross elasticity of demand** indicates the percentage change in demand for a given item resulting from the percentage change in price of some other item, either a complement or substitute. And so on.

The mathematical formula for the price elasticity of demand is as follows:

$$(2.3) \qquad \eta = -\frac{\Delta Q / Q}{\Delta P / P}$$

where η is the traditional symbol for elasticity, $\Delta Q/Q$ is the percentage change in quantity demanded (the symbol Δ means "change in"), and $\Delta P/P$ is the percentage change in price. There is a minus sign in the formula because the demand curve itself is downward sloping; therefore, multiplying through by a negative will yield a positive number for elasticity itself. Note that if we rearrange equation (2.3) slightly, it can also be written as:

$$(2.4) \qquad \eta = -\left[\frac{\Delta Q}{\Delta P}\right]\left[\frac{P}{Q}\right]$$

Now, suppose that we have a demand equation of the form:

$$(2.5) \qquad P = 10 - 0.5Q$$

And, turning this around to express **Q** as a function of **P**, rather than vice versa:

$$(2.6) \qquad Q = 20 - 2P$$

From equation (2.6) it can be seen that $\Delta Q/\Delta P$ (which is the same thing as the slope of this line) will have a value of –2. We can then use this information to construct a numerical example of how elasticity will change along a straight-line demand curve, such as the one in equations (2.5) and (2.6).

The interesting point to notice about Table 2.1 is that even along a straight-line demand curve, elasticity will change depending on the existing combinations of prices and quantities. If prices are relatively high and the quantities demanded are therefore relatively low, we are likely to be in the "elastic" range of demand (with an elasticity of demand greater than one). In this range, a cut in prices will bring about an increase in revenue because quantity demanded increases proportionately more. On the other hand, if the existing situation is that prices are already relatively low and the quantities demand already relatively high, this would be an "inelastic" segment of the demand curve (with elasticity less than one). A further price cut will not be effective in increasing revenue. In fact, the opposite is

Table 2.1:   Elasticity Example

$$\eta = -\left[\frac{\Delta Q}{\Delta P}\right]\left[\frac{P}{Q}\right]$$

P	Q	$\Delta Q/\Delta P$	η
10	0	–2	∞
7	6	–2	2.33
5	10	–2	1
2	16	–2	0.25
0	20	–2	0

true. In this range, a price hike will actually bring in more revenue as the higher price more than offsets the fall in demand.

These ideas are further illustrated in Figure 2.7, which shows the simple straight-line demand curve from equation (2.5) and the associated **marginal revenue** (MR) curve. As can be seen, when prices are at their maximum (and nothing is sold at all), the elasticity of demand is actually infinite. In this case, it is obviously a good idea to cut prices. Then, there is a range with elastic demand ($\eta > 1$) and similarly an inelastic range ($0 < \eta < 1$), at the lower price levels. Between these two ranges, there is one point on the demand curve where elasticity is exactly equal to one. (This would be called **unit elasticity**.) Finally, when the price falls to zero the elasticity of demand also falls to zero. Note that at the exact point where the demand curve is unit elastic, marginal revenue (MR) is zero. This immediately tells us the significance of the MR curve. Roughly speaking, marginal revenue is the *additional* sales revenue that is to be expected when an additional unit of the item is sold. Therefore, it is positive when demand is elastic, and negative when demand is inelastic (as can be seen). When elasticity is equal to unity, marginal revenue must be exactly zero (MR = 0). Marginal revenue is explained in more detail in Chapter 5.

Figure 2.7:   Elasticity along a Straight-Line Demand Curve

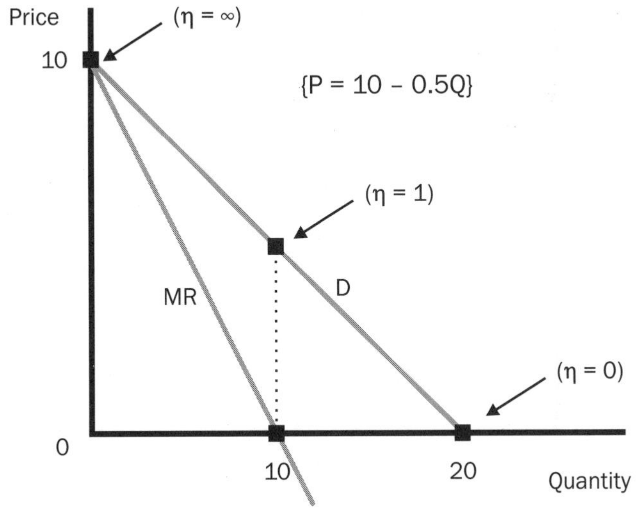

Working with Demand Elasticity

The following examples will give some more insight into the usefulness of the concept of demand elasticity from the point of view of business decision-making. In Figure 2.8 we suggest a case in which the demand curve is simply a vertical line at some given quantity. The demand curve here is **perfectly inelastic**, which means that the consumers always want to buy exactly the same amount regardless of price. It is obviously tempting to think of this product as some sort of (at least mildly) addictive substance. Clearly, there is no point in ever cutting prices in this market. If the price is cut from P1 to P2, the quantity demanded does not increase. All that happens is that an amount of revenue is lost equal to the shaded area in the diagram. To the contrary, if the demand for this product really is perfectly inelastic, prices could be raised by any amount, and the consumers will still pay, thereby increasing revenue.

Figure 2.9, meanwhile, shows the usual type of straight-line demand curve in its elastic range. In this case, as suggested, a price cut will indeed bring in more revenue. If the price falls from P1 to P2, the quantity demanded will increase from Q1 to Q2. It is true that some revenue is lost, as a result of the lower price on the first Q1 units sold (the solid shaded area in the diagram), but this is more than offset by the gain in revenue from all of the new sales (the striped shaded area in the diagram).

Figure 2.8:   A Price Cut Causes a Loss in Revenue

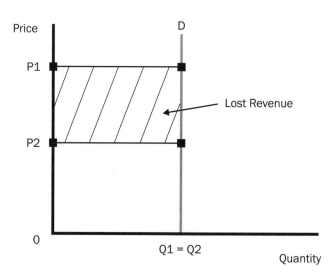

Figure 2.9: **A Price Cut Brings in More Revenue**

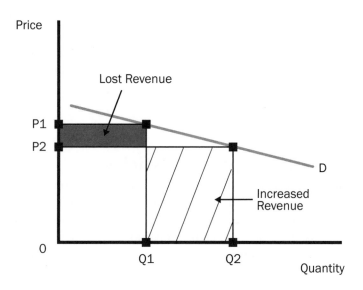

Fig 2.10: **A Demand Curve with Unit Elasticity throughout its Length**

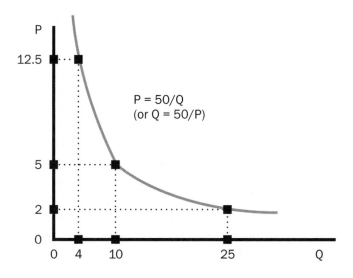

Figure 2.10 departs, for once, from the simplifying assumption that demand curves are roughly linear, and shows a curvilinear example of a demand curve given by the equation $P = 50/Q$. This is, in fact, a geometric form known as a **rectangular hyperbola**, and it has the special property that the price elasticity of demand is equal to one (unit elastic) throughout it's length. In this special case, revenue never changes — it is always equal to $50 regardless of the price charged because the quantity demand changes in the same proportion. Marginal revenue is zero.

Working with Supply Elasticity

As mentioned, the elasticity of supply is an analogous concept to that of the elasticity of demand, and we demonstrate the significance of supply elasticity with a few examples. In Figure 2.11, for example, we reprise a standard textbook discussion of supply conditions. This deals with the market for rental housing units in a particular location or city, in the "short run". The point of this diagram is that in the short run, the supply of rental units in a given location must be very nearly perfectly inelastic (that is, the supply curve will be a vertical line). It takes time to build new apartment buildings, or even to convert existing buildings for residential use. Therefore, if there is noticeable increase in demand, shown in the diagram by a shift of the demand curve out and to the right, in a free market the immediate impact is entirely on prices. Rents will be increased from P1 to P2.

However, over a somewhat longer period of time, in the so-called "long run", supply will be considerably more elastic, as there will then be enough time to convert existing properties, put up new apartment buildings, and so on. This is illustrated by the flatter supply curve in Figure 2.12. Therefore, if the increase in demand is sustained over a period of time, the final result will be a more modest increase in rents, and a greater supply of rental apartments to the market, assuming government land use policies are supportive of new property development.

Economists point to the sequence of events described in Figures 2.11 and 2.12 as a prime example of the role of the price mechanism in optimally allocating resources. There is a greater need for apartments (as shown by the increase in demand), and initially there is a large rise in price reflecting this change. However, precisely as a result of the incentives provided by the higher prices, more rental units are built and more of society's resources are devoted to rental housing. The final result is that more apartments are provided to satisfy the greater need, and the prices themselves return to more reasonable levels. So everything works out according to plan, at least in this example (with supportive institutional structures,

Figure 2.11:   An Increase in the Demand for Rental Housing in the Short Run

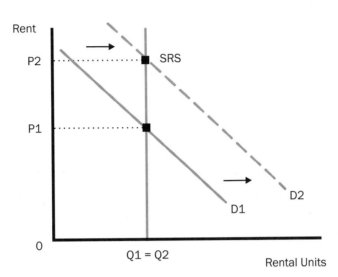

Figure 2.12:   An Increase in the Demand for Rental Housing in the Long Run

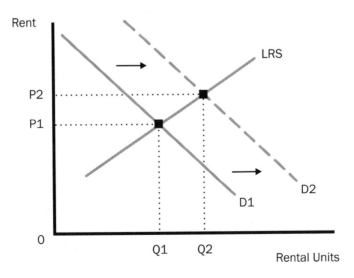

Case Study 3

"An Aging Population and
the Death of Brands"
New York; September 23, 2040

It was a marketer's dream: an aging population with an unprecedented level of wealth. The strategy was simple. Create a wide array of branded products for the "graying" population in the developed countries. Advertising campaigns routinely employed "nostalgia" celebrities to appeal to wealthy retirees. However, the myth of brands was confronted by the reality of longevity. More and more people are living well over 100 years of age. The appeal of brands, with their higher prices, was more than outweighed by concerns about whether retirees would have sufficient income to last beyond 100 years of age. Susan Wright, the president of the luxury goods manufacturer, Gukki corporation, believes that demand has become much more price elastic as the population ages, "People are just more price sensitive than we ever expected."

regulations and capital markets). The *absence* of these mechanisms may explain the high rental prices we see in many big cities, such as London.

Finally, we consider the case of a market with a **perfectly elastic** supply curve, as shown in Figure 2.13. As suggested earlier this might arise, for example, in some large-scale industry with mass production, in which costs per unit are essentially constant over a wide range of output. Hence, there is no need for prices to rise to cover costs when output rises. The result of

Figure 2.13: An Increase in the Demand for Industrial Products

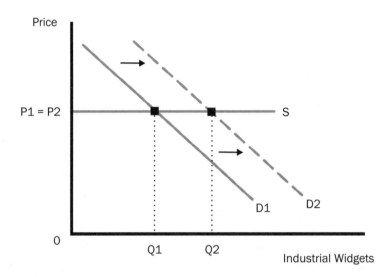

an increase in demand in this case would be simply more resources devoted to the desired product, with no actual increase in price.

Other Applications of the Concept of Elasticity

As mentioned, in addition to the price elasticities of demand and supply, there are some other applications of the concept of elasticity that might be useful to the businessperson. If the symbol **Y** stands for the income of the relevant consumer group, for example, then the formula for the income elasticity of demand is given by:

$$(2.7) \qquad \eta_Y = (\Delta Q/Q)/(\Delta Y/Y)$$

The income elasticity of demand is the percentage change in demand resulting from a given percentage change in income. If $0 < \eta_Y < 1$ (the elasticity is greater than zero but less than one), the item concerned is a **normal good**. An increase in income will cause an increase in the demand

Case Study 4

"Transit in Trouble"
Boston; October 15, 2020

The entire Boston transit system is bankrupt. The government is uncertain as to whether or not the system can be saved, or if it must be shut down in its entirety. Professor Lau, of Harvard University, indicated that the demise of transit is a result of every possible elasticity working against the system. Price elasticity, income elasticity, and the cross elasticity of substitution have all conspired to impact negatively on the Boston transit system. Incomes have risen dramatically in the past 10 years. As a result, commuters prefer to use their own vehicles. The cost of personal transport has fallen dramatically, and vehicles have become more environmentally friendly. As the system lost ridership, it was forced to raise fares to pay for systems operations. One problem with the fare increases was that relatively less well-off consumers, who relied more heavily on the transit system, were increasingly unable to afford riding the system on a regular basis.

for the good, but not by so much as the increase in income ("normal" because this is what is expected to happen in most cases). If $\eta_Y < 0$, the good concerned would be an **inferior good**. When income increases people buy less of it or don't buy it all. A person with a low income, for example, might have a demand for rental accommodation in a basement apartment, but one with a higher income will buy a condo or a detached house. If $\eta_Y > 1$, this is a **superior good**. The demand for this type of product actually increases with income. Wealthy people might serve caviar rather than potato chips at a party, for instance.

For two goods **1** and **2**, the formula for the cross price elasticity of demand, meanwhile, is:

$$(2.8) \qquad \eta_X = [\Delta Q1/Q1]/[\Delta P2/P2]$$

If $\eta_x < 0$, the goods are complements. If the price of butter goes up, the demand for bread goes down. If $\eta_x < 0$, the goods are substitutes. A rise in the price of coffee causes an increase in the demand for tea.

Chapter Summary

- The market price is determined by the interaction of supply and demand.

- An equilibrium price and quantity is determined in the marketplace through the interaction of buyers and sellers.

- Elasticity describes the relationship between a dependent variable (such as quantity demanded) and an independent variable (such as the price of the product, the price of substitutes, or income).

- Businesspeople need to know the relevant elasticity for their goods or services. What if, say, income increases by 10%? Will the demand for my product increase by more, the same, or a smaller percentage than 10%?

Problems

1. Suppose you are in charge of a toll bridge that costs essentially nothing to operate. The demand for bridge crossings, Q, is given by P = 15 − 0.5Q.
   (a) Draw the demand curve for bridge crossings.
   (b) How many people would cross the bridge if there were no tolls?
   (c) What is the revenue associated with a bridge toll of $5?
   (d) Consider an increase in the toll to $7. At this new higher price, how many people would cross the bridge? Would the toll bridge revenue increase or decrease? What does your answer tell you about the elasticity of demand?

2. If both the supply and demand curves shift right, we know the direction of the change in quantity, but not the direction of the price change. If supply shifts right but demand shifts left, we cannot know the direction of either the price or quantity change. Explain why you agree or disagree with these statements.

3. It is generally accepted that the demand for food is relatively price inelastic. If a severe drought reduces production by half, can you determine the effect on farm revenue? If not, what other factors would determine farm revenue?

4. Which of the following events would cause a movement along the demand curve for European-produced clothing, and which would cause a shift in the demand curve?
   (a) Higher costs for producing clothing outside Europe, passed on to consumers in the form of higher prices
   (b) An increase in the income of European consumers
   (c) A reduction in costs in the European clothing industry

5. You have been asked to analyze the world market for wheat. You have estimated the following supply and demand curves:

   $$Qs = 440 + 165P$$
   $$Qd = 1600 - 12P$$

   (a) Calculate the equilibrium price and quantity.
   (b) Calculate the price elasticity of supply and demand at equilibrium.

6. What factors might make demand more elastic?

7. Assume the price of gasoline in 2004 was on the average $1.35 a gallon and 15 million gallons a day were sold. In 2005, the price on the average was $2.15 a gallon and 14 million gallons were sold. Assuming further that the demand for gasoline did not shift between the two years, use the midpoints of these figures to calculate the price elasticity of demand and indicate whether demand was elastic or inelastic.

Case Study Questions | # The Comeback of Caterpillar

Demand

1. Global demand grew by 4.5% in the 1990s. How does this impact forecasts for future demand?
2. Growth in demand was fastest in developing nations. Discuss the implications.
3. Why is the distinction between original equipment and replacement parts important?
4. Why are marketing, distribution, and service so important for this industry?
5. Why was product diversification an important component of Caterpillar's strategy?

Hint: Caterpillar's market has evolved over time. From a focus on the American market, Caterpillar expanded to Canada and Europe. As well, Caterpillar's dominant market position was eroded. Caterpillar has responded by penetrating new markets expanding its marketing efforts, and diversifying the product line.

Supply

1. Discuss the contribution of each of the following elements in the heavy construction equipment industry supply curve:
   - Labor
   - Financial capital
   - Physical capital
   - Technology
2. What is the role of outsourcing in the supply function?

Hint: The case indicates that "Traditionally, Caterpillar functioned as a vertically integrated company that relied heavily on in-

Case Study Questions Continued

house production." Outsourcing, the use of suppliers, can allow a firm to become more productive by focusing on its core competencies.

Elasticity

1. Is the demand for the heavy construction equipment industry elastic or inelastic?
2. Did the entry of Komatsu make the industry demand curve more or less elastic?
3. Did the entry of Komatsu make the industry supply curve more or less elastic?

Hint: The purchase of heavy construction equipment represents a major expenditure. Purchases can be postponed for a time, but equipment must be purchased eventually. The addition of Komatsu alters the industry dynamic. Customers have more choice and the potential for greater negotiating power over price.

Appendix 2.1

Another Method for Calculating Elasticity

Here is another method for calculating price elasticity of demand, in the case where the demand "curve" actually is a curve, and not a convenient straight line.

In Figure 2A.1 we see that if the prices for this particular product drops from $10 to $6, the quantity demanded will increase from 12 to 28. Now remember the elasticity formula:

$$(2A.1) \qquad \eta = (-)(\Delta Q/Q)/(\Delta P/P)$$

Figure 2A.1: Elasticity Calculation using Midpoints

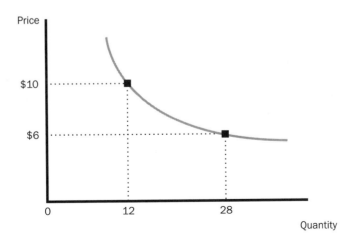

We know that ΔP (the change in price) is –4, and that ΔQ (the change in quantity) is 16. However, what values should be used for the terms P and Q in equation 2A.1? There are two values each of prices and quantity: the starting point and the end point in both cases. The simplest answer is to use the midpoints of the price and quantity ranges. That is:

(2A.2) $P = 8$ (midpoint between 10 and 6)

and also:

(2A.3) $Q = 20$ (midpoint between 12 and 28)

Now use these values in the elasticity formula. The result is:

(2A.4) $\eta = (-)(16/20)/(-4/8) = 1.6$

So, the price elasticity of demand is 1.6 over these prices and quantities, which is in the "elastic" range.

3

The Market Mechanism and the Impact of Regulation and Taxation

Introduction

In the previous chapter we examined the workings of the price system primarily in the context of markets for the output of final goods and services, and also in situations where there were no natural or artificial impediments to the functioning of the market mechanism. In the present chapter, we note that economists tend to apply the same logic in most other economic contexts — for example, to markets for the inputs to the productive process, usually known as **factor markets**, and to markets for **financial assets** and other assets.

It should also be recognized that in reality, there often will be impediments or obstacles to the smooth functioning of markets. These may be either inherent in the situation, in cases of so-called **market failure** (discussed in Chapter 6), or deliberately imposed from outside, for example by public policy. Governments at all levels frequently pass legislation of one sort or another designed to regulate the operation of particular markets. These may be instituted simply to correct for existing market failures, but they may also be deliberately designed to modify the operation of the market mechanism in different ways in the pursuit of public policy goals. For example, there may be price controls legislating maximum or minimum prices in certain situations. Governments also impose taxes of various types, the purpose of which may be simply to raise revenue for the public finances, to pursue other macroeconomic goals, or deliberately to affect behavior in the particular market under consideration in pursuit of social goals. Either way, intentionally or otherwise, the taxes imposed will affect behavior in individual markets, and it is important to be able to understand in what ways they do so. In this chapter, we therefore also consider some examples of different types of market regulation and the ways in which they will likely alter the results of the demand and supply analysis.

Note that we will later examine the impact of other government intervention elsewhere throughout this book. Governments intervene when the market fails in cases of third-party externalities, such as environmental pollution, or because of the accumulation of monopoly powers by business. Also, governments frequently intervene because the market-based outcome is not deemed to be socially or politically desirable — because of the impact on income distribution, for example.

Factor Markets

The markets for inputs to the productive process, such as the market for labor or for raw materials, are usually known as factor markets. They provide classic examples of the situation of **derived demand**. That is to say, the good or service under consideration is only demanded because of its

Figure 3.1:   The Labor Market

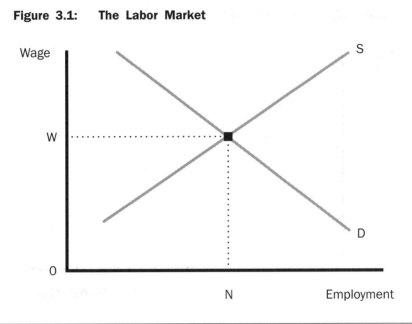

contribution to the ultimate bottom line. For example, although it may be ethically objectionable to many people, neoclassical economists think of the labor market as "just another market" precisely in those terms. As in Figure 3.1, there will be a downward-sloping demand-for-labor curve and an upward-sloping supply-of-labor curve. The intersection of the two will determine the wage rate for this particular type of labor, and the level of employment in the industry. Both variables are determined by market forces, rather than by any notions of what a "fair" wage rate might be.

The demand for labor is thought to arise from the **marginal productivity of labor** in producing a particular final good or service that will yield profit to the employer. It slopes downward because the marginal productivity of labor is believed to decline with increases in employment. Therefore, lower real wages are required to justify further employment from the employer's point of view. The supply of labor, meanwhile, is supposed to arise from the **labor/leisure choice** made by individual workers. It slopes because higher real wages are needed to persuade workers to give up "leisure". Changes in labor market conditions will then lead to changes in both wages and employment in the labor market. For example, a technical change causes an overall increase in labor productivity and will shift the demand curve for labor to the right, and increase both the wage rate and the level of employment.

Figure 3.2:   The Market for "Loanable Funds"

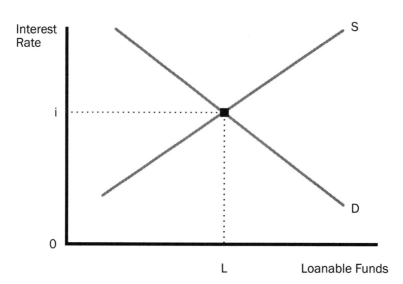

Financial and Asset Markets

Economists also apply the demand and supply logic to the financial markets that bring together borrowers and lenders of money. We illustrate with the standard analysis of the market for "loanable funds" in Figure 3.2. In this case note that it is not the price of a financial asset per se that appears on the vertical axis, but rather the yield or interest rate on the asset. The relation between asset prices and yields is explored in more detail in the appendix following this chapter, as borrowing and lending in particular markets is in fact often organized by the issue of **financial securities**, such as **bonds**. In Figure 3.2, however, the borrowers (for example, firms who want to finance capital investment) simply have a demand for loanable funds that is downward sloping with respect to the interest rate. Similarly, in the diagram there is an upward-sloping supply curve of loanable funds on the part of the lenders. The intersection of the demand for and supply of loanable funds then determines the market interest rate. If there is a change in the motivations of either the borrowers or the lenders, this will cause a change in the interest rate. For example, if there is an increase in the desire to save, this will tend to shift the supply curve of loanable funds down and to the right and reduce the interest rate, and so on.

Figure 3.3 repeats essentially the same analysis, but now in terms of the demand and supply for financial assets such as bonds. This will determine

Figure 3.3:   The Demand for and Supply of Bonds

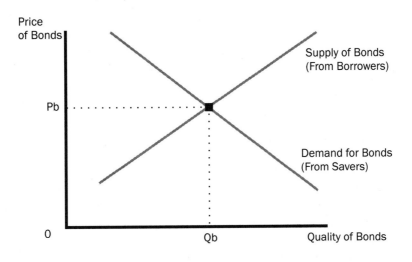

the capital price of the bond, rather than its yield. The lenders are demanding bonds, and the borrowers are supplying them. It is the lenders who are now associated with the demand side in the diagram. An increase in the desire to save, discussed in the context of interest rates above, in this diagram will cause an increase in the demand for bonds, shift the demand curve out and to right, and increase the price of bonds. The price of bonds and the interest rate (or yield) on bonds move in opposite directions.

Further examples of the operation of the price mechanism in assets markets will be given later in the book. For example, the market for **foreign exchange** is discussed in Chapter 12.

The Impact of a "Price Ceiling"

As mentioned, one possible form of market regulation is legislation specifying a maximum price that can be charged in a particular market, a **price ceiling**. Returning to our example of rental housing from the previous chapter, this frequently occurs in such markets. The argument in favor of rent controls will usually be along the lines that tenants in a particular city or other jurisdiction are entitled to "affordable housing". The argument against rent controls is that they distort the market incentives for the provision of such housing, as discussed in that chapter. Figure 3.4 shows the likely result of rent control in the case where it is "binding".

If the maximum price is to be binding (that is, if it is to have any effect) it must be set below the price that market forces would have established anyway; for example, at a level such as MAX in the diagram. In that situation, the supply of rental housing will be "A" units, but the demand will be much higher, at "B" units. Therefore, the effect of the rent controls is to cause a perceived housing **shortage** of (B – A) units. In this situation a proponent of market forces would be likely to argue that the rent controls are themselves the problem. The reason for the shortage of housing is that there is no economic incentive for landlords to provide the extra apartments. The political response may be otherwise, however, to the effect that the existence of the housing shortage itself *proves* the need for rent control.

In the case of rent control, the supply curve can also be affected. At the artificially low price, some landlords cannot survive. They literally "walk away" from the buildings, or attempt to convert the rental units into condominium ownership. This happened, for example, in Toronto in the 1970s. To sustain the supply of rental units, the government was forced to pass legislation that prevented building owners from converting their rental properties to condominiums.

Similar rationing or shortages can also occur in financial markets, of course. Suppose, for example, that in a particular credit market an interest

Figure 3.4:   Rent Control

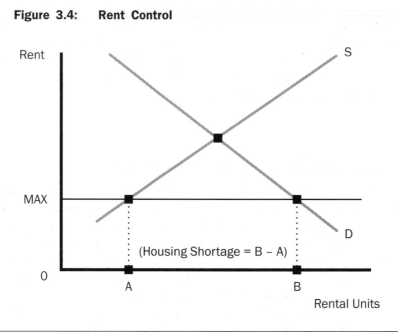

rate ceiling, or a maximum permissible interest rate, is imposed by the relevant authorities. In this case, we may observe the phenomenon of **credit rationing** in the amount (B – A), as illustrated in Figure 3.5. In the field of development economics, this type of situation has sometimes been labeled **financial repression**. The idea is that interest rates in the developing world are often determined by purely administrative or political decisions, and if they are set "too low", the financial sector will not develop (it will be "repressed") because of the lack of incentives for lenders.

The Impact of a "Price Floor"

The opposite of a price ceiling is the imposition of a **price floor**. In such a case the legislation specifies a minimum price to be paid for any good or service. An obvious example would be minimum wage laws (treating the wage rate as the price paid for the services of labor). In practice, of course, minimum wage laws are often applied at the economy-wide or macroeconomic level. However, here we consider the impact in a particular labor market only, such as (to take a contemporary example) workers in fast-food restaurants. This is illustrated in Figure 3.6.

If the minimum wage law is to be binding, it must be set at a level above that which market forces would establish if there were no regulation. At the legislated minimum wage rate (MIN in the diagram), the demand for labor is "H", and the supply of labor would be "G". The supply of labor is greater than the demand for it, and there is unemployment in this particular sector, equal to (G – H). The free market solution would be for wages to fall and employment to rise. However, this is ruled out by the legislation. Therefore, the argument would be that the basic effect of a binding minimum wage law is to cause persistent unemployment in the affected sector. Note that there is something of a conflict of interest here between two groups of workers: those who are employed and those who are unemployed. The workers who *do* have jobs are likely to be happy with their higher wages, which they will lose if employment increases. The unemployed, however, would be happy just to have jobs, even if the wages were lower. The economist interested in the optimal allocation of resources would tend to side with the unemployed workers in this case. The argument would be that if the labor market *is* allowed to clear, society as a whole would be better off and that this would be the efficient solution. Such issues will be discussed in more detail in the section on taxation below. Evidently, however, from the political standpoint such reasoning is not likely to cut much ice with those who would actually lose by the change. Also, from a political standpoint, the actual numbers matter. If unemployment is relatively low, politicians can "buy" many more votes by

Figure 3.5: **Financial Repression**

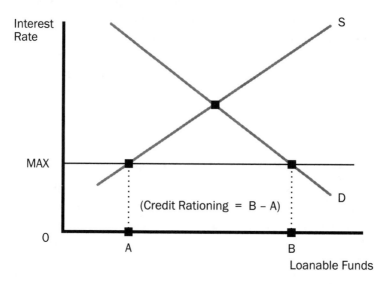

Figure 3.6: **A Minimum Wage**

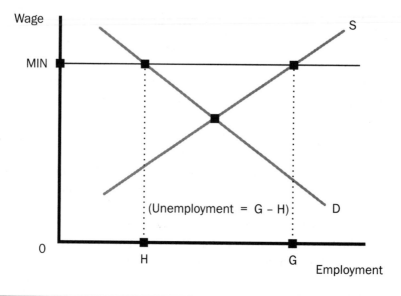

raising the wages of those employed than they can by creating jobs for the relatively few unemployed.

We can sum up the overall discussion of price ceilings and price floors with the observation that a binding maximum price will cause a shortage (in our example above, a housing shortage or credit rationing), whereas a binding minimum price will cause a **surplus** of the good in question (in our example, a "surplus" of workers seeking jobs).

The Impact of Taxation

If a tax is imposed on economic activity in any particular market, this will also affect the price charged and quantities bought and sold of the item. A tax can be imposed on either side of the market. It can be levied,

Case Study 5

"California Abolishes the Minimum Wage" Sacramento; June 10, 2020

Today the governor of the State of California, Mr. Karl Vandenberg, signed a bill to eliminate the minimum wage for the state. The governor argued that the legislated minimum wage created rigidities in the California labor market and, therefore, an unacceptably high level of unemployment. The change will allow all workers to secure meaningful jobs. The governor acknowledged that there will be issues with respect to low wages. Therefore, the government has also introduced legislation to provide income support to working families. Also, there will be new programs to create more affordable housing to meet the needs of lower-income working families.

in the first instance, either on consumers at the point of purchase or on suppliers at some stage of the manufacturing process. An example of the latter was the old Manufacturers' Sales Tax (MST) in Canada, which was later replaced by a tax imposed on consumers known as the Goods and Services Tax (GST).

In the example shown in Figure 3.7, we consider a so-called **specific tax** imposed on the supply side of the market. What is meant by a specific tax is simply an imposition of "x dollars" per unit on the item. From the producers' point of view, if the tax is levied on them, this increases costs at each level of output by the amount of the tax. This is shown by a shift of the post-tax supply curve up and to the left. The new equilibrium price in the market will be higher than it was before the tax, and the level of output will be lower. Price increases from P1 to P2, and output falls from Q1 to Q2. However, producers obviously do not receive the whole of the price P2 for their efforts. Although the consumers pay P2, the producers receive only (P2 – T), where T is the specific tax. The rest of the proceeds represent the total revenue received by the government, equal to the shaded area in the diagram. It is therefore also possible to use the analysis to discuss the **incidence** of this tax, meaning who ultimately pays, regardless of where the tax is first imposed. Actually, both consumers and producers "pay" something. The consumers in effect lose that portion of the rectangle (P2 – T, C, B, P2) above the line (P1, A), whereas the producers lose the

Figure 3.7:   A Specific Tax

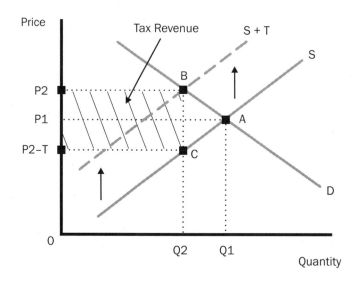

taxation of that portion of the rectangle below the line. These represent parts of lost **consumer surplus** and lost **producer surplus**, respectively. (Consumer surplus is the area under the demand curve and above the original price point; producer surplus is the area above the supply curve and below the original price point.) By reducing output and raising prices, the producers have been able to **shift** some of the tax to consumers, even though the tax was imposed on producers in the first place. The extent to which they will be able to do this clearly depends on the elasticities of demand and supply, as discussed in Chapter 2.

From the point of view of the idea that a market solution represents the most efficient allocation of resources, the main complaint about the tax would be that it distorts market incentives and moves the economy away from the presumed optimum. Prices end up higher, and output is lower than would be the case in a free market with no tax. It is even possible to put a dollar figure on these losses. The amount that society *as a whole* is supposed to lose can be calculated from the area of the triangle (C, B, A) in the diagram. This can be calculated as a dollar sum as it involves both prices and quantities. This is known as the **deadweight loss** of the market distortion. As mentioned, consumers lose some consumer surplus and the producers lose producer surplus, but the shaded portion of these losses is transferred to the government (and, presumably, ultimately to the beneficiaries of government programs) in tax revenue. They are not lost to the society as a whole. The triangle (C, B, A), the area *not* shaded in the diagram, however, consists of lost consumer and producer surplus that is not received by, or transferred to, anybody. This is a net loss to the whole society.

The diagram in Figure 3.8 illustrates the concept of consumer surplus in more detail. The notion of consumer surplus arises because in most markets, all consumers pay the same price, the market price, for all of the units of the item that they purchase. They get some benefit from this circumstance because, as the downward slope of the demand shows, if the supply had been more restricted they would have actually been prepared to pay a higher price for some of these units. In other words, the first Q1 units of the good would have been valued at P1 each, the first Q2 units at P2 each, and so on. Therefore, apart from the "marginal" (last) unit, the subjective valuation of all units sold is greater than the price, P', that all consumers are asked to pay. The total benefit of this can be expressed in dollar terms as the shaded area under the demand curve above P'. This is the so-called consumer surplus. Producer surplus, analogously, would be an area *above* the supply curve, representing the fact that producers also receive the market price on all units sold but that the actual costs of each unit, except for the marginal unit, are typically less than this (in the case of an upward-sloping supply curve).

Figure 3.8: Consumer Surplus

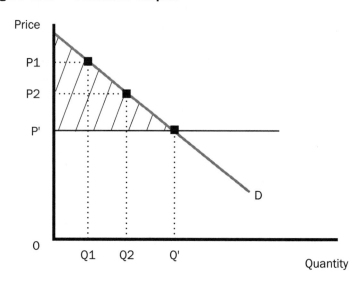

Figure 3.10 shows how it is possible to put some dollar numbers on consumer and producer surplus and, hence, use these numbers rhetorically in debate about various economic changes. In the diagram we see that an increase in price of this product from $8 to $16 causes demand to fall from 18 units to 16 units. By working out the total area of lost consumer surplus we can make statements such as "this change has cost consumers $136".

Note that the idea of consumer surplus, in particular, would have some relevance to the business strategy for a firm that had some **market power** in a particular field, and could split up or **segment** the market in some way so that all or some consumers will pay different prices, reflecting the actual valuation they individually place on the particular good or service, rather than a single market price. An example of this is when home service contractors provide an "estimate" to each individual customer for each individual contract, and therefore some consumers pay a higher price (for roughly the same work), depending on their negotiating skills. This would be an example of so-called **price discrimination**. If there could be **perfect price discrimination**, the seller would be able to extract all the consumer surplus from the customers (i.e., the whole of the area under the demand curve).

Returning now to the issue of taxation, we should also consider the case of an **ad valorem tax**, which is probably a more familiar method of taxation than the specific tax discussed above. This is where the tax is expressed as a percentage of (in this case) the original supply price: in

Figure 3.9: **Producer Surplus**

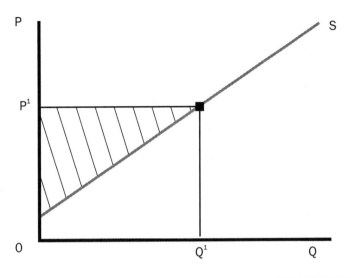

Figure 3.10: **Numerical Example of Consumer Surplus**

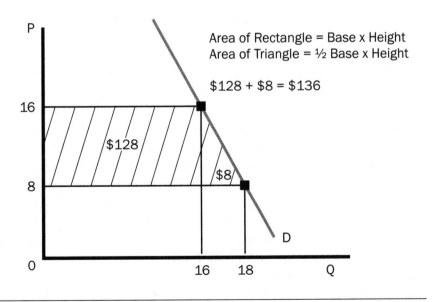

Figure 3.11: An *Ad Valorem* Tax

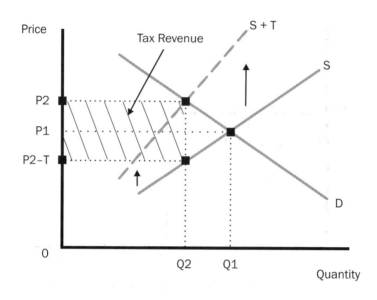

other words, a tax of 10%, 15%, 20%, and so on. This type of tax is shown in Figure 3.11. As can be seen, in this case not only does the post-tax supply curve shift up and to the left, but the slope of the curve also becomes steeper. Otherwise, the analysis remains unchanged.

Finally, note that both a specific tax and an *ad valorem* tax could also be imposed on the demand side of the market in the first instance, thus shifting the demand curve rather than the supply curve, as is assumed in Figures 3.7 and 3.11. Figure 3.12 illustrates the effect of a specific tax imposed on the demand side of the market. This shifts the demand curve vertically upward by the amount of the tax. Note, however, that the final analysis of the price ultimately paid by both consumer and producers, and how the tax is shifted, works out exactly as in the earlier example where the tax was imposed on the supply side. Why then would government tend to prefer to impose a tax on producers rather than consumers? The answer is probably quite simple: more votes. But, on the other hand, why do we often actually see **value-added taxes** (VAT) on demand (i.e., at the retail level), like the GST in Canada mentioned earlier? The explanation here may be the power of the business lobby and the need to maintain international competitiveness if this form of taxation is common among trading partners.

Figure 3.12: A Specific Tax Imposed on Consumers

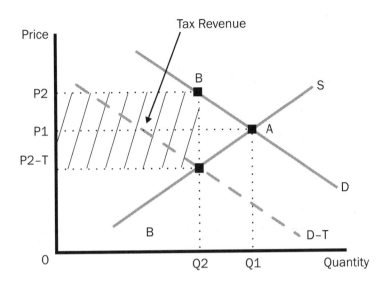

Subsidies

The opposite of a tax (in some sense) is a subsidy, where one level of government or another is willing to subsidize either producers or consumers in a particular market, by literally paying some portion of either the cost or purchase price. Needless to say, however, taxpayers elsewhere in the economy are still being asked to pay for this *largesse*. Subsidies are usually justified on social grounds: for example, that a particular industry may not survive unless a subsidy is granted. As with taxes, there can be either **consumer subsidies** or **producer subsidies**. We illustrate the issue of subsidization with just one example, that of a producer subsidy of "x dollars" per unit, as in Figure 3.13. The impact of the subsidy in this market is to shift the supply curve down by the amount of the subsidy. As they now receive the subsidy, the producers can sell more of the good at a lower price. The impact in the marketplace is that output and the quantity sold increase from Q1 to Q2, and the price paid by consumers falls from P1 to P2. The actual cost of producing Q2 units, however, is (P2 + sub), and the difference must be paid by the government. The total cost to the treasury on Q2 units, therefore, is the shaded area in the diagram. So, the subsidy is beneficial to both the consumers and producers in this particular market, but the costs are paid by other taxpayers. It can also be argued that the market

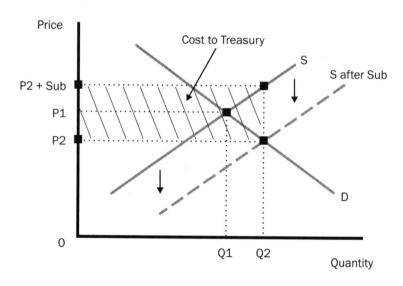

Figure 3.13: A Producer Subsidy

mechanism is distorted, once again. In this case, too *many* resources are devoted to the production of this particular item. Output is inefficiently large because the price paid by consumers does not represent the true costs of production. There is also a case to be made, however, that *assuming* the authorities have indeed decided to intervene in the market mechanism for social reasons, the deadweight loss of achieving their particular goal by the route of a subsidy will be less than by other methods. The reason is that there is no loss of consumer surplus here. Consumers get all they want; it is just the loss to taxpayers from subsidizing inefficient production that causes losses to the society. As suggested previously, however, such niceties probably do not carry much weight in the political arena. Note that this type of analysis can explain such things as the "success" of Airbus, the European commercial jet aircraft venture at the end of the 20th century. It is true that by that time Airbus could be counted as a player in the commercial airline industry; but this was based on an initial deadweight loss of, literally, billions of Euros in subsidies.

Chapter Summary

• Economists apply the logic of the price mechanism to all types of markets, including factor markets and asset markets.

- Any attempt by government to set a price different than that which would be established by the market (e.g., for social reasons) will have a definite impact on the economy.

- Price ceilings (e.g., rent controls) create shortages while price floors (e.g., agricultural price supports) create surplus production.

- Taxes distort equilibrium prices and quantities in the marketplace. Both producers and consumers are given incentives to change their behavior.

- Subsidies are another form of market distortion. Governments take money from one activity, such as education, and use it to support another area, such as steel production.

- Subsidies are defended on the basis of their social benefits. In the case of steel this could include jobs, exports, regional development, research and development, etc.

- Economists always tend to stress the opportunity costs involved and the need for rigorous cost-benefit analysis before a decision to tax or subsidize is finalized.

Problems

1. Ticket prices for sporting and entertainment events are often regulated by municipalities. For example, the city of Los Angeles oversees pricing of events at baseball's Dodger Stadium. If scalping is legal, there will be a market price for scalped tickets, set in the usual way. However, if it is illegal, it is possible to impose a penalty on either the seller (the scalper) or the buyer. Using supply and demand analysis, show that there will be a larger impact on the equilibrium level of scalping if penalties are imposed on both sides of the market.

2. The rent control agency in Bucharest has found that the demand for apartments is $Q_d = 320 - 16P$. Quantity is measured in tens of thousands of apartments. Price, the average monthly rental rate, is measured in hundreds of Euros. The agency also noted that the increase in Q at lower P results in more three-person families coming into the city and demanding apartments. The city's board of realtors acknowledges that this is a good estimate of demand and has shown that supply is $Q_s = 140 + 14P$.
   (a) If both the agency and the board are right about demand and supply, what is the free market price? What would be the change in the population of the city if the agency sets

a maximum average monthly rental in Euros, and all those families who cannot find an apartment leave?

(b) Suppose the agency bows to the wishes of the board and sets a rental rate of €1800 per month on all apartments to allow landlords a "fair" rate return. If 50% of any long-run increase in apartment comes from new construction, how many apartments are constructed?

3. Suppose that a government argues that it can increase revenue from a particular sector by actually *lowering* tax rates. Choose a constant excise (specific) tax, and show a case in which this is possible. Would it make a difference if demand is elastic or inelastic?

4. The city council of a small college town decides to regulate rents in the town order to reduce student living expenses. Suppose the average annual market-clearing rent for a two-bedroom apartment has been $900 per month, and rents were expected to increase to $1,200 within a year. The city council limits rents to the current $900 per month level.

(a) Draw a supply and demand diagram to illustrate what will happen to the number of rental apartments after the imposition of rent control.

(b) Do you think this policy will benefit all students? Why or why not?

5. The market supply and demand functions for milk are:

$$Qs = 800 + 100P$$
$$Qd = 2,000 - 500P$$

To assist milk producers, the government is implementing a price floor of 2.25 per unit. How many units of milk must the government buy at 2.25? How much money must the government spend? What is the increase in producer surplus?

6. How can consumer surplus be determined?

Appendix 3.1

The Relationship between Yields and Financial Asset Prices: An Example

Consider a financial security, such as a bond, which has a **face value F**, attracts an annual **coupon payment C**, and has a term of **n** years to **maturity**. In a competitive financial market the price of the bond should be equal to the present discounted value of the stream of future coupon payments, and the eventual repayment of **principal**, discounted at the market rate of interest, **i**. That is:

$$(3A.1) \qquad P_B = \; C/(1+i) + C/(1+i)^2 + C/(1+i)^3 + ... + \\ C/(1+i)^n + F/(1+i)^n$$

This immediately shows the inverse relationship between the price of bonds and interest rates. When interest rates fall, the price of bonds goes up and vice versa.

For a **zero coupon bond**, that is, a debt instrument that promises only to pay back the principal or face value after a certain number of years, this will reduce to:

$$(3A.2) \qquad P_B = F/(1+i)^n$$

In other words, such a bond will sell only at a discount.

Finally, for a debt instrument that is a **consul** or a **perpetuity** (meaning that the principal will never be repaid, and the holder is simply promised a certain coupon payment in perpetuity), the bond price reduces to the simple expression:

$$(3A.3) \qquad P_B = C/i$$

Suppose, for example, that in equation 3A.3 the coupon is $50. When the market interest rate is 5%, the bond will sell at $1,000 (which is probably its nominal face value). If the interest rate rises to 6.25%, the price of the bond will fall to $800. If, however, the interest rate falls to 4%, the price of the bond will rise to $1,250.

4

The Costs of
Production

Introduction

In Chapter 2, we considered the importance of the concept of the elasticity of demand, and how revenue is likely to change when prices and output change. The other important element in calculations of the bottom line or profit is, of course, the impact of changes in output on the costs of production, and this is the subject of the present chapter.

Strictly speaking, economists insist that the calculation of costs should include all true **economic costs** — that is to say, all the costs of pursuing one course of action rather than another, regardless of whether they can be quantified in money terms (and therefore would appear in any reckoning of **accounting costs**). This is consonant with the basic idea of opportunity cost introduced in Chapter 1. In the present chapter, however, to make the analysis tractable, the assumption will be that all costs are quantifiable accounting costs.

Concepts and Definitions

In Chapter 1 we discussed the production possibility frontier, which showed the trade off between agricultural and industrial production. What determines the position of such a curve? The curve is derived from a **production function**, which, literally, shows the relationship between output and the inputs used in the production process (the factors of production, including capital equipment, labor, and land). That was at the macroeconomic or aggregate level. At the microeconomic level, we can appeal to a similar concept for the output of an individual firm. The basic form of a production function is:

$$(4.1) \qquad Q = F(K, N, L)$$

where $F(...)$ is the functional relationship, Q = output, K = capital equipment, N = labor inputs, or employment, usually measured in **person hours** of work, and L = "land" or natural resources. If the production function exhibits **constant returns to scale**, this means that a doubling of all of the inputs will lead to a doubling of output. A situation of **increasing returns** would imply that a doubling of all inputs will more than double output, whereas a situation of **decreasing returns** means that a doubling of inputs will less than double output. The cost of producing a given level of output will depend on a combination of the technological conditions given by the production function and the money price of the inputs of factors of production. Note also that, in practice, it may not be possible to change all the inputs by the same proportion at the same time. For example, it takes time to build a new plant or install new equipment. Perhaps only a few, or even only one, of the factors can be varied to produce more output in the short run (such as labor working longer hours). In this case, we would speak of **returns to the variable factor**.

The above is the generic textbook form of the production function. Depending on the scope of the analysis being undertaken, it may obviously be useful to employ a more sophisticated or disaggregated version. For some purposes we may wish to disaggregate the natural resources component. For example, the US Bureau of Economic Analysis specifies a KLMS (capital, labor, purchased materials, and services) production function in much of its work. In this chapter we continue with the generic production function, and expand the analysis in Chapter 14.

Figure 4.1 depicts a simplified version of a production function with just one input (labor) and one output. It graphs the relationship $Q = F(N)$. One possible interpretation of this is as a short-run function, as mentioned above, with the other factors of production held constant, and labor as the variable factor. This production function exhibits diminishing or decreasing marginal returns to labor. It is true that each additional input of labor time will increase total output, but at a diminishing rate. This is shown by the curved shape of the production function. Basically, the marginal product of labor (MPN) is given by the slope of the function at each point, and this is gradually declining. The average product of labor (APN), which is equal to

Figure 4.1:   A Production Function with Diminishing Marginal Returns to Labor

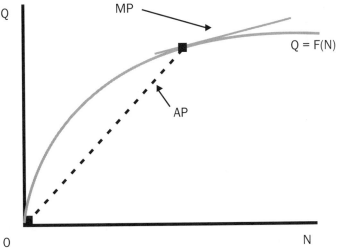

Q/N, meanwhile, is given by the slope of a ray from the origin of the diagram. If marginal product is declining along the length of the production function, average product must obviously be declining also, for reasons explained in more detail later on.

Figure 4.2 then graphs out the average and marginal product curves of labor (both of which are falling with additional labor inputs) as derived from the information about the production function in Figure 4.1.

If we then use the symbol **W** to stand for the wage rate, that is, the price of labor, we can now work out both the marginal and average costs of each increase in output. Given that the marginal and average products of labor are always falling, it follows that marginal and average costs of each additional unit of output will be continually rising, as shown in Figure 4.3. The expression for marginal cost is **W/MPN**, and for average cost the expression is **W/APN**. This graphical analysis has therefore shown how it is possible to derive cost functions from a knowledge of the production function (representing the technical or engineering date on production), plus a knowledge of the prices of the factors of production.

With the above technical background we can now define each of the different cost concepts in more general terms.

The total outlay necessary to produce a given level of output is simply called **total cost** (TC) and, following on from what was said above, it is useful to think of it as being divided into two parts: **fixed cost** (FC) and **variable cost** (VC). Fixed costs are in the nature of overhead costs, outlay

---

Figure 4.2:   Marginal and Average Product of Labor

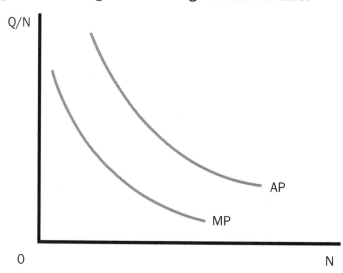

Figure 4.3:   Rising Marginal and Average Cost

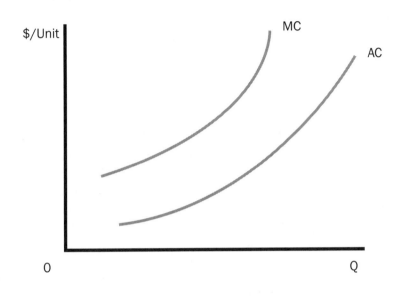

that must be incurred regardless of the level of output. For example, a firm may be renting the building in which manufacturing takes place, and will have to pay the rental regardless of whether any output is actually produced. Variable costs are those that are incurred in actually producing the output (e.g., the wages of workers actually engaged in production, the cost of raw materials, etc.). As the name suggests, variable costs will change with the actual level of output. So, by definition:

(4.2)   **TC = FC + VC**

Now divide through by the actual level of output **Q**:

(4.3)   **TC/Q = FC/Q + VC/Q**

The term on the left-hand side (LHS) of equation (4.3) is the **average cost** (AC) per unit of output (sometimes called average total cost). The terms on the right-hand side (RHS) are **average fixed cost** (AFC) and **average variable cost** (AVC), respectively. Thus, equation (4.3) can be rewritten as:

(4.4)   **AC = AFC + AVC**

In addition to average cost, as previously mentioned, the other important cost concept is **marginal cost**, which can now be defined for our purposes as the additional (hence "marginal") cost of producing one extra unit of output. This means the change in total costs that is brought about by producing one extra unit of output. Formally:

(4.5) $MC = \Delta TC / \Delta Q$

A Cost Example

We now illustrate the cost definitions above with a simple numerical example. Assume that the basic cost data for a firm producing a range of output over 1 to 10 units are as illustrated in Table 4.1. In this example, fixed costs (FC) are equal to $200. As output increases from 1 to 10 units, average fixed costs progressively fall from 200 to 20. Variable costs, meanwhile, progressively increase. For the first unit of output, variable costs increase by $20; for the second, they increase by $30; for the third by $40, and so on. Therefore, as mentioned earlier, we must be assuming **diminishing marginal returns** to the variable factors of production in this particular case. Average variable cost (AVC) therefore also increases progressively. From this data we can also work out the overall average cost (AC) and marginal cost (MC) schedules, as shown in Table 4.2. Average cost is calculated simply by dividing total cost by the number of units of output. It is also equal to the sum of average fixed cost and average variable cost. Mar-

Table 4.1:   Basic Cost Data

Q	FC	VC	TC	AFC	AVC
1	200	20	220	200.0	20
2	200	50	250	100.0	25
3	200	90	290	66.7	30
4	200	140	340	50.0	35
5	200	200	400	40.0	40
6	200	270	470	33.3	45
7	200	350	550	28.6	50
8	200	440	640	25.0	55
9	200	540	740	22.2	60
10	200	650	850	20.0	65

Table 4.2: Average Cost and Marginal Cost

Q	AC	MC
1	220.0	20
2	125.0	30
3	96.7	40
4	85.0	50
5	80.0	60
6	78.3	70
7	78.6	80
8	80.0	90
9	82.2	100
10	85.0	110

ginal cost is the change in total cost for each additional unit of output. Therefore, the MC of increasing output from 4 to 5 units is $60 (200 – 140), from 5 to 6 units it is $70 (270 – 200), and so on. Figure 4.4 then graphs out the average and marginal **cost curves** from this example.

The AC curve falls continuously until a level of output somewhere between 6 and 7 units is reached, and thereafter rises. This is due to two competing forces operating on average cost. The decline in average cost occurs as output increases from its lowest levels when, initially, falling average fixed costs (as output increases) outweigh the simultaneous increase in average variable costs. AFC continues to decline, of course, even after the minimum point of AC is reached; but thereafter, at the higher output levels, the rise in AVC will offset this.

The marginal cost curve is always rising over the range of output we have specified, and it cuts the AC curve at precisely its minimum point. At this level of output, **MC = AC**. The relationship between marginal cost and average cost as shown in this diagram is actually a general one. It exists between any average and marginal relationship. In the case of cost changes, it can be stated as follows:

• When MC < AC, then AC will be *falling*.

• When MC > AC, then AC will be *rising*.

The reason for this is well known to both baseball and cricket fans around the world as the **batting average effect**. We can illustrate with another example, however, which is perhaps a little closer to home for those currently engaged in a business education program. Suppose a student has currently completed four full courses in such a program and has an average mark of 77%. (This would be a B+, and correspond to a grade point average of 6.0 in graduate programs at the Schulich School of Business.) Now, suppose that in the fifth full course — that is the *marginal* course in this context — the student actually receives a grade of 100%. The student's *average* mark will rise to around 82%, which would be in the A– range. In other words, when the marginal mark is higher than the average mark, the average mark rises. Now suppose that, on the contrary, the student performs disastrously in the fifth course, and receives a marginal mark of only 50%. The average mark will plummet to around 72%, which is only a B. Thus, when the marginal grade is less than the average grade, the average grade falls. Evidently, exactly the same sort of principle applies in the case of the AC and MC curves of our example.

Textbook "U-shaped" Cost Curves and Other Configurations for Cost Curves

The cost curves that emerged (by design) in Figure 4.4 are essentially the familiar "U-shaped" cost curves of the textbooks. In other words, in most

Figure 4.4:   Average and Marginal Cost Curves

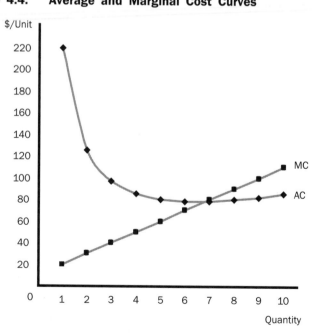

textbook diagrams the general presumption is that average costs do at first decline, then reach a unique minimum point, and thereafter rise. The minimum point is sometimes known as the **"optimal plant size"** or similar. A more stylized version of these textbook cost curves appears in Figure 4.5. These traditionally-shaped cost curves have a long history, going all the way back to the original *Principles of Economics* written by Alfred Marshall well over 100 years ago.[1] It should be made clear, however, that the shape rests on a particular set of assumptions about the behavior of costs and productivity at the level of the individual firm, which may or may not be true in any actual situation. There is no substitute, in other words, for the empirical calculation of costs in each "real world" case. The U-shaped curve does have some plausibility, of course. It is based on the idea that, in many cases, costs will initially be lowered by spreading overheads, but will then rise due to diminishing marginal productivity and organizational issues around the management of large enterprises. However, it is not the only empirical possibility.

In the case of **constant costs**, for example, average costs do not change at all, regardless of the level of output. In this case, the AC and MC will coincide along a horizontal line, as in Figure 4.6.

Figure 4.5: **"Textbook" Cost Curves**

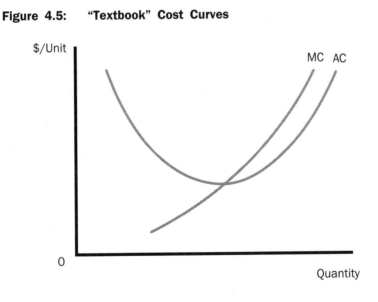

---

[1] Alfred Marshall, *Principles of Economics* (London: Macmillan, 1890).

Figure 4.6: The Constant Costs Case

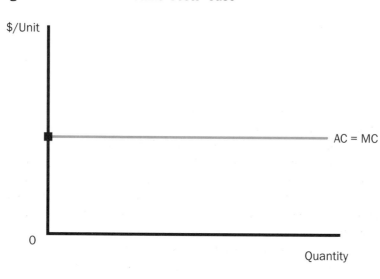

Another possibility is that average costs decline continuously as output increases, due to increasing returns in the production process. In this case, the MC curve must be everywhere below the AC curve, as in Figure 4.7. The type of industry shown in Figure 4.7 is often described as a **natural monopoly**, as there is no effective limit to the size of the firm.

Finally, in Figure 4.8, an **"L-shaped"** AC curve is depicted. The idea here is that costs do fall at first at lower levels of output, but once a certain threshold size is attained, they reach a minimum and, thereafter, are constant. Some economists would assert that this is actually a fairly typical case in industry. In the final analysis, though, how costs actually do behave in any particular firm is an empirical matter, and one on which the manager must be well informed in order to make effective decisions.

Chapter Summary

- Economists examine the costs of production in order to determine optimal resource allocation. Businesspeople need to understand costs in order to make a profit.

- The total costs of production are derived from a production function, which shows the relationship between inputs and outputs on one hand, and the money prices of the inputs on the other.

Figure 4.7: **Decreasing Costs**

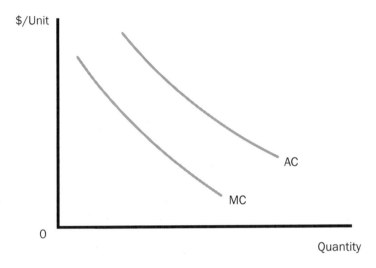

Figure 4.8: **An "L-shaped" Average Cost Curve**

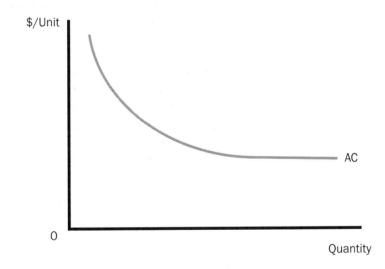

Case Study 6

"Goodbye Economies of Scale,
Hello Network Externalities"
Wall Street Journal; March 23, 2017

The president of Universal Motors, Ms. Sheila Jackson, argues that UM's advantage in the marketplace is now more based on network externalities than on economies of scale in production. "Electronic commerce allows us to create virtual networks with increasing returns to knowledge with our preferred suppliers. This allows us to share knowledge in the design and development of new vehicles over a longer planning horizon." Henry Ford's business model was based on mass production and the application of scientific management to the production process. Companies were vertically integrated, and the most important transaction costs were captured within the firm. With network externalities, the dynamics of production change. This new approach favors collaboration, and revises the notion of transactions costs. As a result, there are greater efficiencies through flexible linkages than there are in attempting to capture economies of scale in production within the firm.

- A production function with increasing returns to scale means that the more you produce the more efficient you become. The businessperson is making more effective use of machines, people, inventory management, etc. (the factors of production).

- Increasing returns implies that the average total costs will decline as output increases.

- However, even in the most efficient industries, at some point average total costs will likely start to increase due to "diseconomies of scale".

- Businesspeople will need to have a good knowledge of the *actual* cost structure in their own industry in order to make effective decisions.

Problems

1. Suppose you are an employer seeking to fill a vacant position in your factory. Are you more concerned with the average product of labor, or the marginal product of labor for the last person hired? If you observe that the average product is just beginning to decline, should you hire any more workers? What does this situation (that AP is beginning to decline) imply about the marginal product of the last worker hired?

2. Suppose a chair manufacturer is producing in the short run with a fixed level of plant and equipment. The manufacturer has observed the following levels of production corresponding to different numbers of workers:

Number of Chairs	Number of Workers
1	20
2	28
3	34
4	38
5	40
6	38
7	35

   (a) Calculate the marginal and average product of labor for this production function.
   (b) Suppose wage rate is $10 an hour. Work out the total variable cost, average variable cost, and marginal cost for each level of output.
   (c) Based on the information obtained above, how would you characterize cost conditions in the chair industry, in general terms?

3. Is it true that constant returns to scale imply constant average and marginal costs, and that marginal and average costs will be equal? Why or why not?

4. Explain why a continuously falling average cost curve might tend to eliminate competition in that particular industry.

5. What is the difference between diminishing returns to a variable factor and decreasing returns to scale?

6. What is the difference between economic costs and accounting costs?

7. If the marginal product of labor is 45 units of output and the marginal product of capital is 56 units of output while the wage rate is $20 per worker and the cost of capital is $28 per machine, are these two inputs being used in the least cost combination? What should be done if they are not?

Case Study Questions | **The Comeback of Caterpillar**

Break-even Analysis
1. Why is this industry considered to be capital intensive?
2. Why do capital-intensive industries have a high break-even point?
3. Why is market share so important to capital-intensive industries?

Hint: The production of heavy construction equipment itself also requires extensive use of machinery and equipment. As a result, this industry has high fixed costs, in the short run, and the short run could be a substantial period of time. High fixed costs imply a high break-even point.

Appendix 4.1

More on Costs and Production*

Time as a Factor in the Determination of Relevant Cost

The time period in which a firm's cost structure is being considered is important in determining which costs are relevant to a particular business decision. In the economic analysis of cost, the time factor is handled by dividing time periods into two basic types: the short run and the long run. Recall that this distinction was also used in the analysis of supply and demand and price elasticity. In the short run, we assume that there are certain resources, such as land, factory space, and machinery, that cannot be changed within the time period allowed. The cost of using these resources is either sunk or fixed. Thus, there will always be certain costs that are irrelevant to a short-run decision. Long-run analysis assumes that there is enough time for managers to vary the costs of utilizing all their resources. Consequently, all long-run costs are either incremental or variable and therefore relevant to a particular business decision.

Production and Costs in the Long Run

The long run is the period in which quantities of all resources used in an industry can be adjusted. Those inputs that had been fixed in the short run — such as machinery, buildings, and cultivated land — can be adjusted in the long run. Because all inputs can vary in the long run, the law of diminishing marginal returns no longer has the same importance as in the short run. In this section, we review the various ways in which a firm can take advantage of this flexibility to reduce its costs over the long run.

---

* Thanks to Dr. Farrokh Zandi for providing the material in this Appendix.

Economies and Diseconomies of Scale

The term **economies of scale** is defined as the decrease in the unit cost of production as a firm increases all its inputs of production. This is opposed to diminishing returns in the short run, when one or more of the factors of production is fixed. This phenomenon is illustrated in Figure 4A.1. The average total cost curve, labeled "Plant 1," represents a certain amount of capacity. At its most efficient point, a firm with this plant capacity is able to produce Q_1 units of output at a unit cost of ATC1. "Plant 2" represents a greater production capacity because it is positioned to the right of Plant 1. In addition, it is located on a lower level than Plant 1, signifying that over a certain range of output, the larger plant is able to produce greater amounts of output at a lower average cost than the smaller one, i.e., the unit cost of ATC2.

Sometimes economies of scale is used interchangeably with the term **increasing returns to scale**. Increasing returns to scale is a long-term phenomenon indicating that the firm's output grows at a rate that is faster than the growth rates of its inputs. For example, a 100 percent increase in inputs results in more than 100 percent increase in output, say 200 percent. In this case, as the firm expands, the per-unit cost drops. The following are the main causes of economies of scale.

Figure 4A.1: Different Plant Sizes

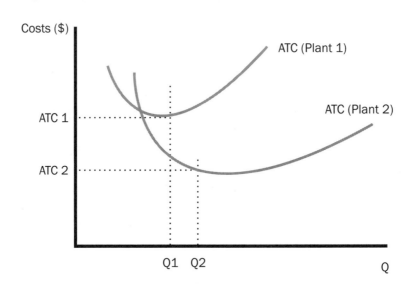

Division of Labor and Specialization

As Adam Smith illustrated over two centuries ago, increases in the scale of production and worker specialization can go hand in hand. Performing fewer tasks allows workers to become more efficient at their jobs. As a result, Smith concluded, quantities of output tend to rise more quickly than the number of workers producing them. The impact of the division of labor is just as prevalent today in labor-intensive production. For example, if a very small restaurant where workers do everything expands, then workers can begin to specialize in either food preparation or service, thus making both sets of workers more efficient in their tasks.

Specialized Capital

In most manufacturing industries, a greater scale of production is associated with the use of specialized machinery. If a car manufacturer raises the quantity of all its inputs, for example, capital equipment can have more specialized functions, so that it performs fewer tasks more efficiently than before. Not every firm benefits from all these factors when it increases its scale of production. For example:

* Firms that have a high level of debt will usually not be able to borrow at the lowest possible interest rate.
* Size may not always offer the firm a cost advantage. Firms that are very large may become bureaucratic and inflexible, with management coordination and control problems.
* Oversized firms experience a disproportionate increase in staff and indirect labor. The resulting increase in these types of cost may cause the average total cost to rise.

These are reasons for diseconomies of scale, or decreasing returns. Decreasing returns occur when a business expands inputs to a product's production by a certain percentage but sees output rise by a smaller percentage. For example, a 100 percent expansion in all inputs may lead to its output rising by only 75 percent. In terms of Figure 4A.1, this can expect the ATC associated with bigger plants to shift up and to the right.

Figure 4A.2 shows how short-run and long-run costs are related. The long-run average-total-cost curve is a much flatter saucer shape than the short-run average-total-cost curve. In addition, all the short-run curves lie on or above the long-run curve. These properties arise because of the greater flexibility firms have in the long run. In essence, in the long run, a firm gets to choose which short-run curve it wants to use. However, in the short run, it has to use whatever short-run curve it chose in the past.

Figure 4A.2 also shows a long-run average cost curve reflecting both economies and diseconomies of scale as well as constant returns to scale.

Figure 4A.2: Long-Run and Short-Run Cost Curves

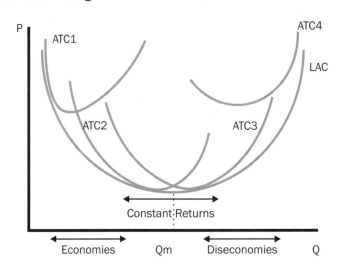

When long-run average total cost declines as output increases, there are said to be economies of scale. When long-run average total cost rises as output increases, there are said to be diseconomies of scale. When long-run average total cost does not vary with the level of output, there are said to be constant returns to scale.

Expressing this differently, assume that our firm (say, an auto-making company) expands its assembly plant three times. Each time, it faces a different short-run average cost curve for each plant size. With each expansion of the plant, the curve shifts to the right, demonstrating the effects of the increased output. When the plant is first expanded, the short-run average cost curve falls from ATC1 to ATC2. This shift results from economies of scale or increasing returns to scale. Recall that average cost is found by dividing total cost by the quantity of output. With economies of scale, output rises more rapidly than the total cost of inputs, so that average cost falls as the scale of production expands.

With the second plant expansion, the shift of the short-run average cost curve (from ATC2 to ATC3) reflects constant returns to scale. Output and the total costs of inputs rise at the same rate when the plant is expanded this second time, so the average cost curve moves horizontally as the output of automobiles rises. With the final plant expansion, the company's short-run average cost curve not only shifts to the right but also rises (from ATC3 to ATC4). This shift reflects diseconomies of scale. Since the plant's output is rising less rapidly than the total cost of input costs, the average cost curve rises as the production of automobiles continues to increase.

Table 4A.1 summarizes the causes of economies of scale and diseconomies of scale.

Economies of Scope

In the long run, it is also possible for managers to identify ways to take advantage of economies of scope. This cost-saving phenomenon occurs when it is possible to produce two or more products together at a lower per-unit cost than for each product separately. A key factor in this form of cost savings is the sharing of a company's fixed cost by multiple products. For example, certain electronic stores that normally sell TVs, VCRs, DVD

Table 4A.1: Economies and Diseconomies of Scale

Reasons for Economies of Scale	Reasons for Diseconomies of Scale
• Specialization in the use of labor and capital	• Disproportionate rise in transportation costs
• Indivisible nature of many types of capital equipment	• Input market imperfections (e.g., wage rates driven up)
• Productive capacity of capital equipment rises faster than purchasing price	• Management coordination and control problems
• Economies in maintaining inventory of replacement parts and maintenance personnel	• Disproportionate rise in staff and indirect labor
• Discounts from bulk purchases	
• Lower cost of raising capital funds	
• Spreading of promotional and research-and-development costs	
• Management efficiencies (line and staff)	

---

players and computers could also sell CDs, videos, DVDs, etc. These latter products are displayed on racks that occupy otherwise unused floor space in the stores. The use of the retail establishment's excess capacity in this manner reduces the average total cost of selling each of the products.

Another way that a company can utilize economies of scope is to produce goods or services that require similar skills and experience. For example, when PepsiCo expanded into the snack and fast-food business, it was able to utilize its background in one type of fast-moving consumer item (soft drinks) to another (chips, tacos, and fried chicken). The product development, channels of distribution, and marketing know-how are very similar in these two product groups.

The Learning Curve

As pictured in Figure 4A.3, the learning curve shows that a firm's unit cost decreases as its total cumulative output increases. Its rationale is that you improve with practice. Over the long run, as a firm produces more of a good or service, its workers are expected to get better at what they are doing. This increase in labor productivity will then decrease the unit cost of

Figure 4A.3: A Learning Curve

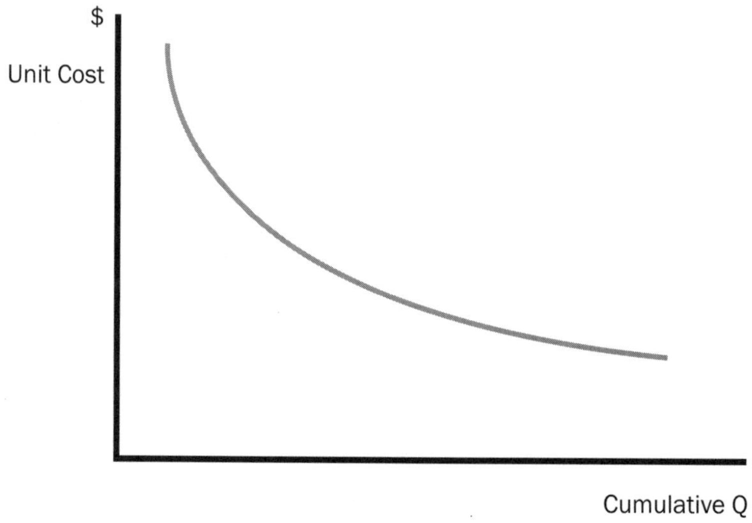

production. But other people besides the direct labor involved in the production process are also expected to improve with practice. For example, researchers may find less costly substitutes for raw materials currently used; engineers may develop more efficient production processes or product designs.

The learning curve has played an important part in the strategic approach called learning-curve pricing. This approach advocates that a firm should set its price at a relatively low level to stimulate demand, even though there is the possibility that it will earn minimal profit or even incur a loss at the outset. The greater demand will accelerate the learning effects that accompany the higher accumulated volume of production. As the company's costs are brought down the learning curve, the company will start to become profitable.

Break-Even Analysis

What is to be done about those costs that are not relevant to a marginal decision? After all, even if they are ignored as sunk costs, they must still be paid for. However, this, in fact, is the logic of designating a cost as irrelevant. By definition, an irrelevant cost is one that must be incurred, regardless of the alternative selected by the decision maker. The question of how this cost is recovered is a separate issue altogether. To understand this aspect of the problem, we can turn to a commonly used technique called break-even analysis.

Break-even analysis is perhaps the most widely used application of the concept of "relevant cost". This analytical technique addresses the basic question: 'How many units of a particular product does a company have to sell to cover *all* its costs of production: that is, to 'break even'? Another name for break-even analysis is cost-volume-profit analysis. This label describes the break-even problem more explicitly. That is, given the company's fixed and variable cost, how much volume does it have to sell to break even? Moreover, once it passes the break-even point and becomes profitable, how much profit will it earn as its volume increases?

Let's look at an example. You own a seafood store. How many kilograms of seafood per month must be sold to break even? To answer this, we first divide the monthly costs into their fixed and variable components. Fixed cost is presented as a total figure, while the variable cost is shown on a per-unit basis. Variable cost per unit is also referred to as average variable cost (AVC) (See Table 4A.2).

To find the break-even point, we use the following equation:

$$(4A.1) \qquad Q_{BE} = \frac{TFC}{P - AVC}$$

Table 4A.2: Fixed and Variable Cost Data

Total Fixed Cost		Variable Cost per Unit (Average Variable Cost per Unit	
Rent	$1,200	Average wholesale price	$3.00
Utilities	400	per kilogram of seafood	
Wages	2,350		
Interest Payment on Loan	1,500		
Insurance	400		
Miscellaneous	150		
Total	$6,000		

Where:

Q_{BE} = the break-even quantity of product sold
TFC = Total fixed cost
P = Selling price of the product
AVC = Average variable cost of the product
P – AVC = 'Contribution margin' per unit of product sold

that must be incurred, regardless of the alternative selected by the decision maker. The question of how this cost is recovered is a separate issue altogether. To understand this aspect of the problem, we turn to break-even analysis (see Figure 4A.4).

The logic of break-even analysis is very straightforward. The amount by which the selling price exceeds the average variable cost is called the contribution margin per unit of product sold. When the amount of product sold reaches the point where the total contribution margin covers all the fixed costs of a product, the firm breaks even. The break-even concept can also be shown graphically. In Figure 4A.4, the break-even point occurs when the firm's total cost line crosses the total revenue line. Although our example is quite simple, we do not want to imply that break-even analysis applies only to small and uncomplicated business operations. To be sure, larger and more complex businesses might have a more difficult time dividing their costs into fixed and variable components, particularly when fixed and variable costs have to be determined for many different products. But no matter how complicated the situation, there still remains the basic concept of generating enough sales so that the contribution margin covers fixed cost.

Figure 4A.4: Break-Even Analysis

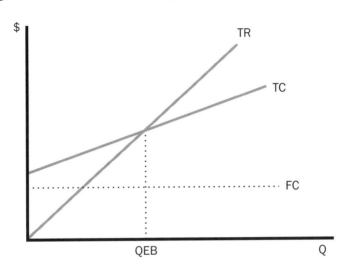

Limitations of Break-Even Analysis

As useful as this technique can be, it is still subject to several shortcomings. First, break-even analysis selects only one price for a particular product and then proceeds to determine how much a firm has to sell at this price to break even. In order to consider the possibility of different amounts demanded by consumers at different prices (i.e., the price elasticity of demand), a whole schedule of prices and break-even points would have to be constructed. Break-even analysis determines how much a firm with a given price and cost structure needs to sell in order to break even. However, it does not provide any indication of how many units it will actually sell. Second, and more important, this analysis assumes that a firm's average variable cost is constant. In certain circumstances, it is quite possible for a firm's average costs to either decrease or increase as more of a good or service is produced.

5

Two
Benchmarks
for Business
Strategy: Perfect
Competition
versus Monopoly

Introduction

The notion of **market structure** is a particularly important concept from the point of view of business strategy. Much of the training of the business executive is focused on how to gain strategic or competitive advantage in the particular industry in which they are operating. The success of these activities will depend to a large extent on the existing market structure. In this chapter, we discuss two extreme benchmarks for market structure, on which economists have focused a lot of attention, but which, in reality do not offer much scope for strategic decision making: **perfect competition** and **monopoly**. As will be seen, these notions are in the nature of "ideal types",[1] as most real world market structures must, presumably, be some mixture or combination of the two. However, the point of the current discussion is that an understanding of these extreme cases is nonetheless a prerequisite for understanding any actual situation, which will have elements of both.

The Firm in a Perfectly Competitive Industry

The notion of perfect competition is in some sense the economists' ideal because of the argument that such a structure will indeed ensure the optimal allocation of resources. It is questionable, however, whether participation in such an industry would be ideal from the business point of view. The argument about social optimality rests on the premise that, in the long run, firms in such an industry will only be covering their costs, and all profit will be competed away. True, it is usually argued that such costs should properly include the opportunity costs of the manager's time in supervisory duties, and hence some sort of "normal profit". However, these will hardly be the kind of rewards to stimulate entrepreneurship and innovation. Moreover, the implication is also that there is not much that can be done about this situation in terms of business strategy. Firms just have to accept the going price for their output, and will automatically produce the optimal amount of that product at this price.

The basic characteristics of a perfectly competitive market are the following:

• There are many firms, each of which is too small in itself to impact the market price by its own activities.

---

[1] Max Weber, *Economy and Society*, volume 1, edited by G. Roth and C. Wittich (Berkeley: University of California Press, 1978).

- Each firm is therefore a **price-taker**.

- Because of its small size, each firm will assume it can sell all it wants at the **going price**.

- There are no "barriers to entry" to the industry; additional competing firms can enter the industry whenever they see an opportunity to do so.

It can easily be seen, therefore, that there can be no meaningful business strategy under such conditions. The only rule guiding the firm's conduct would be the simple idea that in order to maximize profits at any given time (even if these profits will disappear eventually), each firm should expand output up to the point where the market price equals their marginal cost of production. In other words, the rule that they should follow must be:

(5.1)   **P = MC**

The meaning of this rule is further illustrated in the diagram in Figure 5.1. Because the firm will always accept the going market price, in effect it faces an individually horizontal demand curve at the market price **P**. The only decision left is how much output to produce. The firm assumes that it

Figure 5.1:   Profit Maximization under Perfect Competition

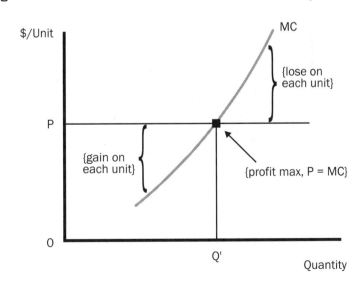

is so small in relation to the market as a whole that it can sell any amount it chooses. The diagram also shows the firm's marginal cost curve for producing additional units of output, with an upward slope as in the "textbook" cost curves discussed in the previous chapter. Note that in every situation in which the price is greater than marginal cost, the firm should always decide to produce an extra unit of output. The price that it will receive for this extra unit is greater than the marginal cost of producing it, and therefore the additional production must add to total profits. Conversely, in every situation in which price is less than marginal cost, the firm should cut back production, as it is making a loss on that unit. Following the logic of these choices, it is clear the profit-maximizing level of output must be at **P = MC**. Only at this level of output will the firm have no incentive to change. Initially, this may seem counter-intuitive. How can you maximize profits when price *equals* marginal cost? The key is the "marginal" component of cost. That is, the *extra* cost to produce one extra unit. When MC equals price it means the greatest difference between Total Revenue and Total Cost and, therefore, the largest profit.

In Figure 5.2, a similar analysis is repeated, but now we add the average cost curve (which in this case is a textbook-style U-shaped AC curve) to the mix. If the market price is as high as **P** in this diagram, and the firm adheres to the **P = MC** rule, it will actually be making profits in

Figure 5.2:   The Firm Earns Profits in the "Short Run"

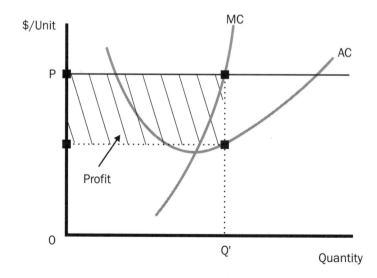

the short run. Profits are equal to price less average cost, multiplied by the quantity sold **Q'** or, in other words, the shaded area in the diagram. Given the perfectly competitive market structure, however, it is clear that this favorable situation cannot last. There are literally no barriers to entry to this industry, and the mere existence of the profits might therefore be very attractive to new entrants. As new firms come into the market, total supply increases, and (as previously shown in the simple demand and supply analysis in Chapter 2) the market price will fall. This process must continue until prices fall so low that all profits are eliminated, with none of the firms making any money but just covering their costs.

The long-run situation of each perfectly competitive firm is represented in Figure 5.3. In the long run, the profits of the perfectly competitive firm are "competed away", and the level of output chosen corresponds to the minimum point of the AC curve. As mentioned, this price/quantity combination would be regarded as the social optimum from the point of view of rational resource allocation. The price of every unit of output corresponds to exactly what it is "worth". As against this, however, it is a very common argument that the profit motive is the most important incentive mechanism in the capitalist economy. From this point of view, it might be thought that it is something of an anomaly that profits apparently disappear in this supposedly ideal situation. As mentioned, it is reasonable to argue that the costs covered by the market price include a normal rate of return to the

Figure 5.3: The Perfectly Competitive Firm in the "Long Run"

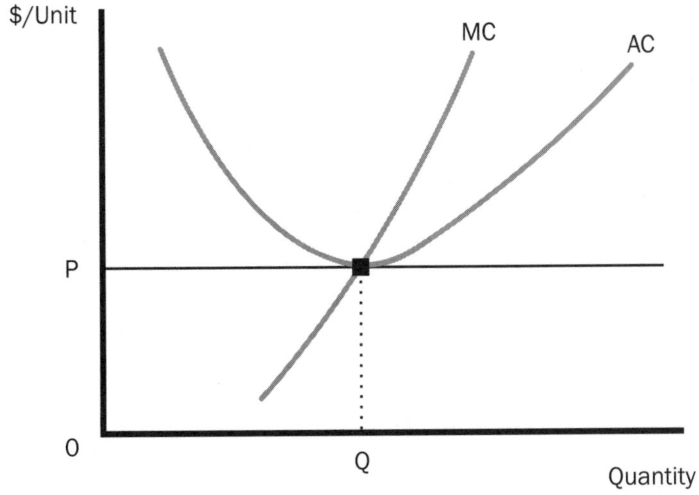

managers of the firm. However, there are definitely no economic profits or excess profits, such as might be thought to provide incentives for innovation and change. The perfectly competitive equilibrium is essentially a static rather than a dynamic concept.

The Firm as a Monopolist

The polar opposite to the perfectly competitive market is the case of a monopoly, in which there is only one firm in any given market. From the point of view of market efficiency, this situation would be frowned on by the economist concerned with resource allocation. The owners or managers of the firm concerned, however, will presumably be much happier with the potential profits. Even so, if the monopolist's position is genuinely not **contestable** by new entrants or competing products, then, just as in the case of perfect competition, there would not really be very many strategic decisions for the managers to actually make. Once again, it would just be a question of picking the profit-maximizing level of output from the point of view of the firm. (In practice, clearly, no real world monopoly situation is likely to be as solid as all that, and in reality potential or existing "monopolists" will usually be vitally concerned with how to either achieve or maintain their monopoly.) The basic characteristics of an absolutely uncontested monopoly, however, would be the following:

- A single firm controls the whole market.

- Therefore, the firm is itself a **price-maker**.

- The firm must face a downward sloping demand curve (the market demand curve as a whole).

- "Barriers to entry" to this industry are completely effective, so the monopoly situation will persist.

For the monopolist, the concepts of **marginal revenue** (MR), and **average revenue** (AR) become all-important. The **total revenue** (TR) received from the sale of any given level of output is simply price times quantity, or:

$$(5.2) \qquad TR = PQ$$

Average revenue is then just TR divided by output, which is the same thing as price:

$$(5.3) \qquad AR = PQ/Q = P$$

In short, the average revenue curve for the monopolist will coincide with the market demand curve. Marginal revenue in this context can then be defined as the increase in revenue that will be obtained by the sale of one additional unit of output. That is:

(5.4) $\mathbf{MR = \Delta TR/\Delta Q}$

In order to further illustrate these concepts, we can revert to the device of a simple linear relationship between the quantity demanded and the price, as employed earlier in Chapter 2. For example, suppose that the relationship between quantity demanded and price is given by the equation:

(5.5) $\mathbf{Q = 20 - 2P}$

The market demand curve as usually drawn will therefore be:

(5.6) $\mathbf{P = 10 - 0.5Q}$

With this data it is therefore possible to construct a numerical example (shown in Table 5.1) for TR, AR, and MR over a range of output from $\mathbf{Q = 1}$ to $\mathbf{Q = 12}$. The AR and MR curves can then be exhibited graphically, as in Figure 5.4 (with the range extended to $\mathbf{Q = 20}$ — not to scale). This obviously replicates the diagram illustrating the concept of demand elasticity along a straight-line demand curve from Chapter 2. We can now explicitly see the connection between price elasticity and the behavior of

Table 5.1:   Total, Average, and Marginal Revenue Example

Q	AR (=P)	TR (=PQ)	MR
1	9.5	9.5	9.5
2	9.0	18.0	8.5
3	8.5	25.5	7.5
4	8.0	32.0	6.5
5	7.5	37.5	5.5
6	7.0	42.0	4.5
7	6.5	45.5	3.5
8	6.0	48.0	2.5
9	5.5	49.5	1.5
10	5.0	50.0	0.5
11	4.5	49.5	−0.5
12	4.0	48.0	−1.5

Figure 5.4:   Average and Marginal Revenue Curves

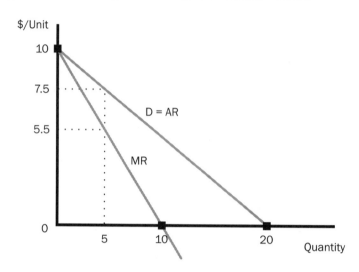

marginal revenue. For example, it would evidently be no good at all to expand output into the range where MR becomes negative. The firm would only be losing money in that case. However, the profit-maximizing level of output for the monopolist will be still further to the left of the point where **MR = 0**. Costs have also to be taken into account. By analogy with the discussion of perfect competition (in which we compared the market price to marginal cost), the monopolist must compare the marginal revenue of producing one additional unit of output with the marginal cost of that additional unit of output. The difference is that unlike the perfectly competitive firm, the monopolist must take into account the potential impact of falling prices on their own revenue. For the monopolist, if **MR > MC** then this is the signal that output should be increased; but if **MR < MC** then output should be cut back. The profit-maximizing level of output must be at the point where marginal revenue is equal to marginal cost:

(5.6)   **MR = MC**

This is shown in Figure 5.5, in which the AR and MR curves are compared with the firm's cost curves.

With the profit-maximizing output at **MR = MC**, the price level at this volume of output can then be read directly off the demand (AR) curve.

Figure 5.5:   Monopoly Profit

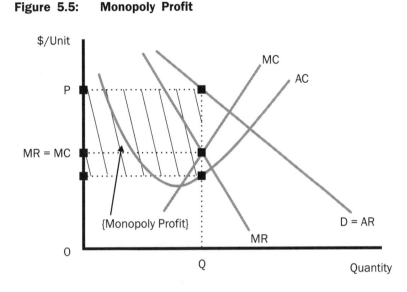

Average cost is given by the corresponding point on the AC curve. The profit, in this case **monopoly profit**, will be the distance (P − AC) multiplied by the quantity sold, or in other words, the shaded rectangle in the diagram. There is an important difference between this monopoly profit and the economic profit sometimes earned by perfectly competitive firms in the short run. The latter will soon disappear as new firms enter the market, whereas, in principle, the monopoly profits continue indefinitely, or at least for as long as demand conditions in the marketplace remain unchanged.

As suggested, the perfectly competitive industry is frequently held up as the ideal market structure because of the argument that it will ensure the optimal level of output, from the social point of view, in the long run. From this perspective also comes one of the main criticisms of a monopolistic organization — it will fail to produce the optimal level of output. This argument is most easily seen by repeating the above analysis of monopoly profit, but in an industry with constant costs (i.e., with **AC = MC** throughout).

Once again, the monopoly output will be given at the point where **MR = MC**, and monopoly profit is represented by the shaded area in the diagram shown in Figure 5.6. The price charged by the monopolist will be **Pm**, and the output produced will be **Qm**. Recall, however, that the demand curve in this diagram is the demand curve for the entire market.

Figure 5.6:   Monopoly Profit in the Constant Costs Case

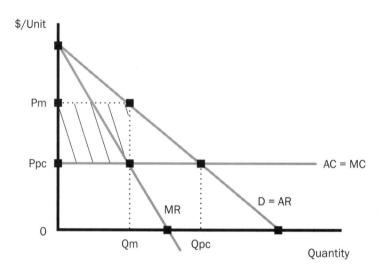

Therefore, it can be inferred that the output of this same industry, if it was perfectly competitive, would be where **P = MC** in the diagram. In other words, the perfectly competitive price would be **Ppc**, and the perfectly competitive output would be **Qpc**. The conclusion that can be drawn is that prices will be higher, and output will be lower, under monopoly than under perfection competition. Moreover, as prices and output under the latter are held to be the social optimum, it follows that the monopolist must be producing a socially sub-optimal level of output. As will be seen in Chapter 6, in many jurisdictions with "capitalist" economic systems this argument is taken very seriously by the defenders of free markets, to the point where it is an important influence on public policy. In the present chapter, however, the objective has been simply to point out the contrast.

Chapter Summary

- Economists greatly favor the perfectly competitive model. It produces a standard product at the lowest per unit cost of production, with no excess profits. This is supposed to be the perfect example of "optimal resource allocation".

Case Study 7

"Macrosoft: A Bankrupt Monopoly"
Redmond; August 14, 2016

Macrosoft™ filed for bankruptcy protection today. For many years, Macrosoft captured a monopoly in both the operating system and applications software for personal computers. At one time, Macrosoft was the richest and most powerful company in the world. Macrosoft dealt very aggressively with any and all potential competitors, real and imagined. In fact, there was such a high level of concern with respect to this behavior that the US government instituted antitrust action to break up the corporation. At one time, there was consideration of breaking Macrosoft into two companies: one for the operating system and the other for applications software. For a variety of reasons, this action was never undertaken. As it turned out, however, the market accomplished what the government was unwilling or unable to do. Professor Stephen Glauber of the University of Washington noted: "The Macrosoft monopoly was never really sustainable. Technological change was always going to ensure that Macrosoft's monopoly could not be maintained. New innovators have attacked Macrosoft from many directions, and Macrosoft's strategic response was inappropriate. Instead of innovating itself, Macrosoft focused on trying to keep out new entrants to maintain its so-called monopoly."

- Of course, businesspeople might have a different attitude to the purely competitive model. There is no room for business strategy (and perhaps no need for people with an MBA qualification!), and no opportunity to make economic profits.

- Governments and consumers have mixed emotions. It is beneficial to have the maximum possible output at the lowest possible price. But standardization implies no product differentiation. Everything would look the same.

- In a monopoly, the entire market is controlled by one firm, possibly a businessperson's dream.

- Economists, citizens, and some governments dislike the higher prices, lower quantities, and the control of the marketplace by one dominant firm.

- However, monopoly markets may be contestable. The threat of new entrants may force the monopolist to behave in a more competitive manner.

- If the world economy really was composed of only purely competitive markets, it would truly be a static (unchanging) equilibrium. It is difficult to see how major innovations would occur. There would be little incentive for research and development as all new initiatives would be replicated by competitors, eliminating all excess returns.

- Most governments feel compelled to regulate monopolists to modify the behavior of the dominant firm.

Problems

1. You notice that the fans get thirsty at a soccer game. Therefore, you set up a refreshment stand. After raw materials, you clear 500 Pesos for the afternoon. Are your economic profits 500 Pesos? Why or why not?

   Now suppose your friends hear about your success. What are your chances for a repeat success at the next game? If the stadium officials auction off refreshment stand rights to the highest bidder, what would you be willing to bid? Under the bidding system, who gets the profits? Comment on how easy, or difficult, it might be to earn positive economic profits.

2. Suppose you are a regulator of the local public electric utility, a natural monopoly with decreasing average costs throughout the relevant range of production. What is your job? What information do you need in order to carry it out? How would you obtain such

information? Would you rather price according to marginal or average cost? Why?

3. Consider an industry dominated by a single monopolist. The demand for the product is given by $Q_d = 12 - 0.2P$. Costs per unit of output are constant, and the firm estimates these to be $35 per unit.
   (a) What will be the profit-maximizing quantity of output produced by the firm, and what price will the firm charge?
   (b) What will be the total revenues, total costs, and total profit at the profit-maximizing level of output?
   (c) Suppose that this industry was perfectly competitive instead of a monopoly, would the market price and level of output be any different from the above? If so, what would they be?
   (d) Suppose the government decides to regulate this industry, and the price is set at $40 per unit. Will this change the firm's profit from the pure monopoly case? How will it affect the total of output produced by the industry?

4. Why do firms enter an industry when they know that in the long run economic profit will be zero?

5. Zeon Industries is a monopoly provider of electricity. The demand for electricity is:

   $$Q_d = 49 - 0.7P$$

   The marginal revenue curve is:

   $$MR = 70 - (20/7)Q$$

   The marginal cost is:

   $$MC = 10 - 0.02Q$$

   The average cost function is:

   $$AC = 10 - 0.01Q$$

   If a price ceiling of $10 per unit is implemented, will social welfare increase? Will Zeon Industries remain in operation?

6. Under what conditions should a competitive firm shut down in the short run?

| # The Comeback of Caterpillar

Rate of Return

1. In 1986 Caterpillar invested $1.8 Billion US dollars in a plant-modernization program. The program focused on:
   - Just-in-time inventory systems
   - Factory automation
   - A network of computerized machine tools
   - Flexible manufacturing systems

Hint: A rate of return calculation compares capital expenditures to the future stream of revenue generated by this expenditure. However, we must recognize that future revenues are of less value than current revenues (think about inflation, risk, and the wait time required). Caterpillar must use a rate of return calculation to justify this significant capital investment.

Appendix 5.1

Price Discrimination*

Price discrimination describes in general a method that can be used by some sellers, in particular those who have some degree of monopoly power, to tailor their prices to the specific purchasing situations or circumstances of their buyers. Specifically, price discrimination is defined as the practice by a seller of charging different prices to the same buyer at different times or to different buyers for the same good or service at the same time, without corresponding differences in cost. For analytical purposes, it is convenient to distinguish among three degrees of differential pricing.

First-Degree Price Discrimination

In differential pricing of the first degree, the seller charges the same buyer a different price for each unit bought, thereby extracting the consumer's maximum willingness to pay **reservation price**. By shading the price down to the buyer for each additional unit purchased, the seller obtains larger total revenue than if the same price per unit were charged for all units bought. Unfortunately for managers, first-degree price discrimination (also called perfect price discrimination) is extremely difficult to implement because it requires the firm to know precisely the maximum price each consumer is willing and able to pay for alternative quantities of the firm's product.

Nonetheless, some service-related businesses, including car dealers, mechanics, and lawyers, successfully practice a form of first-degree price discrimination. For example, when a firm sells a product at an auction, it is attempting to get consumers to bid up the price so that the consumer with the highest reservation price purchases the good. Also, most car dealers post sticker prices on cars that are well above the dealer's actual marginal

---

* Prepared by Dr. Farrouk Zandi.

cost, but offer "discounts" to customers on a case-by-case basis. The best salespersons are able to size up customers to determine the minimum discount necessary to get them to drive away with the car. In this way they are able to charge different prices to different consumers depending on each consumer's willingness and ability to pay. This practice permits them to sell more cars and to earn higher profits than they would if they charged the same price to all consumers. Similarly, most professionals also charge rates for their services that vary, depending on their assessment of customers' willingness and ability to pay.

Figure 5A.1 shows how first-degree price discrimination works. Each point on the market demand curve reflects the maximum price that consumers would be willing to pay for each incremental unit of the output, i.e., reservation price. Consumers start out with 0 units of the good, and the firm can sell the first incremental unit for $100. Since the demand curve slopes downward, the maximum price the firm can charge for each additional unit declines, ultimately to $80 at an output of 80 units. The first unit goes to the customer with the highest reservation price, $100. The firm would sell the first unit for $100 and capture all of the consumer surplus. The second unit is sold to the person with the second-highest reservation price of $99, and similarly, the third unit goes for $98, etc. This way, the seller charges each customer his or her highest reservation price for that unit, which is the height of the demand curve. The difference between each point on the demand curve and the firm's marginal cost represents the profits earned on each incremental unit sold. Thus, the shaded area

Figure 5A.1: First Degree Price Discrimination

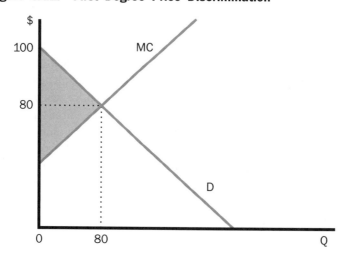

between the demand curve and the firm's marginal cost curve reflects the firm's total profit when it charges each consumer the maximum price he or she will pay for small increments of output between 100 and 80 units. This strategy allows the firm to earn the maximum possible profits. Notice that consumers receive no consumer surplus on the 5 units they purchase: the firm extracts all surplus under first-degree price discrimination. This practice is also referred to as *perfect price* discrimination.

Second-Degree Price Discrimination

More practical and common is second-degree price discrimination. Differential pricing of the second degree, more commonly known as volume discounting or quantity discounting, involves the same underlying principle as first-degree differential pricing, except that the seller charges different prices for blocks of units instead of for individual units. By doing so, the firm will extract part, but not all, of the consumer surplus. By charging a higher price for smaller quantities, the seller receives higher total revenue than if a single price were charged. This practice is very common in the electric utility industry, where firms typically charge a higher rate on the first hundred kilowatt hours of electricity used than on subsequent units. Thus, the firm charges different prices to different consumers, but does not need to know specific characteristics of individual consumers.

For example, suppose that the firm of Figure 5A.2 sets the price of $24 per unit on the first 6 units of the product and the price of $18 per unit on the next batch or block of 6 units of the product.

The total revenue of the firm would then be *$144* ($24 × 6) from the first batch of 6 units of the product and *$108* ($18 × 6) from the second batch or block of 6 units, for the overall total revenue of *$252 and profit of $132* (TR − TC = $252 − $10 × 12), as compared to *$160* with first-degree price discrimination and *$100* without any price discrimination. Thus, consumers end up with some consumer surplus, which means that second-degree price discrimination yields lower profits for the firm than it would have earned if it were able to perfectly price discriminate. Nonetheless, profits are still higher than they would have been if the firm had used the simple strategy of charging the same price for all units sold. In effect, consumers purchasing small quantities (or alternatively, those having higher marginal valuations) pay higher prices than those who purchase in bulk.

Third-Degree Price Discrimination

The final type of price discrimination is commonly practised by firms that recognize that the demand for their product differs systematically across

Figure 5A.2: Second Degree Price Discrimination

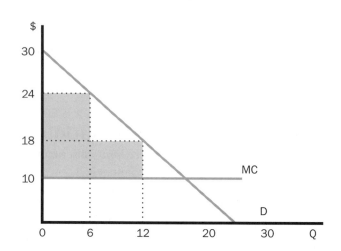

consumers in different demographic groups. In these instances firms can profit by charging different groups of consumers different prices for the same product, a strategy referred to as *third-degree price discrimination.*

Differential pricing of the third degree occurs when the seller segregates buyers according to income, geographic location, individual tastes, kinds of uses for the product, or other criteria, and charges different prices to each group or market despite equivalent costs in serving them. Thus, as long as the demand elasticities among different buyers are unequal, it will be profitable to the seller to group the buyers into separate classes according to elasticity, and charge each class a separate price. This is what is referred to, more generally, as *market segmentation* — that is, the carving up of a total market into subgroups from the standpoint of pricing.

There are many examples of third-degree price discrimination. One of these is provided by electrical power companies, which usually charge higher rates to residential than to commercial users of electricity. The reason for this is that the price elasticity of demand for electricity is higher for the latter than for the former because the latter could generate their own electricity if the price rose above the cost of building and running their own power plants. This choice is generally not available to households. Other examples of third-degree price discrimination are the higher air fares charged by airlines to business travellers than to vacationers, the higher price charged by telephone companies during business hours than at other times, and the higher prices charged for many services to all customers, except children and the aged.

To practise price discrimination effectively, two conditions must be satisfied:

1. **Market Segmentation.** The seller must be able to partition (segment) the total market by segregating buyers into groups or submarkets according to elasticity. Profits can be enhanced by charging a different price in each submarket.
2. **Market Sealing.** The seller must be able to prevent — or natural circumstances must exist that will prevent — any significant resale of goods from a lower-priced submarket to a higher one. Any resale (leakage) by buyers between submarkets tends to neutralize the effect of different prices and narrow the effective price structure toward a single price to all buyers. To see how the third-degree price discrimination enhances profits, we will consider a firm with market power that can charge two different prices to two groups of consumers and the marginal revenues of selling to group A and group B are MR_A and MR_B, respectively. The basic profit-maximizing rule is to produce output such that marginal revenue is equal to marginal cost. This principle is still valid, but the presence of two marginal revenue functions introduces some ambiguity. The condition for maximum profit using price discrimination is that the marginal revenue be the same in all markets and equal to marginal cost. That is, the additional revenue gained from selling one more unit in market A shall be equal to the additional revenue obtained

Figure 5A.3: Third Degree Price Discrimination

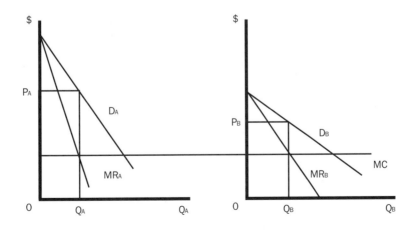

by selling one more unit in market B. If the MRs are not equal, the firm can increase its revenue and profit by selling more to the market with the higher MR.

Figure 5A.3 illustrates that the customers are willing to pay a higher price than those in market B, perhaps because there is less competition in market A. Less competition implies higher mark-up. In contrast, in market B the lower price represents lower mark-up, which is the symptom of a weaker market power, which in turn can be a function a greater competition in that market.

6

Alternative Market Structures, Business Strategy, and Public Policy

Introduction

In the previous chapter, the discussion revolved around two possible forms of market structure that were at opposite poles. In perfect competition, there were many sellers, each producing a standardized (commodity-type) product, and there was complete freedom of entry to, and exit from, the industry. Firms would have no market power; they must simply accept the going price for their product, and no real issues of business strategy would arise. In monopoly, on the other hand, there was a single seller producing a unique or essential product, and barriers to entry to the industry were completely effective. The firm therefore had total market power, constrained only by demand conditions. In effect, the firm could simply "charge what the market will bear". Again, though, there would no important issues of business strategy. In this case, presumably, the managers of the firm could live with this situation. They would just sit back and rake in the profits.

In the present chapter, we look at some other intermediate forms of market structure where strategic issues do arise. These would include situations of **monopolistic competition**, **oligopoly**, and **duopoly**. The chapter also provides a brief introduction to so-called **game theory**, which is one of the economist's primary tools for analyzing strategic situations, and looks at potential public policy solutions — both in situations in which less than perfectly competitive market structures have arisen, and where no market solution seems possible at all.

Monopolistic Competition

One type of possible market structure that is usually mentioned in economics textbooks is the case of so-called **monopolistic competition**.[1] Obviously this is a hybrid of our extreme two types. The basic idea is that of a **differentiated product**. By advertising different production methods, style and design characteristics, or whatever, each firm in the industry is able to convince consumers that its particular product is unique or special, even though it performs much the same kind of function as the products of other firms. For example, toothpaste Brand A "whitens teeth", toothpaste Brand B "prevents cavities", and so on. So each firm is a "monopolist" in a sense, in terms of its own unique product. At the same time, however, such firms must be aware of competitors who also have a "unique" product, but is actually a close substitute for their own. The following are characteristics of a monopolistically competitive industry:

---

[1] Edward Chamberlin, *The Theory of Monopolistic Competition: A Re-Orientation of the Theory of Value* (Cambridge, MA: Harvard University Press, 1933).

- There are many potential competitors.

- Each firm produces a differentiated product.

- There is freedom of entry to and exit from the industry as a whole.

- Firms have market power over their own particular product line but must be aware of competition from rivals who produce similar items.

There will now be a number of strategic issues for managers to deal with, primarily in terms of positioning the product and establishing a brand name. However, a key element here is that there is still freedom of entry to, and exit from, this industry. There are no effective barriers to entry to the industry for any similar (albeit differentiated) products. Presumably, therefore, entry will indeed occur if existing firms are earning excess profits, and eventually the profits must get competed away after all. This is the "competitive" part of monopolistic competition. Much of the retail sector in the developed world exhibits the characteristics of monopolistic competition. Restaurants are an excellent example. It is relatively easy to enter and exit the industry, but very few restaurants seem to make a substantial profit over the longer term.

Given a downward-sloping demand curve, and the associated marginal revenue curve, the short-run equilibrium position of the monopolistic competitor will be just the same as that of the monopolist, as illustrated in Figure 6.1. Positive short-run profits will be earned.

However, the very existence of short-run profits will attract other firms (producing differentiated but similar products) into the market, and the market share of the original firm will be reduced. This is shown by a shift in the downward-sloping demand curve back and to the left. The final outcome is that it will shift all the way over to the left until it is just tangent to the average cost curve, as shown in Figure 6.2. The firm is still keeping the MR = MC rule (marginal revenue equals marginal cost) at this point, but the price is only just covering average costs, and no profit is being made. Also, the firm is producing a level of output *below* the optimal plant size (which would be at the minimum point of the AC curve).

From the point of view of the neoclassical economist, even though the firms will be making no economic profit in the long run, this does not mean that the level of output and average costs that emerge in a monopolistically competitive industry will be the social optimum. Once again, output will be lower and costs higher than in the equivalent perfectly competitive industry. This is because the effort that the individual firms are making to differentiate their products must cost something and use up resources. The "sub-optimal" level of output reflects precisely these spurious costs of product differentiation. A possible counter-argument is that consumers are at least given choices, such as different types of restaurants, clothing, etc. It can be argued that choice offers social value (utility).

Figure 6.1: Short-Run Equilibrium for the Monopolistic Competitor

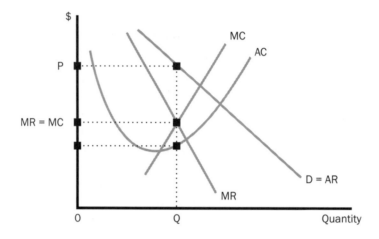

Figure 6.2: Long-Run Equilibrium for the Monopolistic Competitor

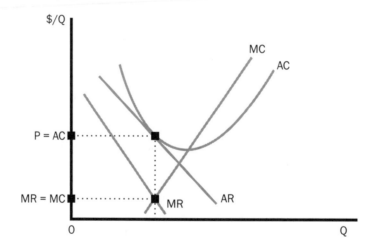

Oligopoly

Perhaps the more general case of what is generically called **imperfect competition**,[2] however, is that of **oligopoly**, which literally means an industry with only a "few sellers". Ironically, this would be an industry in which there actually is head-to-head competition in the everyday sense of this term, rather than in the specialized meaning that it has in economics. An extreme case of oligopoly would be **duopoly**, meaning an industry with only two competitors. The characteristics of an oligopolistic market structure are:

- only a few sellers, each with substantial market share

- either a standardized or differentiated product

- relatively effective barriers to entry to the industry, at least in the short run

- strategic interaction between the players becomes the key issue

Oligopoly encompasses a wide range of large capital- and knowledge-intensive industries, such as automotive, steel, petrochemicals, and pharmaceuticals. Such things as capital and knowledge intensity, as well as control of distribution channels, act as barriers to new industry entrants.

Moreover, the above characteristics obviously do seem to describe the type of environment that business students typically learn to deal with in their courses on strategic management. The way in which economists tend to deal with these strategic issues is by drawing on the concepts of game theory, as discussed in the next section of this chapter.

An Introduction to "Game Theory"

The use of game theory to study strategic behavior is often introduced with a famous non-economic example known as the **prisoner's dilemma**, first introduced by the Hungarian mathematician John von Neumann.[3] We imagine two individuals who have been arrested for collaboration in some crime, and are in jail in separate cells. The situation is that if neither of the prisoners confesses to the crime, there will be no evidence against them and they both go free. A prisoner who confesses will have a reduced sentence of five years, and a prisoner who does not confess and is nonetheless found guilty will serve a sentence of 10 years. The prisoners cannot

---

[2] Joan Robinson, *The Economics of Imperfect Competition* (London: Macmillan, 1933).

[3] John von Neumann and Oskar Morgenstern, *Theory of Games and Economic Behavior* (Princeton: Princeton University Press, 1944).

collude with each other, so this is an example of a **non-cooperative game**. What should each prisoner do to maximize their individual self-interest, taking into account the fact that they do not know what the other person's strategy will be? One way of analyzing this situation is to construct a **pay-off matrix** for each of the different strategies, as in Table 6.1.

Obviously, the best solution for both prisoners A and B is for neither of them to confess; then neither will stay in jail. Their payoff is **{0, 0}**, and zero is a good thing here. However, they have no way of communicating an agreement with each other not to confess. Now, suppose that A decides *not* to confess (hoping that B will do the same). If B then confesses (in order to get a reduction in the sentence to five years), A will actually serve 10 years. The payoff is **{-5, -10}**. A similar situation would arise if B confesses and A does not. A conservative strategy for both players, to minimize the damage regardless of what the other player does, is actually for both to confess. Technically, this is known as a **maximin** strategy. If both players follow such a strategy, their payoff is **{-5, -5}**.

The equilibrium reached in this game, which is not actually the best solution that could be obtained in other circumstances (e.g., in a **cooperative game**), is an example of a so-called **Nash equilibrium**, named after the famous American mathematician John Nash, whose life and "beautiful mind" were once the subject of a Hollywood movie.[4] This is a very common, indeed ubiquitous, idea in game theory and economics. The Nash equilibrium is the equilibrium reached when all players pursue the best

Table 6.1:   The Prisoner's Dilemma

		Prisoner A	
		Confess	Don't Confess
Prisoner B	Confess	-5, -5	-5, -10
	Don't Confess	-10, -5	0, 0

[4] Sylvia Nasser, *A Beautiful Mind: A Biography of John Forbes Nash Jr.* (New York: Simon and Schuster, 1998).

strategy for themselves, in the sense of minimizing the downside *regardless* of what the other players do. Therefore, the solution to the prisoner's dilemma is a clear example of a Nash equilibrium.

We now turn to a more specifically economic example. Suppose we have an example of a duopoly (two firms) in a particular industry, and they reach a **collusive agreement** with each other to "fix" prices in the industry. In principle, the idea is that both players understand that there are effective barriers to entry to this market. They therefore realize that if they get together on price they can jointly maximize profits, rather than beating each other up in active competition. In a case where there were more than two firms as parties to such an agreement, it would be called a **cartel**. (For example, OPEC, the Organization of Petroleum Exporting Countries, is a cartel, albeit involving producing *nations* rather than firms per se.)

The problem is that, once such an agreement has been reached, there are powerful incentives for both parties to "cheat". If firm *A* decides to undercut the agreement with special discounts negotiated "under-the-table" with their customers, and *B* faithfully sticks to the agreement, *A* will gain market share and hence profits, and *B* will lose out. It will be the other way around if *B* decides to cheat and *A* does not. Suppose the payoff matrix in this situation looks something like that in Table 6.2, where we have inserted some arbitrary numbers.

Again, the best overall solution would be the cooperative result, where both firms stick to the agreement and carve up the market between them; both enjoy profits of **+4** (say $4 million). However, if *A*, for example, decides to cheat, and *B* does not, *A* will get the whole market and will make twice the profit, at **+8**, while *B* will be wiped out with losses of **−4**. Similarly, if *B* decides to cheat and *A* does not, *B* will gain large profits, and *A* will be the loser. So the Nash equilibrium remains the most likely

Table 6.2:   A Collusive Pricing Agreement

		Firm A	
		Cheat	**Don't Cheat**
Firm B	**Cheat**	0, 0	+8, −4
	Don't Cheat	−4, +8	+4, +4

result. Both players cheat and end up with zero profits (but at least no losses). Something of this kind is thought to explain why cartels and collusive agreements do frequently break down in practice.

Another fairly realistic situation is that of a duopolistic industry, in which both of the players might be able to increase their market share by advertising expenditure. Soft drink A "tastes better" than soft drink B, and so on. We suppose that advertising will determine which brand consumers will buy, but not the total amount spent on the product. A pay-off matrix in this case might be like the one illustrated in Table 6.3. The best strategy (collectively) would be to not spend any money on advertising. The firms would then share the market, and both make profits of {+6, +6}. However, if one firm does not invest in a marketing campaign and the other firm does, the non-spending firm will lose out and their rivals will make all the profits. What will be likely to happen, then, is that they both compete in an expensive advertising blitz. They will both make some profits at {+1, +1}, but most of their gains are chewed up by "wasteful" advertising expenditures. Some would argue that this is exactly what happens between well-known brands of soft drinks in reality. Stop the advertising campaigns and everyone would be better off — the companies, consumers, and society as a whole — with resources reallocated to more productive and socially useful activities.

At this point the reader will be wondering whether, looking at matters from the point of view of a business executive, there is any possibility of escape from the underlying prisoner's dilemma. One constructive point that can be made is that all of the examples above are implicitly **one-shot games**, in which there is no chance for learning behavior. In a **repeated game**, the prospects for a cooperative solution may not be so dismal. If a game is "played" over and over in each period (say each accounting period,

Table 6.3:   An Advertising Game

		Firm A	
		Advertise	**Don't Advertise**
Firm B	**Advertise**	+1, +1	+9, −4
	Don't Advertise	−4, +9	+6, +6

such as a quarter or a year), then, for example, a so-called **tit-for-tat strategy**, elaborated by the Canadian mathematician, Anatole Rapoport, might work. This means a **credible threat** will follow whatever **strategic move** is made by the rival in the current period, the next time the game is played. For example, in the collusive pricing game, if the rival cheats the first time, threaten to "punish" them by following the same strategy in the next round; but, if they do not cheat, then "reward" them by also not cheating. In this way, presuming that one of the rivals does not go under at some point, it is possible to learn about the other player's intentions. Some game theorists have claimed, in fact, that this tit for tat strategy, if feasible, is the optimal course of action most of the time.[5]

At the risk of being repetitious, however, we return now to the Nash equilibrium concept one more time, as a means of leading into the subject matter of the next section of this chapter. We now introduce the notion of a **contestable market**. Imagine that there is currently a monopolist operating in a particular market, and that the firm could therefore, in principle, extract monopoly profits from the consumers. However, further suppose that the barriers to entry are not really all that severe, and that if high prices are charged and large profits are made, a rival firm may be tempted to enter the industry to get a piece of the action. This is what is meant by a contestable market. Consider the pay-off matrix in this situation, as indicated in Table 6.4. In this example, the incumbent, *A*, has two strategic choices. These are to set a high price in the hope of earning "monopoly" profits, or to set a low price in the hope of forestalling entry by *B*. The challenger, *B*, also has two choices, to enter or not to enter. Suppose *A* sets a high price, and *B* enters at a relatively lower price and takes away the market. The payoff might be {**+10, −15**} with *B* a winner and *A* a

---

Table 6.4:   A Contestable Market

		A	
		High Price	**Low Price**
B	**Enter**	+10, −15	−10, −5
	Don't Enter	+5, +15	+5, +5

---

[5] Robert Axelrod, *The Evolution of Cooperation* (New York: Basic Books, 1984).

loser. If *A* sets a high price, and *B* decides not to enter, the payoff is {+5, +15} with *A* the winner, and *B*'s gains coming from whatever other industry they were in to begin with. If *A* sets a low price, and *B* enters, the payoff is {–10, –5}; they wipe each other out in a price war. The Nash equilibrium is therefore the couplet {+5, +5}, where *B* does not enter the industry but *A* sets a low price and receives relatively low profits. Again, this is not the most satisfactory result from the point of view of *joint* profit maximization, but is likely to occur because of the incentives each player separately faces.

Case Study 8

"OPEC Disbands"
Geneva; February 7, 2023

The Organization of Petroleum Exporting Countries (OPEC) officially disbanded today. In many respects it is a direct result of their own initial successes. The period of instability in the early years of this century saw oil prices increase dramatically. The process was accelerated by the rapid economic growth of China and India. The interplay of market forces then resulted in the development of new sources of supply. Also, technology identified alternative energy sources. Oil is now at its lowest price, in real terms, in more than a century. As a result, there is little need for OPEC, essentially because of the inability of OPEC to control the price of oil. Oil can now be considered as one among many other commodities that have experienced systematic declines in relative prices over a prolonged period of time, such as cocoa, tea, and coffee.

There is another point of interest in this example in that although this industry is superficially a monopoly, because the market is contestable, the market price does end up closer to what it would presumably be under perfect competition. The suggestion therefore seems to be that the *actual* competitive situation in a particular market cannot be judged by market share alone. Nonetheless, this is what is quite often done in practice in public policy decision making, especially in the area of competition policy, which is the subject of the next section.

Competition Policy

As we have seen from the above discussion, a key idea of neoclassical economics is that a competitive market is in the best interests of consumers, and in the public interest generally. On the other hand, in practice, the situation in many industries is actually that of imperfect competition. One development in the regulation of the marketplace in many jurisdictions, therefore, has been actually to put legal remedies in place to prevent the development of a monopoly or oligopoly. This type of action falls under the rubric of **competition policy** and, from the point of view of management, is one more strategic issue to be dealt with. That is say, business executives must be aware of what the legal rules are in their particular jurisdiction, and make sure that the various strategic actions taken to enhance their firm's position do not fall foul of the law. In a sense, where competition policy is strong, this is a question of economic theory being taken very seriously indeed, to the point of affecting both the legal and business environment. One awkwardness in the application of competition policy, however, is that market share per se often tends to be the main criterion of whether legal remedies should be applied. That is to say, if a particular firm does achieve a large market share, it is regarded as *prima facie* evidence that this is against the public interest. The contestable market example above, however, has shown that this assumption may not always be warranted. We will discuss another argument along these lines in our discussion of the concept of **creative destruction**, below.

Competition policy is usually called **"antitrust policy"** in the USA because of the historical resonance of the term, and it is usually thought to be fairly active in that country as compared with other nations. Two examples that most people will have heard of are the breakup of the *AT&T telephone monopoly* in the 1980s, and the *Microsoft case* in the 1990s. The Microsoft case was also interesting because it involved a number of the key issues raised in this book — for example, that economics is now global. Microsoft experienced as many, or more, problems with European competition policy as it did with actions in the USA.

119

Case Study 9

"Global Warming: The Crisis That
Never Happened"
Kyoto; February 23, 2024

At the time it seemed like a real crisis.
It was supposed to be a classic case
of economic externalities, or third-party
effects. Negative externalities occur
when market activity creates impacts
on participants who are not directly
affected by the particular transaction,
in this case "global warming" caused
by industrial pollution. The science
seemed very secure at the time and
appeared to provide a basis for action.
An international treaty was formulated,
the Kyoto Accord, which required all of
the major countries to sign on. A treaty
was necessary because, at that time,
there were few international institutions
with enforcement powers. The former
United States of America, now the
Northland Republic, and Russia, now a
province in the Euro Union, refused to
sign the agreement. In retrospect, this
was the correct decision. As Dr. Smith
of Potsdam University has indicated, "It
was an example of a problem where
international institutions were unable to
undertake the proper scientific analysis
or to mobilize the international community effectively around what seemed to
be a critical international issue."

Externalities, Public Goods, and Natural Monopolies

If the main goal of competition policy is to enforce a market solution, or at least to move as far as possible in the direction of the perfectly competitive ideal, there are also some scenarios in which a market solution may not actually be possible. In this section, we discuss the concepts of **externalities** and **public goods**, which traditionally, even for supporters of *laissez-faire*, have provided respectable grounds for "government intervention" in the operation of market forces, at least in some cases.

An externality exists where the production or consumption of a good creates either a benefit or a cost for some third party not directly involved in its consumption or production. If there is a benefit, this is a **positive externality**; if there is a cost, it is a **negative externality**. If my neighbor keeps a nice backyard (e.g., with a lawn, flowers, trees, etc.), that is a positive externality to me as I can enjoy seeing it without having to do the work. On the other hand, if my neighbor plays loud rock music at 3:00 a.m. every morning, that is a negative externality. Pollution would be an example of a negative externality in production. A positive externality in production might be, for example, if a number of firms using a particular technology set up in the same location. Among other things, this will attract a suitably qualified workforce to the area. So a firm's private decision to locate in a particular area benefits all the other firms to some extent, without their having to pay for it.

From the point of view of the optimal allocation of resources and static efficiency, the problem is that market prices obviously do not reflect either the benefits or costs of externalities. Therefore, there is probably too little produced of a good or service with positive externalities (from the point of view of the social optimum), and too much of a good or service with negative externalities. In these cases, it can no longer be claimed that market forces are optimally allocating resources. There is, therefore, at least in principle, a case for government intervention in the marketplace in these situations. For example, it may be possible to levy fines or taxes on firms who pollute the environment, or pay subsidies to other firms to locate in a particular area. There must be some doubt, however, as to how far the system of taxes and subsidies actually in place in many jurisdictions really does move the economy any closer to the elusive optimum.

A **public good**, meanwhile, is a good or service that has the twin characteristics of **non-excludability** and **non-rivalry** in consumption. That is to say, once it exists, no one can be prevented from consuming it; but also, when one individual consumes the good, this does not prevent all other individuals from consuming it at the same time. The problem is that even if a particular public good is a "good thing" from society's point of view, it will not be provided by the market, as no one can charge a price

Case Study 10

"The United States Closes Its Last Public Hospital"
Washington, DC; February 7, 2042

Senator Rappaport announced today that the last public hospital would close this month. He said that this is a significant milestone, "Hospitals used to be considered a public service, but our view of these institutions has changed dramatically over the past few years. Services can be delivered faster, cheaper, and with better quality by private-sector providers. This is particularly true with the application of telemedicine, which allows services, including sophisticated operations, to be undertaken from anywhere in the world." Senator Rappaport suggested that the new role of government is to provide a regulatory environment and selected funding to ensure that the medical system functions well, is properly financed, and provides reasonable access for all American citizens.

for it. The classic example that is usually given is that of national defense. Because all citizens benefit from this service, they could not be excluded from receiving it even if they refuse to pay. The textbooks also frequently quote the example of a lighthouse on a rocky shoreline. All the ships in danger can see the light at the same time, and they cannot be prevented from seeing it in order that they might be charged a price for this service. Evidently, the existence of public goods in this sense tends to suggest that they should be provided by the state, with the costs defrayed by general taxation. On the other hand, it is obvious that not all items that are actually provided by the state fall into this category. For example, postal services are not non-rival or non-excludable. There are evidently also a number of other political or social reasons for various industries being included in the public sector at any point in time. The argument that a particular good or service is a public good would simply make a strong addition to the case. Note that if public goods do exist, another alternative to actual state provision is for the government to provide the funds, but then to license the actual activity out to the private sector. This might be the preferred method of dealing with the question of public goods on the part of those economists who generally favor "market" solutions, but would bring in its own set of problems in terms of accountability and the public interest.

Another situation in which it may not be possible to find a market solution (at least not a *competitive* market solution) is the case of so-called natural monopoly, defined earlier (in Chapter 2) as a situation in which both average and marginal costs are continually declining.

It is often suggested that industries requiring large capital investment, such as utilities like electricity, natural gas, water, etc., and some types of transportation, such as railroads, fit into this category. In fact, the natural monopoly, if it exists, could operate perfectly well on its own terms as a private monopoly. The managers would just apply the MR = MC rule, and the price charged would be the monopoly price **Pm** in Figure 6.3. The firm would then earn permanent monopoly profits. However, as already discussed, this private monopoly solution involves a higher price and lower level of output than would be regarded as the social optimum. Therefore, as there cannot be more than one firm in the industry, there are likely to be demands either for it to be nationalized (taken over by the government) or, if left in the private sector, regulated in some way. In short, the existence of natural monopoly would be another argument, in addition to those about externalities and public goods, for there to be some sort of government intervention.

There is a problem, however, if the firm is forced to supply the socially optimal level of output at P = MC with price **Pmc**. As marginal cost is everywhere below average costs, the firm must definitely make losses in this case. For a nationalized industry, it would be theoretically possible to force the enterprise to use **marginal cost pricing**, and make up the losses via subsidies from general taxation. However, the political difficulties with this are obvious. Another solution, which is actually seen in many jurisdictions (e.g., for utilities) is to regulate (rather than nationalize) the industry and to mandate **average cost pricing.** This means to set prices at **Pac** in Figure 6.3 (perhaps with some small mark-up to allow the firm to make some profit). This will not yield the socially optimal level of output, but will make the industry come closer to it, and is much more likely to be acceptable politically.

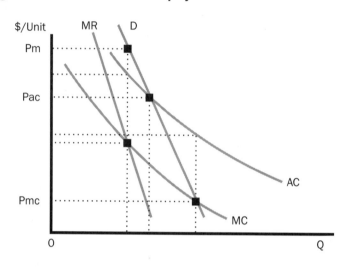

Figure 6.3:   A Natural Monopoly

Schumpeter's Defense of Monopoly/ Imperfect Competition

As noted, the basic idea of competition policy (and even of some of the government interventions required to correct for externalities, etc.) is to try to make actual markets work in a way that is as close as possible to the perfectly competitive idea. However, we should also point out that not all economists, including some of the staunchest defenders of capitalism, have believed that this idea of static efficiency is actually the most conducive to a dynamic capitalist economy. Famously, Joseph Schumpeter, for example, who is well known for his theory of economic development, focusing on innovation and entrepreneurship,[6] defended monopoly and imperfect competition on the grounds that any excess profits earned in a given industry would serve to stimulate innovation by other entrepreneurs, designed to bypass the original monopolists and make their product obsolete. This is known as the process of **creative destruction**.[7] For example, if there is a monopoly in railroads, this will stimulate someone to invent the automobile,

---

[6] Joseph Schumpeter, *The Theory of Economic Development: An Inquiry into Profits, Capital, Credit, Interest, and The Business Cycle*, edited by J.E. Elliot (New Brunswick, NJ: Transactions Publishers, 1983 [1934]).

[7] Joseph Schumpeter, *Capitalism, Socialism and Democracy* (London: Routledge, 1994 [1942]).

Case Study 11

"Schumpeter Wins the First
Posthumous Nobel Prize in Economics"
Stockholm; November 20, 2015

Joseph Schumpeter was awarded this year's Nobel Prize in economics. The key contribution for meriting the prestigious award is his work in the field of economic sociology and the theory of economic development. Schumpeter's work implies that the standard neoclassical model of economic behavior is limited in its capacity to understand and predict behavior. Recent work in the field of neoclassical economics has become ever more mathematical and is predicated upon notions of rational behavior and optimization. These notions have led to very sophisticated mathematical modeling of economic processes. However, Schumpeter's work shows that a deeper understanding of economic behavior must involve an evolutionary or sociological perspective. Economic activity depends on complex social structures and motivations that have evolved over long of periods of time, and on the institutions and incentives that are associated with them. Economic growth is dependent on processes driven by profit seeking, development, innovation, adoption, adaptation, and diffusion that are, in some respects, generic. Economic development is based not only on static optimization, but also on the complex motives of economic agents as they interact with subsets of other

Case 11 continued

agents and, above all, on the spirit of entrepreneurship. Nonetheless, the Committee noted that there are continuing efforts to provide solid mathematical foundations for Schumpeterian economics, which are in some respects consistent with the traditional neoclassical approach. The committee suggested that Dr. Joseph Schumpeter may have been the greatest economist of all time, which justifies this first posthumous award.

and so on. Note that the argument is *not* that the monopoly profits earned by the incumbent will be spent on R & D, but that *others* will always be searching for innovative ways to get around the existing situation. In any event, the argument suggests that a regime of static efficiency may not actually be the best launching pad for growth and innovation.

There are counterarguments to the above, of course. It could alternatively be argued that a regime of many competitors *is*, in fact, the most stimulating environment for innovation, as expressed in the phrase, "Innovate or die".[8] Maybe such a regime also stimulates innovation in the sense that the more enterprising firm is attempting to *escape* from a situation of perfect competition.[9] Even these arguments are inherently dynamic, however, and quite far moved from a situation of "equilibrium" in which the status quo is maintained, where nothing changes and all firms earn zero profits.

[8] Michael Porter, *The Competitive Advantage of Nations* (New York: The Free Press, 1990).

[9] Peter Howitt, "Endogenous growth, productivity and economic policy: a progress report", *International Productivity Monitor* (Spring 2004) 8: 3–12.

Chapter Summary

- Monopolistic competition and oligopoly are more realistic models of the marketplace.

- In both cases, there can be some product differentiation.

- The key difference between these two models is in the ease of entry into the industry. It is easier in monopolistic competition, and more difficult in oligopoly.

- It seems that almost anyone can start, for example, a restaurant, or food stall, in either the developing or developed world. Ease of entry makes life very difficult for the businessperson. It is very hard to earn excess profits if anyone can copy your concept and open a similar restaurant right next door.

- In an oligopoly, entrepreneurs see the opportunity, but barriers to entry make it difficult to act. For example, the pharmaceutical industry is very profitable, and the industry looks desirable; but the entry barriers are enormous (high research and development costs, regulatory approval processes, and access to distribution channels).

- Game theory is used by economists to study strategic behavior in oligopolistic markets.

- While many businesspeople have never studied game theory, they apply the principles every day. Businesspeople are always concerned with the reactions of competitors. For example, if I lower the price for my consulting services in Mexico, how will my competitors respond?

- A free market is a powerful tool for producers and consumers to independently arrive at an equilibrium price and quantity that clears the market. However, "market failure" is also possible.

- Negative externalities are third-party effects to a transaction. When the air becomes polluted due to industrial production, I am, literally, a third-party bystander to the transaction. Although not directly involved in this market, I am harmed by both the production and the sales process.

- It is possible that the market produces too little of a good or service that has benefits to society. It might be argued, for example, that society produces a less than optimal level of research and development and training, which in itself would be a positive externality.

- The existence of positive and negative externalities provides a rationale for government intervention. However, government intervention might also make the situation worse.

- It is usually conceded that some activities need to be undertaken by government. These public goods cannot or should not be left to private producers, public parks, national defense, nuclear power, etc.

- However, not all goods provided by the public sector are strictly "public goods". The degree of government involvement differs from society to society. In the USA, much of the healthcare system is delivered by the private sector. In many other parts of the world, healthcare is regarded as an entitlement provided by the state.

Problems

1. Suppose all the firms in a monopolistically competitive industry were merged into one large firm. Would that new firm produce as many different brands? Would it produce only a single brand?

2. Why has the OPEC oil cartel succeeded in raising prices substantially, while the CIPEC copper cartel, for example, has not? What conditions are necessary for a successful cartel? What organizational problems must a cartel overcome?

3. What is a "strategic move"? Can the development of a certain kind of reputation be a strategic move?

4. Do you agree with the following statement?

   The Schumpeterian concept of *creative destruction* is the main explanation offered by economists as to why monopoly or imperfect competition is an undesirable market structure from the social point of view.

5. Two firms are in the market for chocolate confectionery. Each can choose to go for the high end of the market (high quality) or the low end (low quality). Resulting profits are given by the following payoff matrix:

		Firm 2	
		Low	High
Firm 1	Low	−20, −30	900, 600
	High	100, 800	50, 50

    (a) What outcomes, if any, are Nash equilibria?

    (b) If the manager of each firm is conservative and each follows a maximin strategy, what will be the outcome?

    (c) What is the cooperative outcome?

    (d) Which firm benefits most from the cooperative outcome? How much would that firm need to offer the other to persuade it to collude?

6.   What is the difference between monopolistic competition and perfect competition?

7.   How can economies of scale in production result in an oligopoly?

8.   What is a Nash equilibrium?

9.   Assume firm A and firm B are competing for customers and that if they both advertise, they would each earn $30 million in profit. If neither advertises, they each earn $50 million in profits. But if one advertises and the other doesn't, the firm advertising earns $40 million in profit while the other earns $20 million in profit. What is each firm's dominant strategy and the result of this choice?

Case Study Questions | **The Comeback of Caterpillar**

Differentiation

1. Caterpillar broadened its product line: from 150 to 300 models and lightweight machines for small-scale owner-operators. Why was this differentiation important for the revitalization of Caterpillar's strategy?

2. How would this impact Caterpillar's demand function and the elasticity of demand?

Hint: "Caterpillar needed to reevaluate its product mix because heavy equipment was not selling well." A broader product line can increase demand and give Caterpillar greater control over its market.

Case Study Questions Continued

Market Share

1. Why is market share critical for large, capital-intensive industries such as Caterpillar?
2. How did Caterpillar lose market share to Komatsu?
3. What strategies did Caterpillar use to regain market share?

Hint: Capital intensive industries have high fixed costs. Volume demand is required to spread fixed cost overhead over as many sales units as possible.

Market Structure

1. Is it reasonable to argue that Caterpillar had a near monopoly prior to the arrival of Komatsu?
2. Which market structure currently best describes this industry (purely competitive, monopoly, monopolistic competition, and oligopoly)?
3. Use the language of game theory to describe the interaction between Komatsu and Caterpillar.

Hint: In purely competitive markets firms are "price takers." As a result, firms pay little attention to the behavior of other firms in a purely competitive market. By definition, the firm in a monopoly industry maintains full control over the market. The other market structures require firms to evaluate decisions on the basis of the potential responses of rivals. In a real sense this is equivalent to a sporting team evaluating the behavior of the opposing team in a competitive game.

Case Study Questions Continued

Theory of the Firm

1. What role has outsourcing played in Caterpillar's strategy?
2. Why are joint ventures an important component of Caterpillar's strategy?
3. Caterpillar uses a network of distributors. Should Caterpillar consider establishing its own distribution system?
4. How has the employee involvement program impacted the structure of Caterpillar and its competitive position?

Hint: The use of joint ventures and networks permits Caterpillar to focus internal resources on areas of highest priority. Alternative organization structures involve different concepts of employee involvement in the firm's decision-making process.

Externalities

1. Discuss Caterpillar's efforts to transform itself into an "energy technology" company to address pollution problems produced by diesel generators.

Hint: Becoming an "energy technology" company can make Caterpillar more productive by lowering the cost of inputs and using resources more efficiently. Customers may prefer energy-efficient solutions to be more productive and to meet emission requirements.

Appendix 6.1

Notes on Regulation

Societies and governments regulate many forms of human behavior. Regulation is a legal restriction by government administrative agencies. There can be legal penalties for non-compliance. Societies regulate for social as well as economic purposes. Examples of social regulation include age of majority for voting/ driving/consumption of alcoholic beverages, slander/libel, etc.

Economic regulation addresses issues of perceived market failure. Economic regulation can be direct, which is normally industry specific, such as rent control in the residential housing sector. Indirect, or social, regulation is designed to influence the behavior of industry in general. Examples of social regulation include: consumer protection, health and safety and environmental protection.

Market Failure

Economists argue that the "invisible hand" of the purely competitive marketplace results in optimal market outcomes: this is referred to as "Pareto efficient" when no individual can be made better off without another being made worse off. However, most economists agree that free markets can fail due to the following:

- *Monopoly power*: economies of scale result in falling average total cost of production. Examples include utilities.
- *Oligopoly power*: anti-competitive behavior, such as predatory pricing, due to market power.
- *Externalities*: third-party effects that can be positive or negative. Negative third party effects include environmental pollution, while workplace training is an example of a positive externality.
- *Imperfect or asymmetrical information*: the qualification of medical doctors is an example of imperfect information between the consumer of the service and the service provider.

- *Market absence*: there is no market for households to purchase clean air.
- *The absence of public goods*: examples include public parks and national defense.

Approaches to Regulation

There are a number of regulatory strategies:

- *Command and control*: the government sets standards for behavior. An example is health and safety regulation in the workplace.
- *Self-regulation*: in some countries medical doctors establish self-regulating professional review procedures.
- *Incentives*: differential taxes on leaded versus unleaded petrol/gasoline
- *Competition policy*: review of proposed mergers and acquisitions to assess potential abuses of power due to market size.
- *Tradable permits*: governments establish limits on the amount of a pollutant that can be emitted. Companies receive credits or allowances that represent the right to emit a specific level of pollutant. Companies that pollute beyond their allowances can purchase credits from those who pollute less than their allowances. Economists prefer emission permits to command-and-control approaches because firms are able to respond to market forces. This results in fewer distortions to equilibrium market outcomes.
- *Public ownership*: the government controls the means of production to achieve socially desired outcomes. Public utilities, such as water systems, are examples of public ownership.
- *Access to the legal system*: tort law permits legal action to address perceived market failure. In some countries individuals can take legal action against firms that pollute the environment.
- *Subsidizing positive externalities*: providing funding for research is an example of subsidizing a positive externality.
- *Consumer protection legislation*: food labelling is designed to address the information imbalance between producers and consumers.

Coase Theorem

Coase has argued that, under restrictive assumptions, the parties affected by negative externalities can achieve a mutually satisfactory resolution.[1] Suc-

---

[1] Ronald Coase, "The problem of social cost" *Journal of Law and Economics* (1960) 3, 1–44.

cessful negotiations occur when there are zero negotiating costs. Both parties attain an efficient outcome irrespective of which party is legally responsible for, as an example, pollution.

Appendix 6.2

Theory of the Firm

The theory of the firm sets out to explain the nature and limitations (or boundaries) of the firm or corporation as an economic institution. The theory of the firm can be located within the broader analysis of economic organization, which attempts to explain the observed diversity of institutional arrangements in the economy. Some transactions occur in markets, others in firms, and still others in hybrid structures, such as franchises, joint ventures, and strategic alliances. The study of economic organization seeks to understand the conditions that create this diversity.

All theories of the firm share a common set of assumptions about the following:

1. The need for exchange arising from specialization.
2. The need for coordination and cooperation among economic agents.
3. The assumption of efficiency in economic organization.

Central questions in the theory of the firm are the following:

1. What constitutes a firm's identity?
2. What is the purpose and rationale of a firm: why do different activities have to be integrated?
3. What determines the boundaries of the firm?
4. How does the co-ordination of activities in and between firms take place?
5. What other forms of organization of economic activities are there, besides the firm, and how do they differ from the firm?

Transaction Cost Approach

The transaction cost approach to the theory of the firm was created by Ronald Coase.[1] Transaction cost refers to the cost of providing for some

---

[1] Ronald Coase, "The nautre of the firm" *Economica* (1937), 4, 386–405.

good or service through the market rather than having it provided from within the firm.

In order to carry out a market transaction it is necessary to discover who it is that one wishes to deal with, to conduct negotiations leading up to a bargain, to draw up the contract, to undertake the inspection needed to make sure that the terms of the contract are being observed, and so on.

More succinctly, transaction costs are:

- search and information costs
- bargaining and decision costs
- policing and enforcement costs

Coase contends that without taking into account transaction costs it is impossible to understand properly the working of the economic system and have a sound basis for establishing economic policy.

The object of a business organization is to reproduce the conditions of a competitive market for the factors of production within the firm at a lower cost than the actual market. But if an organization exists to reduce costs then why are there any market transactions at all? Coase gave two reasons:

- The costs of organizing additional transactions rise with scale and are equated with the costs of additional market transactions.
- The organization of bigger firms may not reproduce the effects of market conditions.

Resource-Based Approach

The resource-based perspective (RBV) argues that a firm's ability to attain and keep a profitable market position depends on its ability to gain competitive advantage in the resources required for production and distribution.

The Input-Output Model

The major emphasis of the input-output model is the "structure-conduct-performance" hypothesis: that is, industry structure determines firm conduct, which determines economic performance. The principal limitation on size and scope is government regulatory intervention. The motivation for firm expansion is to increase monopoly/oligopoly power, or to prevent other firms from gaining monopoly control.

The Schumpeterian Approach

Schumpeter argued that the purpose of the firm is to seize competitive opportunity by creating or adopting innovations that make the position of rivals less competitive.

Monopoly power is seen as an incentive to develop revolutionary innovations (since innovation is inherently risky). The firm is then able to capture scale and scope economies.

The Firm as Contract Manager

This theory views the "firm" as a manager of contracts between economic agents.

A firm could be characterized as "team production" in that the services of several specialists are required to produce an end product. In some cases this phenomenon is called a "virtual firm". The Baranti Group case study (see page 138) is an example of a virtual organization.

Knowledge Theories

All knowledge-based theories of the firm start from the premise that knowledge is the most important strategic asset that a firm possesses. The literature makes a strong distinction between explicit knowledge in the public domain and tacit knowledge. Tacit knowledge cannot be easily codified and can only be learned through observation and practice. Tacit knowledge is a valuable resource because it cannot be directly appropriated and attempts at imitation will be costly. Explicit knowledge is easier to transfer and contracts protecting this type of knowledge are difficult to enforce.

Business Strategy Implementation

One of the main responsibilities of the chief executive officer/president of a firm is to establish the boundaries of the organization. In diversified firms, the key question is which strategic business units to invest in and which to harvest, or divest.

Case A

The Baranti Group

The Baranti Group is a business network that in many respects exemplifies and suggests future trends in manufacturing in North America.

The Baranti Group is a manufacturing network — a "virtual company". The group comprises five separate companies, all located in the Toronto area:

1.   A design and engineering firm in Toronto that employs 15 people.
2.   A plastics injection molding company located in Richmond Hill that employs 34 people.
3.   An electronics firm in Markham that employs 23 people.
4.   A machining firm in Ajax that employs 30 people.
5.   A business services company in Toronto that employs 10 people.

The five companies are interconnected through a computer network and contract their services to each other on a project-by-project basis. Each firm retains its own corporate identity. Rights to products developed by the group are held by the services company, the ownership of which is split four ways among the owners of the four enterprises. Together the Baranti Group acts as a "virtual company" — as if the group of companies were a single enterprise, each undertaking the function in which it adds the greatest value in an integrated production system.

The Baranti Group currently has 35 projects underway — 25 of them with international customers. Of those 25, 12 are with US companies; seven are with Japanese firms; and six are with European customers.

The group's first major contract was with a US firm in 1989. Baranti Group obtained an exclusive worldwide contract for the design and production of Procter-Silex coffeepots (for sale at Canadian Tire, a well-known retail chain in Canada, for $39.95). The contract was won on the strengths of design and the flexibility that Baranti Group was able to offer in the production and delivery.

The coffeepot is itself a product of a set of global business contracts:

- Plastics are imported from the US, where they are produced by a subsidiary of a British firm.
- Electronic components are produced by a Japanese company in Taiwan.
- Copper wiring originates in Malaysia, where it is produced by a Canadian-based subsidiary of a French firm.
- The technology used in plastic injection molding comes from the UK. Machining technologies are from Germany. Electronics technologies are from Japan.
- Investment financing is provided by a Swiss band and by Japanese equipment suppliers.
- The Procter-Silex contract was brokered by a Canadian agent living in the US.
- Procter-Silex markets the coffeepot under its own name and trademark.

The technology employed by the Baranti Group also indicates the rapid pace of change affecting modern manufacturing:

- Computer networks and advanced software allow the design process to be integrated directly into production, marketing, and customer services — in the process of "concurrent engineering".
- R&D occurs primarily in the design and on the shop floor. Production technologies are acquired — not developed in-house.
- Technological applications are diverse and can be readily changed on a product-by-product basis, given a change in software and programming.
- There is a high reliance on advanced manufacturing technologies — CAD-CAM, materials handling systems, robotics, plastics injection systems, laser stereolithography — all keeping up with new generational capabilities.
- Production systems are composed of interchangeable components that can be easily disassembled and reassembled according to the project at hand.
- Software accounts for about 40% of Baranti's investment in its production technologies.
- Expert skills are required to make the system work.

Operations control technologies are the glue that hold the networks together. New aspects of management are also apparent:

- Focus on quality control, workforce participation, joint decision-making — Total Quality Management is a priority.
- Organization of technology and all employees in project teams.
- Emphasis on in-house technology and information management skills.
- Management of the network defines the operations of companies that are part of the network.
- Emphasis is on flexibility and timeliness to market.
- Project planning is a crucial consideration in allocating resources within the group.

Manufacturing in the Baranti Group is based on a project-by-project basis. Products are developed to order for customers, and can be produced in high volume or small batch jobs. However, the production process itself represents a relatively small share of Baranti's total operating costs. Overheads and salaries are high — reflecting the level of investment technology and the group's reliance on the skills and creativity of its employees.

Baranti's costs are budgeted at the group level. Profits are reinvested according to project requirements, or divided in the form of dividends among participating firms according to a formula based on the number of employees in each.

The Baranti Group is planning to expand its activities in the US by incorporating a California software company into the network. The FTA facilitates such a relationship by providing for the freer movement of professionals between Canada and the US. NAFTA further eases entry requirements to the US for Canadian businesspeople. It harmonizes intellectual property protection on industrial designs and computer software. In addition, NAFTA guarantees access to, and use of, telecommunications networks across North America, and it provides for future compatibility of standards for telecommunications equipment in Canada, the US, and Mexico.

Problems

1. Which form of market structure best describes the Baranti Group?

2. Organizations, such as the Baranti Group, are often called "virtual companies". What do you think is the meaning of this concept?

3. Baranti's cost structure is unusual. Why might overhead costs be high relative to the costs of production?

4. Do you think Baranti has higher fixed or variable costs?

5. Use the language of game theory to discuss the strategic options facing Baranti in negotiations with its global business contractors.

6. Use the language of game theory to discuss the strategic options facing Baranti in negotiations with the large Canadian retailer, Canadian Tire.

7

The Global
Economy I:
The Debate over
Free Trade

Introduction

In this chapter we look at some of the key issues of international economics and, specifically, the debate over **free trade** versus **protectionism**. This is simultaneously one of the oldest, and also the most up-to-date topics in political economy, and this fact alone is perhaps sufficient indication of its importance. Back in the earliest days of capitalism, it was the decisive issue between the **mercantilists** and the **classical economists**. The former advocated various restrictions and regulations on international trade, including **tariff barriers**, **excise taxes**, and any other measures they could think of, all with the objective of improving the **balance of payments** of their own particular nation, if necessary at the expense of others. The classical economists, on the contrary, argued that the welfare of all would be enhanced with no restrictions at all on trade (literally free trade). Using the language of game theory, trade was seen as either a zero sum game or a positive sum game.

If we fast forward to the 21st century, it is quite obvious that this debate is still very much alive in modern times. We hear a good deal, for example, about the crucial importance of **international competitiveness**. There is also bitter debate about the impact of so-called **globalization**, meaning not only increased trade, but also increasing **economic integration** between the various nations of the world, and whether this trend is a good or bad thing for economic, social, and political development. Finally, particularly in the economically developed nations, there are continual complaints about the **international outsourcing** of jobs and production to regions with cheaper labor costs.

Differing Degrees of Economic Integration

The classical free-traders, in fact, were advocates of **unilateral** free trade. The argument was that a nation would be better off simply by opening their own markets to trade, eliminating all tariff and other barriers, regardless of what was happening elsewhere. There was no discussion of strategic trade issues. In this view, those countries that kept trade barriers intact would just be "shooting themselves in the foot". They would, perhaps, enhance the income of some individual producer groups within their own borders, but at the expense of the well being of the nation as a whole.

Perhaps needless to say, the above has not been the approach of modern free-traders, presumably for political reasons. For more than half a century now, the main push for global (as opposed to regional) free trade has been institutionalized in a series of multilateral trade negotiations, or "rounds", under the auspices of international bodies: the General Agreement on Tariffs and Trade (GATT) from 1947, and the World Trade Organization (WTO) after 1995. Another prominent development, which, however, would have an ambiguous status from the point of view of purist free-traders, has been the development of major **trading blocs**, such as the North American Free Trade Agreement (NAFTA), the European Union (EU), the Association of Southeast Asian Nations (ASEAN), and Mercosur in South America. Such agreements presumably increase trade between their members, but possibly also lessen trade with the rest of the world. The issues of **trade creation** versus **trade diversion**, and **regionalization** (rather than globalization) clearly arise. The different types of trading blocs, arranged by increasing order of economic integration, are listed below:

(a) *A Free Trade Area*
   - eliminates internal tariffs, but does not impose a common external tariff, or allow free factor movements

(b) *A Customs Union*
   - adds a common external tariff

(c) *A Common Market*
   - adds free factor movements

(d) *Economic and Monetary Union (EMU)*
   - adds a common currency

The last, of course, is characteristic of the contemporary EU, and this type of organization brings up many political issues that go far beyond the purely economic sphere. In the case of the EU, the question is whether this group of nations will (or perhaps must) eventually become a European "superstate". This is also a matter of politics rather than just a question of trading arrangements.

The Case for Free Trade

There are two main types of arguments in favor of a regime of free trade, which may loosely be described as the **static** and **dynamic** arguments. The static argument asserts that there are gains to trade even if this leads to no further gains to the economy in terms of improving productivity, encouraging innovation, and so on. This is the traditional concept of **comparative advantage**, first enunciated by David Ricardo almost 200 years ago.[1] The dynamic case for free trade would go still further and assert that

---

[1] David Ricardo, *The Principles of Political Economy and Taxation*, edited by D. Winch (London: J.M. Dent & Sons, 1973 [1817]).

Case Study 12

"Finally, an Economic Union"
Brussels; October 20, 2025

The European Union is now finally an economic union, said Dr. A. Nasser, President of France. Of course, economics was always an issue with respect to European integration. However, it must be acknowledged that the original impetus for the European Union was primarily issues of collective security and the need to avoid future European wars. The process of economic integration has been long and painful. The addition of the transitional economies with different infrastructure capabilities and cultural values was difficult. However, as Dr. Nasser indicated, "We are now at the stage where economies of scale have finally taken effect. Europe is now large enough, and its social, political, and economic institutions integrated enough, for us to take full advantage of our one-billion-person society." Costs of production are now equivalent to those of Asia and North America. Europe is now able to reinvest effectively in research and development, as well as to repair the social welfare institutions, which have tended to deteriorate over the past 30 years.

engaging in international trade will, in fact, make the domestic economy itself more productive. For example, domestic firms with access to global markets will be able to improve productivity through **economies of scale**.

Also, being forced to compete in international markets will have a salutary effect on existing local monopolies. They must become more competitive, or go under. It goes without saying, however, that these latter arguments do rest heavily on the presumption that it will be the domestic firms, rather than the foreign firms, that win out in the competitive struggle.

Comparative Advantage and the Gains from Trade

In the light of the contemporary focus on "competitiveness", it is important to realize that the static **"gains from trade"** do *not* arise from **absolute advantage**, but, as mentioned, only from comparative advantage.[2] Absolute advantage would exist when one country is more productive than another in every industry across the board. In such a circumstance, in fact, it might seem that there is no basis for trade between them. Such a conclusion would be erroneous, however. What is important is comparative advantage, which involves only a relative comparison, and invokes the basic idea of opportunity cost, as discussed in a previous chapter. Comparative advantage exists when the opportunity cost of producing one product rather than another differs across countries. The main case for trade is based on this sort of comparison rather than absolute advantage or general competitiveness.

We can illustrate with a simple example involving trade between two imaginary countries: "Ecoland" and "Pecunia". They each produce two products, wheat and steel, with one productive input: namely, labor. The production data for these two economies are given in Table 7.1. From this information it is easy to see that the domestic exchange ratios of wheat for steel must be as follows:

> Ecoland: **1 wheat = 0.5 steel**
> Pecunia: **1 wheat = 0.8 steel**

What we are looking at here is the domestic opportunity cost of shifting resources (in this case labor inputs) from wheat to steel in each country. On this basis, wheat is *relatively* cheaper in Ecoland than in Pecunia. To get one unit of wheat in Ecoland, it is necessary to give up only 0.5 units of steel. To get the same amount of wheat in Pecunia, it would be necessary to give up 0.8 units of steel. By the same token, steel is relatively cheaper in Pecunia. We would say that Ecoland has a comparative advan-

---

[2] Paul R. Krugman, "What do undergrads need to know about trade?" *American Economic Review* (1993) 83(2): 23–26.

Table 7.1:   Production Data for Ecoland and Pecunia

(labor inputs required to produce
1 ton of steel and 1 bushel of wheat)

	Ecoland	Pecunia
Wheat	30	20
Steel	60	25

---

tage in wheat, and Pecunia has a comparative advantage in steel. It is clear, therefore, that a deal is possible at any intermediate price ratio between 0.5 and 0.8, which would benefit both sides. For example, they would both benefit from a ratio of **1 wheat = 0.7 steel**. Note that a deal is possible even though *both* the steel and wheat industries are more efficient in Pecunia than in Ecoland. What matters is comparative advantage, not absolute advantage.

The next step in the argument is to construct the production possibility frontier for Ecoland. (Recall that this concept was first introduced in Chapter 1.) Suppose that there are 15,000 workers in Ecoland, and that there is full employment. Then the production possibility frontier will be as in Figure 7.1. It is a straight line in this case, because we have assumed (admittedly unrealistically) that there is no decline in efficiency of the single input as resources are increasingly devoted to one product or the other. If all resources are devoted to wheat production, the maximum amount of wheat attainable is 500 bushels; whereas, at the other extreme, if all resources are devoted to steel, the maximum output of steel is 250 tons. Any intermediate combination of wheat and steel along the frontier is also attainable. If Ecoland is in a state of **autarky**, meaning that it undertakes no trade with the rest of the world, both production and consumption possibilities will have (at best) to be somewhere along the frontier. Suppose, for example, that domestic market forces would lead to a choice of 250 bushels of wheat (both produced and consumed) and 125 tons of steel. This can be illustrated by the tangency of the **social indifference curve** with the production possibility frontier, as shown in Figure 7.2. In this diagram, it may help to think of the production possibility frontier as the country's "supply side", while the social indifference curve represents the collective set of preferences or demand conditions in the society.

Now, carry out a similar exercise for the case of Pecunia. Suppose that Pecunia has 25,000 fully employed workers. This means that as well as being more efficient, Pecunia also has more resources. It is the "larger"

Figure 7.1:   Production Possibility Frontier for Ecoland

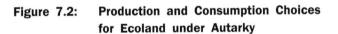

**Figure 7.2:   Production and Consumption Choices
for Ecoland under Autarky**

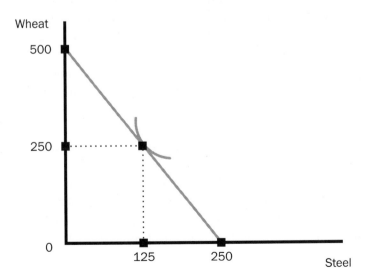

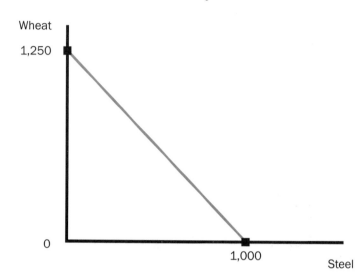

Figure 7.3:   Production Possibility Frontier for Pecunia

economy in every sense. The production possibility frontier for Pecunia is shown in Figure 7.3. If Pecunia is also operating under conditions of autarky, once again the production and consumption choices will be limited to what is available. One possible choice for them in that situation is, therefore, a combination of 500 bushels of wheat and 600 tons of steel, as shown in Figure 7.4.

The discussion so far has set out what the situation of both countries would be if they did *not* trade with each other. Now we can compare this with what becomes available when trade opens up. Suppose that trade does start to take place, and a **world price** of 1 wheat = 0.7 steel is, in fact, established. The possibilities now open to Ecoland, for example, are immediately improved, as shown in Figure 7.5.

As Ecoland has a comparative advantage in wheat, it may as well specialize entirely in wheat — that is, not produce any steel at all. If the country needs steel, it can trade for it on the world market at the world price. In the limit, by trading all the wheat away, Ecoland could acquire a maximum of 350 tons of steel, which is far more than if it had concentrated all productive resources in steel under autarky.

Once again, market forces will decide the particular consumption choices the residents of Ecoland will actually make. Suppose, however, that they turn out as in Figure 7.6. This diagram shows the gains from trade

Figure 7.4:   Production and Consumption Choices for Pecunia under Autarky

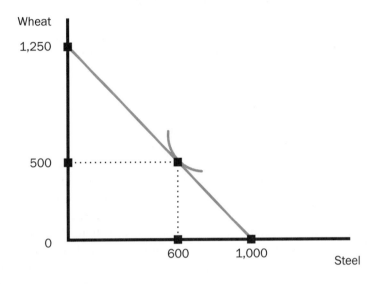

Figure 7.5:   Trading Possibilities for Ecoland

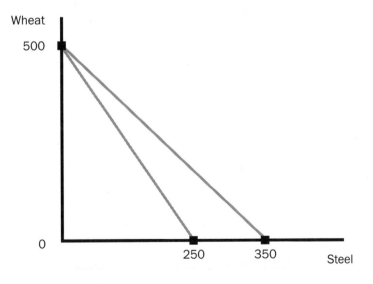

for Ecoland, given its particular consumption choices. Under autarky, Ecoland would both produce and consume 250 bushels of wheat, and produce and consume 125 tons of steel. Now the country produces 500 tons of wheat and consumes 280 bushels of it. The rest they trade away in exchange for 154 tons of steel. So now Ecoland produces no steel at all, but actually consumes more of it than when a domestic steel industry was in existence. It also consumes more wheat than before. The total gains from trade for Ecoland are:

(7.1)   **280 − 250 = 30 wheat**

(7.2)   **154 − 125 = 29 steel**

In other words, the country has 12% more wheat, *and* 23.2% more steel.

Evidently, the "small" economy, Ecoland, does benefit quite substantially by trade. However, its trading partner, Pecunia, does not lose by trade either. It also makes some gains. The point is, again, that trade is *not* a zero sum game. Pecunia is a bigger country than Ecoland, with a much higher real income, and because of this disparity, Ecoland will not be able to satisfy Pecunia's entire demand for wheat. So Pecunia will not be able to specialize entirely in steel. It must retain a domestic wheat industry. However, it can transfer 3,850 workers from wheat production to steel production to produce the 154 tons of steel to trade to Ecoland,

---

Figure 7.6:   **Gains from Trade for Ecoland**

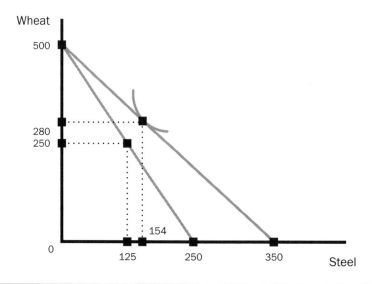

---

thereby giving up 192.5 bushels of wheat from its own production. But in return, Pecunia gets 220 bushels of wheat from Ecoland. So, Pecunia's gains from trade are:

(7.3)   **220 – 192.5 = 27.5 wheat**

Therefore, Pecunia also gains around 5.5% more wheat compared to its initial level of consumption of 500 bushels, without having to give up any of its previous steel consumption.

Demand and Supply under Free Trade

In addition to the device of the production possibility frontier, it is also possible to use the apparatus of demand and supply curves (introduced in Chapter 2) to gain insight into the effects of free trade. Figure 7.7 shows the domestic demand and supply curves in two trading countries, and also the world price of a given traded good. The focus here is on the impact of trade on both of the *domestic* markets for this particular item.

Note that country A would actually have had a lower market price (P_A) for the good under autarky than now exists in the global economy. Under globalization, consumers in country A are paying a higher price and con-

Figure 7.7:   Demand and Supply under Free Trade

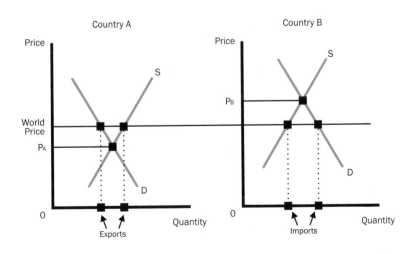

suming less of the commodity than they would otherwise have done. However, producers in country *A* are getting a higher price. The difference between the amount firms are producing at the world price and the amount consumers are willing to buy at this price is what is going for export. In country *B*, meanwhile, the world price under globalization is lower than the national price (P_B) that would have existed under autarky. With free trade, country *B* consumers are able to buy more at a lower price than they otherwise would have been able to. Country *B* producers, however, have seen their industry downsize and are getting a lower price for their efforts, while the gap in the domestic markets is made up by imports.

It can well be imagined that consumers in country *A* and producers in country *B* will be against free trade or globalization, and consumers in country *B* and producers in country *A* will be in favor of it. The neoclassical economist, however, would still argue that both countries *taken together* are better off with free trade, and therefore the world economy as a whole is better off with free trade. This is illustrated in Figure 7.8, using the device of consumer and producer surplus triangles first introduced in Chapter 3.

In both countries *A* and *B*, the net gains from trade are illustrated by the triangular shaded areas. The gains are "net" in the sense that this is the surplus that remains over and above any of the purely distributional transfers that have taken place (e.g., from consumers to producers or vice

Figure 7.8:   The Overall Gain in "Welfare" from Trade in Countries A and B

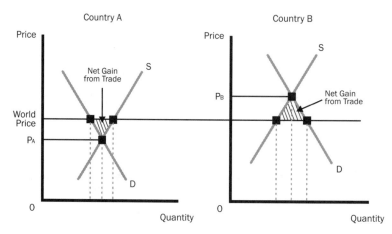

versa). Therefore, although it cannot be denied that there may be losses to particular groups in each society in moving toward freer trade, the proponents of free trade would argue that the existence of the net gains means that *in principle* any losers can always be financially **compensated** for their losses, and there will still be net benefits left over for all to share. We discuss this question of compensation in more detail later on.

Tariff and Non-Tariff Barriers to Trade

If the argument in favor of moving to free trade is that there will be economic gains for the society as a whole, then the converse of that argument must that any barriers to trade that are newly introduced will make society worse off, even if they do benefit particular groups. Figure 7.9, for example, illustrates the case of a tariff (a tax on imports) imposed on a particular product in the domestic market.

Before the tariff, the good is trading at the world price **Pw**. Domestic consumption of the good is at **Qd1** and domestic production at **Qs1**. Imports are therefore equal to **Qd1 – Qs1**. After the tariff the price paid by domestic consumers rises to **Pw + t**. More domestic firms can be competitive at that price, so domestic production increases to **Qs2**. Meanwhile, because of the higher price, demand falls off to **Qd2**. Therefore imports fall to **Qd2 – Qs2**. Who gains and who loses from this change? The pur-

Figure 7.9:   The Effect of a Tariff

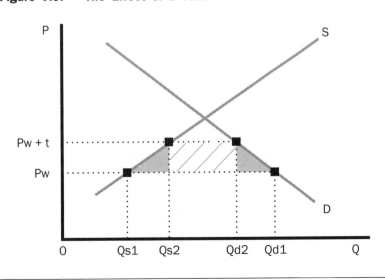

pose of the tariff was to protect domestic firms and increase their output —
and this works — the domestic firms gain producer surplus, equal to the
blank area above the supply curve and below the final price point. Consumers lose, because they are buying fewer goods at higher prices. The government, of course, will get something: tax revenue equal to the striped area
in the diagram. There is, however, a deadweight loss to the society as a
whole, shown by the two shaded triangles in the diagram. These represent
the net loss in consumer satisfaction, and the inefficiency of domestic production of the item as compared to foreign production.

In addition to tariff barriers there are as many **non-tariff barriers** to
trade as human ingenuity can devise. They can be a simple as increasing
bureaucracy and "red tape" at the customs office (filling in forms, etc.) so
that the goods cannot get through, or the classic device of requiring imports to have rigorous health and safety inspections, and appointing too few
inspectors. Figures 7.10 and 7.11 look at just two examples of non-tariff
barriers: the imposition of an import quota, and subsidies to the domestic
industry, respectively.

An import quota, arbitrarily limiting the amount of import into the
country, turns out to have an effect very similar to that of a tariff. At
the world price, Pw, imports were equal to **d − a**; now they are reduced to
the amount of the quota, **c − b**. Obviously, the amount of production by
the domestic industry goes up (to ba), and domestic firms gain producer

Figure 7.10: An Import Quota

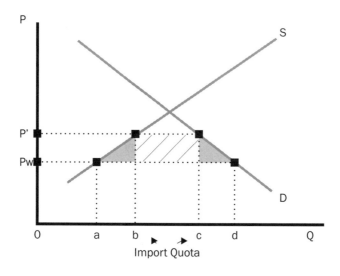

surplus. However, prices go up also, to P', because of the restriction in the total availability of goods, and demand falls off to point **c**. There is a dead-weight loss to society as a whole, again as shown by the two shaded triangles. One interesting feature is that the government will actually get no revenue from this exercise (no tariffs or excise taxes are involved). The striped rectangle in Figure 7.10 actually goes to the foreign importers. Therefore, they may not be too unhappy to collaborate with the quota regime.

Figure 7.11 shows a case where the government tries to "protect" a domestic industry by subsidizing it. The subsidy does enable the industry to compete more effectively on the world market as shown in the diagram.

The subsidy shifts the domestic supply curve down by its full amount, and allows the domestic firms to get a greater share of the market at the world price, with the costs of the subsidy borne by the treasury. Domestic output increases from **Qs1** to **Qs2** and imports fall to **Qd** – **Qs2**. As with other cases of subsidization (e.g., as discussed in Chapter 2), there is no loss of consumer surplus in this case, as the consumers are still getting all the goods they want. There is still an overall loss to society, however, as the subsidy is clearly encouraging inefficient levels of production in the domestic industry. The same goods could have been had at a cheaper price elsewhere.

Figure 7.11:   A Subsidy to the Domestic Industry

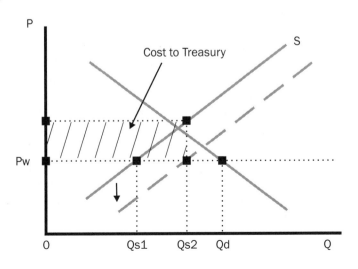

The "Compensation Principle" of Welfare Economics as Applied to Free Trade

In effect, as has been shown in the previous discussion, the political case for free trade rests on the idea that, in the aggregate, all parties will be better off in economic terms. This being the case, however, it might well be asked, if the benefits are so clear, why is there any debate at all over free trade, globalization, or international outsourcing? The obvious answer is that the parties concerned, nations or regions, are far from homogenous entities. As shown in the previous discussion of supply and demand in two countries, there are different interest groups *within* each nation, such as producers (in turn, divided into management, shareholders, and workers), and consumers. The government itself, and its bureaucracy, can also be considered an interest group from this point of view.

Implicitly, the argument in favor of free trade rests on the so-called **compensation principle** of **welfare economics**, and this may be of dubious value in the realm of actual political economy, as opposed to pure economic theory. Welfare economics is precisely that branch of economics that attempts to apply a **cost-benefit analysis** to various proposed economic changes. The compensation principle says, in effect, that if there are net gains to any economic change *sufficient* to compensate any losers, then it should go ahead, *regardless of whether or not the compensation is actually paid*. As applied to trade, we have seen that there are always net *gains* to trade, and therefore, on this principle, a free trade agreement is always a "good deal". However, there is an obvious flaw in this from a political point of view. Clearly, unless there is some guarantee that the compensation actually *will* be paid, there is every reason for any group that would be likely to lose out from a change in the trading regime to oppose it.

Consider the steel industry in Ecolard, for example. As we have shown, this industry would be wiped out in a free trade regime. It is true that the country as a whole will benefit by more than enough to make good all these losses, and still have something left over. From the point of view of entrepreneurs and workers in the steel industry, however, this is no good unless they have cast-iron guarantees that the compensation will be paid. Realistically, they have every reason to be suspicious and, hence, to oppose moves to a freer trading environment. Presumably, many of the **trade disputes** observed in reality have this sort of motivation at their core.

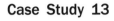

Case Study 13

"The End of an Era"
Milan; August 25, 2033

Well, it finally had to happen. Today in Italy, the last clothing manufacturer finally closed its doors. All of Italy's high fashions are now physically produced in Asia. The head of the Italian Textile Industry Association (ITA) said that it was the end of an era. Paradoxically, however, Milan is busier than it has ever been. The design industry is booming, and the city has added five new showrooms this year. As well, the software industry is booming. More and more young Italian designers are using computers for fashion design. In fact, the Italian government has created two new technical institutes devoted entirely to computer-aided design software. Meanwhile, the Italian design house, Roma™, has just announced the opening of a new manufacturing facility in India. One thousand new jobs will be created in India as a result of this investment. Roma noted that there is also a major spin-off benefit for Italy. More than 200 new high-technology jobs have been created in Milan as a result of this investment. The company stated that this is the best time for Italian fashion, and that the industry has never been stronger.

Some Arguments Against Free Trade

In what follows, having set out the case in favor of free trade in some detail, we list some of the other arguments, in addition to the distributional question already discussed, that are typically made on the opposite side. We take it that the reader will investigate each of these and make a judgment as to how cogent or otherwise they may be in particular circumstances. A non-exhaustive list would include the following:

- the "infant industry" argument

- the impact on environmental protection

- social and cultural issues

- questions of national sovereignty and national defence

- the loss of government revenue from tariffs

- situations where one trading partner has global market power in a particular commodity

All of the above have been raised at one time or another in each of the real-world examples of trade debates, and certainly have been influential politically. Many of these arguments can be found in the anti-globalization literature. This discussion includes social, political, and cultural issues, as well as the purely economic. It would be fair to say, nonetheless, that most economists have an instinctive bias in favor of free trade and are usually found on the other side of the argument.

Chapter Summary

- The benefits from trade seem obvious. Every day we all make multiple transactions or "trades": we purchase a paper, pay a telephone bill, etc. International trade simply takes this principle across national borders.

- Specialization arises through comparative advantage. Even if the CEO of a major company was a highly skilled driver, it would still pay her to hire a chauffeur or take a cab (perhaps driven by someone with less skill). Why? Because her time is better spent running the company. That is her "comparative advantage". Another good example could look at trade between countries. For example, say Australia produces computers five times more efficiently than Pakistan, but produces footwear three times more efficiently. Consequently, Australia exports computers to Pakistan but imports footwear (so it can spend more time making and selling computers). This initiates more trade and business between merchants in both countries and creates more competitive prices. The comparative advantage of Australia is in computers and the comparative advantage of Pakistan is in footwear (in this hypothetical example).

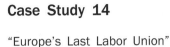

Case Study 14

"Europe's Last Labor Union"
Paris; May 1, 2048

Today, the last labor union in Europe officially disbanded. At their inception in Europe in the 1800s, unions were seen as an important source of countervailing power against corporations and, to some extent, governments. However, the rise of international labor markets and the creation of international labor standards have resulted in stronger national and international regulations. The leader in this process has been the World Trade Organization (WTO). Although its original mandate was to establish freer trade, the WTO has recently taken on a greater role in dealing with issues such as the harmonization of labor and environmental standards. Essentially, governmental institutions, both domestic and international, have replaced the need for an organized trade union movement. The principle of collective bargaining has been replaced by comprehensive national and international regulatory mechanisms. As such, there now seems to be no need for the intervention of third parties such as labor unions.

- Some economists argue that the benefits of trade are so great that a country should unilaterally move to free trade. But for political and social reasons, countries usually maintain some degree of protection.

- The reasons for protection range from the somewhat defensible, such as the idea that farmers are the "backbone" of the nation, to the indefensible, such as the awarding of monopolies to the families and cronies of influential politicians, which then must be protected from international competition.

- Countries try to move toward freer trade while trying to protect key sectors or segments of society. A number of trading blocs have been created to allow nations to gain the benefits of trade while maintaining some protection.

- Trade creates overall benefits to a society, but there are winners and losers. For economists, the solution is simple: have the winners compensate the losers. To some extent this actually occurs, mainly in developed countries. Government programs, such as employment insurance, welfare, and re-training, are designed to assist those negatively impacted by change. However, opponents to freer trade can argue that these programs and other forms of compensation are usually insufficient for those displaced by international competition.

- There are many other arguments against freer trade, such as environmental impacts and the loss of national sovereignty. It is easy to criticize international trade. However, the counterfactual is not very appealing. If trade is bad, then no trade should be ever be undertaken. But every nation trades to some extent. The empirical results are clear. By and large, the more open a nation is to trade, the better it performs economically.

Problems

1. "I oppose a free trade agreement with Bolivia because Brazilian workers will lose jobs to lower-paid Bolivian workers." Explain whether you agree or disagree with this statement.

2. South Africa can produce 1,000 shoes if it specializes in shoe production. Alternatively, it can produce 500 shirts. Egypt can produce 500 shoes or 200 shirts. Explain which country will specialize in shoe production, and which in shirt production. What is the possible range of the terms of trade?

Table 1

Price per TV ($)	Q_d in Canada ('000s)	Q_s in Canada ('000s)	Q_d in Japan ('000s)	Q_s in Japan ('000s)
100	100	10	100	25
200	85	20	85	50
300	70	30	70	70
400	60	40	60	80
500	50	50	50	90
600	40	60	40	100
700	30	70	30	110
800	20	80	20	120

3. Table 1 presents the demand and supply schedules for television sets in Japan and Canada. If there is no trade between these countries, what are the equilibrium price and equilibrium quantity in Canada?
    (a) P = $100, Q = 100
    (b) P = $200, Q = 85
    (c) P = $300, Q = 70
    (d) P = $400, Q = 60
    (e) P = $500, Q = 50

4. Table 1 presents the demand and supply schedules for television sets in Japan and Canada. If there is no trade between these countries, what are the equilibrium price and the equilibrium quantity in Japan?
    (a) P = $100, Q = 100
    (b) P = $200, Q = 85
    (c) P = $300, Q = 70
    (d) P = $400, Q = 60
    (e) P = $500, Q = 50

5. Table 1 presents the demand and supply schedules for television sets in Japan and Canada. If Japan and Canada trade with each other, what will be the equilibrium price in the world market for television sets?
    (a) $100
    (b) $200
    (c) $300
    (d) $400
    (e) $500

6. Table 1 presents the demand and supply schedules for television sets in Japan and Canada. If Japan and Canada trade with each other, which country will export television sets, and how many?
    (a) Japan will export 20,000 television sets to Canada.
    (b) Japan will export 30,000 television sets to Canada.
    (c) Canada will export 20,000 television sets to Japan.
    (d) Canada will export 40,000 television sets to Japan.

7. Table 1 presents the demand and supply schedules for television sets in Japan and Canada. If Canada and Japan trade with each other, what will happen to the output of television sets in Canada?
    (a) TV production in Canada will fall by 10,000 units.
    (b) TV production in Canada will fall by 20,000 units.
    (c) TV production in Canada will fall by 30,000 units.
    (d) TV production in Canada will increase by 10,000 units.

161

8. Table 1 presents the demand and supply schedules for television sets in Japan and Canada. If Canada and Japan decide to trade with each other, what will happen to the output of television sets in Japan?
    (a) TV production in Japan will fall by 10,000 units.
    (b) TV production in Japan will fall by 20,000 units.
    (c) TV production in Japan will fall by 30,000 units.
    (d) TV production in Japan will increase by 10,000 units.

Case Study Questions | # The Comeback of Caterpillar

Competitive Advantage
1. How has international trade benefitted Caterpillar?
2. During the early 1980s, how did Komatsu gain its competitive advantage in international trade?

Hint: Competitive advantage is created. Komatsu instituted a comprehensive business strategy to "encircle Cat," which included improved quality while reducing costs.

Economies of Scale
1. Why are scale economies so important for capital-intensive industries?
2. Why might we expect to find a relationship between economies of scale and oligopolistic industries?
3. How could the Caterpillar investment in Information Technology enhance scale economies?

Hint: Capital-intensive industries imply high fixed costs which, in turn, impose a bar-

Case Study Questions Continued

rier for firms attempting to enter the industry. Information technology was used to maintain Caterpillar's commitment to have the most comprehensive and fastest parts delivery system in the industry and to monitor machines remotely (reducing the need for an extensive, and expensive, parts inventory).

8

Economic
Indicators and
the Basic Data
of the
Macroeconomy

Introduction

The concept of an **economic indicator** refers to a statistical series that illustrates one aspect or another of macroeconomic performance.[1] More than one hundred of such indices are reported on a regular basis by the national statistical agencies, and by such international bodies as the **Organization for Economic Cooperation and Development** (OECD)[2] and the **International Monetary Fund** (IMF).[3] From the point of view of the business executive, the reason to have some awareness of these numbers is simply to be able to judge, in a general sense, which way the economy is headed. If it seems likely that the economy is headed for a recession, for example, it may not be the right time to undertake a major expansion of productivity capacity. In this book, we focus on just a few of the more important indicators; in particular, the following:

- gross domestic product (GDP)

- the aggregate price level

- the unemployment rate

- the interest rate

- the supply of money

- the foreign exchange rate

- the balance of payments

In the present chapter, in fact, we will concentrate on the first five of these, leaving questions of the exchange rate and the balance of payments for a later discussion.

Gross Domestic Product

The most common measure of aggregate economic activity is **gross domestic product** (GDP), which attempts to measure the value of all output produced in the domestic economy during a given accounting period, such as a quarter or a year. Another way of expressing this is that GDP measures the total **value added** in the nation's economy during the accounting period. We should distinguish between **nominal GDP**, which is simply the dollar value of domestic output, and **real GDP**. The latter concept is an attempt,

---

[1] The Economist, *The Economist Guide to Global Economic Indicators* (New York: John Wiley & Sons, 1994).

[2] http://www.oecd.org

[3] http://www.imf.org

via the device of a **price index**, to measure the actual *volume* of output. The real **economic growth rate** is then usually defined as the percentage rate of change of real GDP. Let the symbol **Y** stand for real GDP, and **P** for the aggregate price index (a measure of the average level of prices in the economy as a whole). Then, by definition:

(8.1)   **Nominal GDP = PY**

(8.2)   **Real GDP = PY/P = Y**

Also, using the lower-case symbol **y**, to stand for the growth rate of real GDP:

(8.3) $y = \dfrac{Y - Y_{-1}}{Y_{-1}} \times 100\%$

The most common breakdown of GDP is given by the familiar expression:

(8.4)   **Y = C + I + G + (X − IM)**

or, expressing this in nominal (dollar) terms:

(8.5)   **PY = \$C + \$I + \$G + (\$X − \$IM)**

(The dollar sign in front of a variable in the previous equation indicates a nominal sum of money.) The symbol **C** stands for **consumption expenditure**, on both durable and non-durable consumption goods, and **I** for **investment expenditure**. This, to an economist, means investment in physical plant and equipment, and in inventories. Meanwhile, **G** is total **government expenditure**. Finally, the symbol **X** stands for **exports**, and **IM** is **imports** (both priced in domestic currency). The expression **(X − IM)** therefore means **net exports**.

The definition of GDP as value added, or the total of **final goods and services** produced during an accounting period, such as a quarter or a year, means that not everything that the average person would think of as "economic activity" is included. Obviously it *excludes* all trades in existing assets, whether these are shares on the stock market, real estate transactions involving existing homes or raw land, or (e.g.) used bicycles. All such trades in existing assets clearly should not be included in a measure of *current* production. In fact, if you sell your existing home, the only part of the transaction that should in principle be included in GDP (whether or not it is in practice) is the commission to the real estate agent. That does represent payment for services rendered in the current period. If you then buy a new home rather than another existing home, that transaction would, however, be counted in the GDP, as it does represent production in the current period.

The definition of GDP as value-added also means that GDP does not measure the total value of *transactions* during the period, even of those related to current production. To avoid double counting, transactions in **intermediate goods** must be excluded. If I buy a new car this year, for example, I cannot count the tires on the car separately as part of GDP, as they are already included in the price of the car. On the other hand, if I buy news tires for my 10-year-old truck, those tires *are* a final good in that case, and should be counted. Table 8.1 gives a simple example of a value-added calculation for illustrative purposes, the value added in a loaf of bread.

Obviously, we cannot count the total value of transactions ($10.20 in Table 8.1) as measuring the value of economic activity — this would double count several times. The total of value added in the example is, in fact, equal to the value of the good sold to the final consumer ($3.95). They are the same thing. The GDP calculation applies this principle to the whole economy.

Why are net exports **(X – IM)** included in the GDP definition, and not just exports, X? As mentioned, GDP is supposed to capture the total value added of items produced in the domestic economy during the relevant accounting period. In principle, then, assuming that the categories of consumption expenditure, investment expenditure, and government expenditure are exhaustive, what GDP should measure is the total of **C** plus **I** plus **G** all *produced domestically*, plus the value of exports (**X**). However, in practice, the statistics for consumption, investment, and government spending do not specify whether any individual item purchased was produced domestically or abroad. That is why it is necessary to subtract the total value of imports (**IM**) to arrive at the correct figure.

We can illustrate the breakdown of GDP in Table 8.2 with some arbitrary figures for the imaginary economy of Ecoland, for a particular year. These numbers, and the ones to follow in subsequent sections, are "fic-

Table 8.1:   Value Added in a Loaf of Bread

	Value of Transactions	Value Added
Farmer sells grain to Miller	$0.85	$0.85
Miller sells flour to Baker	$2.05	$1.20
Baker sells bread to Retail Grocer	$3.35	$1.30
Grocer sells bread to Consumer	$3.95	$0.60
Total	$10.20	$3.95

tional". Ecoland does not exist, and (at the time of writing) the year under consideration is some time in the future. We have been careful, however, to make these numbers plausible in the sense that they are in orders of magnitude and proportions that could well occur in an actual medium-sized industrial economy. The reader will wish to look up the analogous numbers for any particular real economy that is of interest.

What we see in Table 8.2 is, in fact, known as the **expenditure breakdown** of GDP. It is always possible to break it down in a number of other ways, also — for example, by the income generated (**wages, profits, interest,** etc.). By definition, **income = expenditure**; what is expenditure for the buyer in any transaction is income for the seller. For readers familiar with the principles of accounting, this is the equivalent of double-entry bookkeeping. In fact, this reporting of national income is called **national income accounting**.

Price Indices and Inflation

An aggregate price index attempts to measure the average level of prices in money terms during any given accounting period. There is no one "correct" method of calculating this average; hence, a number of different such indices are reported, each one giving a slightly different answer to the question of how prices have changed "on average". In the IMF publication *World Economic Outlook*,[4] for example, the agency reports both a **consumer price index** (CPI) and a **GDP deflator** for each country. In Table

---

Table 8.2: **Illustrative Numbers for Nominal GDP**

Nominal GDP For Ecoland (2025)
(billions of Ecodollars)

$C	1,312.4
$I	399.2
$G	498.6
$[X – IM]	100.6
Statistical discrepancy	– 0.9
GDP (nominal Ecodollars)	2,309.9

---

[4] International Monetary Fund, *World Economic Outlook*, annual (Washington, DC: IMF).

8.3, we do the same for the hypothetical country of Ecoland. Many jurisdictions also report a **chain index**, which is a sort of hybrid of the two.

As can be seen, a price index arbitrarily defines the average level of prices in a particular year as equal to 100 (or 100%), and expresses prices in other years as some percentage of this. For the CPI in Table 8.3, the **base year** is 2019, and therefore prices in that year have a value of 100. In 2015, the index has a value of 86.4. The implication of this is that prices on average in 2015 were only around 86% of what they were to become in 2019. By the same token, the CPI in 2027 was 112.2, meaning that prices were around 12% higher by 2027 than they had been in 2019. The base year for the GDP deflator is 2025, and according to this calculation prices were, for example, only 96% of the 2025 levels three years earlier, in 2022. Similarly, by 2027 prices had only risen by about 1% from the base.

This treatment will not go into all of the details of how the different indices are calculated by statisticians. Suffice it to say that a CPI, for example, as the name might suggest, attempts to measure changes in the **cost of living** of the average consumer or household. This is done by defining a standard "bundle" of goods and services consumed by this average unit in

---

Table 8.3:   Illustrative Numbers for the Consumer Price Index and the GDP Deflator

Year	CPI	GDP Deflator
2015	86.4	79.6
2016	91.0	84.1
2017	95.4	88.0
2018	98.5	93.3
2019	100.0	94.2
2020	101.8	95.0
2021	103.6	95.8
2022	103.6	96.0
2023	105.8	97.3
2024	107.3	98.6
2025	109.2	100.0
2026	110.2	99.6
2027	112.2	101.3
2028	115.2	104.0
2029	118.2	106.5
2030	120.9	108.6

---

the base year and working out what this same bundle would have cost in all past and future years. It can be updated by moving the base year forward and by changing the composition of the bundle of goods (e.g., DVDs for VCRs).

To quickly illustrate how a consumer price index might be constructed, consider trying to calculate an index of a bundle of goods consisting of just three items — apples, wool, and wood — over a period of four years. The prices charged and quantities consumed in this example are shown in Table 8.4.

First we must choose a base year, say 2027. The actual quantities of the bundle consumed in that year will then be the "weights" used in the price index. Essentially what the index will do is work out what that same bundle of goods (23 apples, 35 wool, and 30 wood) would have cost in the prices of each of the other years. The calculation is as follows:

$$2025 \quad \frac{(14 \times 23)+(12 \times 35)+(10 \times 30)}{(18 \times 23)+(20 \times 35)+(12 \times 30)} = \frac{1042}{1474} \times 100 = \mathbf{70.7}$$

$$2026 \quad \frac{(20 \times 23)+(15 \times 35)+(11 \times 30)}{(18 \times 23)+(20 \times 35)+(12 \times 30)} = \frac{1315}{1474} \times 100 = \mathbf{89.2}$$

$$2027 \quad \frac{(18 \times 23)+(20 \times 35)+(12 \times 30)}{(18 \times 23)+(20 \times 35)+(12 \times 30)} = \frac{1474}{1474} \times 100 = \mathbf{100.0}$$

$$2028 \quad \frac{(25 \times 23)+(20 \times 35)+(15 \times 30)}{(18 \times 23)+(20 \times 35)+(12 \times 30)} = \frac{1635}{1474} \times 100 = \mathbf{110.9}$$

The CPI in this case would therefore be reported as shown in Table 8.5.

Table 8.4:   **Price and Quantity Data for Consumer Goods**

	Apples		Wool		Wood	
	P	Q	P	Q	P	Q
2025	14	22	12	31	10	40
2026	20	22	15	35	11	25
2027	18	23	20	35	12	30
2028	25	30	20	40	15	35

Table 8.5: **CPI for a Bundle of Three Goods**

Year	CPI
2025	70.7
2026	89.2
2027	100.0
2028	110.9

A GDP deflator will differ from the CPI in two main ways. First, the weights in the statistical calculation are changed each year. (They are the quantities consumed or purchased in the year for which the index is being calculated, rather than the base year.) Second, typically the coverage extends to the whole of GDP rather than just those items important for the cost of living. Evidently, given different methods of calculation, the rival indices will not give exactly the same answer for estimates of either the aggregate price index or of its rate of change, the **inflation rate**. For example, consider the results for the years 2025–2026 in Table 8.3. According to the CPI, there was a slight *rise* in prices between those years, whereas the GDP deflator is recording a slight *fall*. However, the emphasis should be on the adjective *slight*. If properly calculated, the different indices will not give a dramatically different picture of what is going on. In the years 2025–2026, the truth is that prices were not changing very much, so whether this comes out as a slightly negative, or a slightly positive change, the basic message is that prices were flat. Similarly, a period of persistent inflation will show up clearly enough in both indices even if the exact numbers differ, as will a period of persistent **deflation** (i.e., falling prices). So, although there is plenty of scope for arguing which is the "best" method of calculating inflation, in practice, for judging the basic trends, the choice may not matter very much as long as they are competitively calculated.

Whatever method is chosen for calculating the price index, the inflation rate is given by the formula in equation (8.6). Letting the symbol **p** (lower case) stand for the inflation rate, the inflation rate is just the percentage rate of change of the price index itself.

$$(8.6) \qquad \mathbf{p} = \frac{\mathbf{P} - \mathbf{P}_{-1}}{\mathbf{P}_{-1}} \times \mathbf{100\%}$$

The importance of the distinction between **real** and **nominal** variables in macroeconomics is further illustrated in Table 8.6, which highlights data for a period in which there was a **recession** in Ecoland. Technically, a

Table 8.6:   A Recession in Ecoland

Year	PY	P	Y	y (%)
	($b)	(2012 = 100)		
2015	1211.8	109.6	1105.7	—
2016	1301.6	114.9	1132.8	2.5
2017	1339.5	118.5	1130.4	−0.2
2018	1349.6	121.6	1109.9	−1.8
2019	1376.5	123.3	1116.4	0.6

recession occurs in the economy when real GDP falls (i.e., growth is negative) for at least two successive quarters. In Ecoland, the data actually show a recession for two full years, in 2017 and 2018. What is interesting in Table 8.6 is that if we look simply at the numbers for nominal GDP in the left-hand column, it would seem (falsely) that there were no economic difficulties in those years. The dollar value of GDP increases in every year without exception. However, also included in the table is an aggregate price index (this time with a base year of 2012). If we shift the decimal point in the price index two spaces to the left, so that 109.6, for example, becomes 1.096, and then use the results to deflate the dollar values, it is possible to arrive at an estimate of the real GDP, recorded in the third column. This is an estimate of the GDP in each year expressed in the prices of the base year. It is therefore sometimes called GDP in **"constant dollars"** (in this case "2012 dollars"). These numbers represent at least some sort of approximation to the actual volume of output. The picture of economic activity in Ecoland then seems very different from that suggested by just looking at nominal values. Real GDP does increase between 2015 and 2016, but then actually falls for two successive years in 2017 and 2018. Only in 2019 does the economy begin to grow again, and then only in a very weak recovery. The growth rate of real GDP (which is what is usually meant by the **rate of economic growth** as reported in the financial press) is shown in the extreme right-hand column of Table 8.6.

The Business Cycle, Inflation, and Unemployment

One of the most politically sensitive of the economic indicators is the **unemployment rate**, which many people take as *par excellence* the barometer of how well the economy is doing. There is some presumption that the GDP growth rate and unemployment are negatively related. That is to say, when the growth rate improves, the unemployment rate will fall. On the otherhand, there is also sometimes discussion in the financial press of a so-called "jobless recovery" — that is to say, a situation in which economic growth measured by real GDP is improving, but does not translate into a growth in employment opportunities. On a longer view, however, this situation tends to occur in the early stages of an economic recovery, when much of the growth is simply an increase in labor productivity. A sustained period of economic growth does tend to improve employment prospects, for obvious reasons. As discussed later in Chapter 11, this relationship was quantified many years ago, and is known as **Okun's Law**, after the economist who first developed the relevant equation.

The definition of what actually constitutes employment and unemployment also tends to be controversial. A particular problem is what happens to the so-called **discouraged workers**. An unemployed person is usually defined as someone who does not have a job but is "actively seeking" work. In practice, this often means someone who is officially registered with the relevant state agency, and is collecting unemployment benefits. But what happens when the benefits run out, or if the people concerned are so discouraged that they do not even present themselves to the government agency? They just disappear from the statistics, even though, clearly, they do remain unemployed in any meaningful sense of the term. Another problem is the definition of what it actually means to be "employed" in any given time period. For example, suppose during a particular quarter an individual works at a part-time job for 10 hours a week for three weeks, and does not work for the rest of the time. Is that person employed or unemployed during the quarter? It depends entirely on the definitions and cut-off points the government or statistical agency chooses to employ. These can and do differ across jurisdictions. With these caveats in mind, in each country there is a certain definition of the **labor force** (**LF**), meaning those employed plus those actively seeking work, and a definition of **employment** (**N**), each of which is more or less arbitrary. The unemployment rate (**u**) is then given by the formula:

$$(8.7) \qquad \mathbf{u} = \frac{(\mathbf{LF} - \mathbf{N})}{\mathbf{LF}} \times \mathbf{100\%}$$

Given the vagaries in calculating the figures, this number in itself may not, therefore, be very meaningful, but (at least if the definitions are consistent) *changes* in the unemployment rate will give some clues as to what is happening in the economy. It may not mean very much to say that, for example, the unemployment rate was 7% last year. However, if this year it goes up to 10%, that is obviously in the wrong direction. It is also true that some of the international organizations do try to provide harmonized definitions, so that it becomes more meaningful to compare the unemployment rate of, say, Denmark with that of Mexico, at least within the database of each agency.

Having defined the inflation rate, the unemployment rate, and the growth rate, now suppose that over a period of years the figures in Ecoland for each variable work out as in Table 8.7. It is now possible to observe the phenomenon of the **business cycle** in Ecoland by graphing the behavior of GDP growth, as in Figure 8.1. The term **cycle** is something of a misnomer, as the ups and downs of the economy are not all that regular or symmetrical. However, this usage is by now so well established that we must stick with it. A period in which the rate of growth of GDP is increasing, such as from 2018 to 2021, is the **expansionary** phase of the cycle. When the rate of growth is falling, as from 2021 to 2023, this is the **contractionary** phase. A local maxima, such as in 2026, is known as the business cycle **peak**, and a local minima, as in 2028, is the **trough**. As mentioned, when growth is negative, as in 2017 and 2018, this is a recession.

Business people would like to forecast, or anticipate, changes in the business cycle. Economists have created indices of leading indicators to estimate future economic activity. These indicators include factors such as average weekly hours worked by manufacturing workers, average number of initial applications for unemployment insurance and the number of manufacturers' new orders for consumer goods and materials. Unfortunately, however, these indices sometimes tend to be more useful in recording past economic activity than in actually predicting future changes in the business cycle.

Another issue, which is always front and center in economic debates, and is also controversial, is the relationship between inflation and unemployment. To the extent that unemployment is (negatively) related to the business cycle, this debate is also about the relationship between economic growth and inflation. Figure 8.2, for example, shows the relationship between inflation and unemployment according to our data for Ecoland. The reason that this relationship is controversial can be illustrated, for instance, by the behavior of the inflation rate and unemployment rate between the years 2016 to 2019. In this period (which coincides with a recession in Ecoland), inflation is falling and unemployment is rising. As the preferred economic policy in orthodox policy-making circles is usually to keep the inflation rate as low as possible (and certainly to take steps to reduce inflation after it has risen), the question naturally arises whether this objective is pursued at the expense of employment and economic growth. This is vigorously denied by the policy establishment. As will be discussed in later chapters, it is argued that any apparent trade-off between inflation and unemployment is only short term. In the longer run (it is argued) there is no reason why a low inflation rate is incompatible with a healthy

Table 8.7: Inflation, Unemployment, and Growth in Ecoland

Year	Inflation	Unemployment	Growth
2015	4.6	7.8	4.8
2016	5.3	7.5	2.4
2017	4.8	8.1	−0.2
2018	3.2	10.3	−1.8
2019	1.5	11.2	0.6
2020	1.8	11.1	2.2
2021	1.8	10.3	3.5
2022	0.0	9.4	2.8
2023	2.1	9.6	1.6
2024	1.6	9.1	4.2
2025	1.6	8.3	4.1
2026	0.9	7.6	5.4
2027	1.8	6.8	4.5
2028	2.7	7.2	1.5
2029	2.6	7.6	3.4
2030	2.3	7.6	2.8

Figure 8.1: The Business Cycle in Ecoland

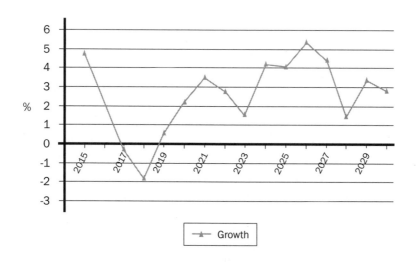

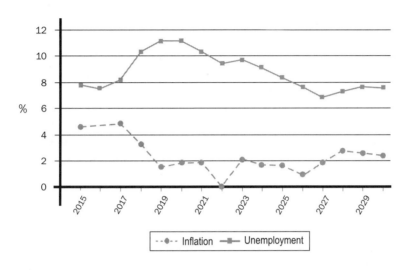

Figure 8.2: **Inflation and Unemployment in Ecoland**

economic growth rate and low unemployment. Some would go even further and argue that a low inflation rate is actually a prerequisite for economic prosperity (again from a longer-term perspective).

Interest Rates

Economics textbooks often talk about "the interest rate" as if this is just one thing, but in practice, there are many different types of interest rates on many different types of debt instruments and for different time periods. There are interest rates on mortgages, interest rates on credit card balances, interest rates on bank loans, etc. Moreover, not every individual will get the same interest rate for the same purpose. Individuals who pose a higher credit risk (from the bank's point of view) may have to pay a higher interest rate on a loan. To be fair to the textbooks, however, it is true that (very roughly speaking) all interest rates do tend to move up and down together. In general, no one is in any doubt as to whether the period they are currently living through is one of "high" or "low" interest rates.

One important issue is to be able to distinguish between **nominal interest rates** and **real interest rates**. The nominal rate is simply the rate actually quoted in the marketplace. It is the percentage return, in terms of money, on a loan of money. If there is a loan between two individuals of \$100 for one year, and the interest rate is 5% *per annum*, then the lender will have to repay the borrower \$105 (principal plus interest) at the end of the year. The concept of real interest, however, takes account of the fact that usually inflation is going on, and that the \$105 received one year hence will typically buy less in terms of goods and services than the same sum of money would do today. For example, suppose that inflation is also 5%. Then \$105 in one year's time will only buy the same amount of goods and services as \$100 will do today. In this case, with a nominal interest rate also of 5%, the effective cost of borrowed money is zero. That is to say, the real interest rate is zero. Similarly, if the nominal interest rate is, for argument's sake, 16% and the expected inflation rate is 12%, the real interest rate is actually 4%. The relationship between the two is, therefore, as follows:

$$(8.8) \qquad r = i - p^e$$

In this expression, i stands for the nominal interest rate, r for the real interest rate, and p^e for the expected inflation rate. So, the real interest rate is equal to the nominal interest rate less the expected inflation rate. In terms of economic decision-making, it is presumably the real rate, rather than the nominal rate, that matters, as the real rate represents the real cost of borrowing. Adjusting the nominal interest rate for expected inflation in this way is sometimes known as the **"Fisher effect"**, after the famous American economist, Irving Fisher.

Another distinction that needs to be made between different types of interest rates relates to the time period for which the loan contract is in force. The expressions **short rates** and **long rates**, for example, are commonly used, even though the dividing line between what is "short" and what is "long" tends to be a bit vague. The relationship between interest rates on securities with different terms to maturity is known as the **yield curve**, and this is a concept with which business students may be familiar from their courses in finance. We illustrate the different types of interest rates with some numbers for nominal interest rates with different terms to maturity in Table 8.8. This table documents three different types of interest rates that each play a role in the economy of Ecoland. The first is the **policy-related interest rate**, which is a (very) short-term interest rate, essentially determined by the **central bank** in its implementation of monetary policy. The central bank is a government agency (although typically operating at arm's length from the rest of the government, such as the Ministry of Finance) which, in the modern world is the lynchpin of the financial system and is responsible for the conduct of monetary policy. In the USA the central bank is known as the **Federal Reserve Board**; in Japan it is the **Bank of Japan**; in the Euro-zone it is called the **European Central Bank**; in Canada it is the **Bank of Canada**; and so on. Typically, the policy-related

Table 8.8: **Nominal Interest Rates in Ecoland**

Year	Policy Rate	Short Rate	Long Rate
2015	8.8	8.9	10.2
2016	10.9	11.3	9.9
2017	11.6	12.6	10.8
2018	9.0	9.0	9.8
2019	6.6	6.7	8.5
2020	4.6	5.0	6.9
2021	5.1	5.4	6.9
2022	5.8	6.7	7.2
2023	3.0	4.3	6.5
2024	4.3	3.2	5.7
2025	5.0	4.7	5.8
2026	4.8	4.9	5.9
2027	5.8	5.8	6.0
2028	2.3	3.4	5.5
2029	2.8	2.9	5.4
2030	2.5	2.9	5.3

interest rate is an overnight rate on inter-bank settlement balances among the major commercial financial institutions that participate in the **clearing house** operated by the central bank. In the USA, the policy rate is called the **federal funds rate**, in Japan the **overnight call rate**, in the Euro-zone the **main refinancing rate**, and in Canada the **overnight rate**. Second, short rates are usually defined as interests on debt instruments with less than one year to maturity. Very often in the compilation of statistics, the rate on **three-month treasury bills** is used as the benchmark for short rates. Finally, long rates are usually represented by a **10-year bond rate** or longer. When the figures are presented on an annual basis, as above, the figure given is obviously the annual average level of each interest rate. To get some idea of the inter-relationships between interest rates with different terms to maturity, the numbers from Table 8.8 are now also graphed in Figure 8.3.

As can be seen, the short rate of interest basically follows the policy rate, so it is reasonable to conclude that monetary policy decisions generally determine the overall level of short-term nominal interest rates in the economy. The long rate, however, is much less "volatile" than the short rate.

Figure 8.3: Nominal Interest Rates in Ecoland

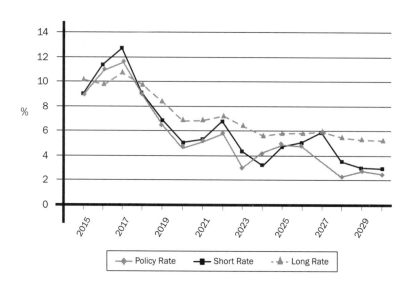

Even though, over the long haul, it moves in the same general direction as the policy rate, it certainly does not follow every twist and turn. This is because, according to the **expectations theory** of the **term structure of interest rates**, the long rate is basically a geometrically weighted average of *expected* future short rates, and there must always be some uncertainty about the direction of short-term rates in the future. If the short rate falls in the current period, for example, this may just be a "blip", and it might go up again very soon. So, it is unlikely that long interest rates will begin to respond to changes in short rates until a trend is well established. Long rates can even move in the opposite direction to short rates, at least for a while.

The yield curve itself would be represented by a vertical cross section in Figure 8.4. A so-called **normal yield curve** exists in 2028, for example, with short rates lower than long rates. Indeed, this is usually the case, as can be seen. However, it is also possible for an **inverted yield curve** to exist, with long rates lower than short rates, as occurs in 2017, for example. When this happens, it is usually taken by the financial markets as a sign that a recession is imminent, as indeed did occur in the imaginary Ecoland economy around that time.

Table 8.9 illustrates some of the behavior of real interest rates in Ecoland. This is a more difficult task than it sounds because the calculation

Figure 8.4: Ex-post Real Interest Rates in Ecoland

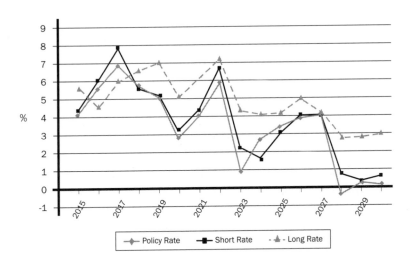

Table 8.9: Ex-post Real Interest Rates in Ecoland

Year	Ex-post Real Policy Rate	Ex-post Real Short Rate	Ex-post Real Long Rate
2015	4.2	4.3	5.6
2016	5.6	6.0	4.6
2017	6.8	7.8	6.0
2018	5.8	5.6	6.6
2019	5.1	5.2	7.0
2020	2.8	3.2	5.1
2021	4.0	4.3	5.8
2022	5.8	6.7	7.2
2023	0.9	2.2	4.4
2024	2.7	1.6	4.1
2025	3.4	3.1	4.2
2026	3.9	4.0	5.0
2027	4.0	4.0	4.2
2028	−0.4	0.7	2.8
2029	0.2	0.3	2.8
2030	0.2	0.6	3.0

of what real interest rates actually were in any *past* period is a complicated exercise. The definition of the real interest rate is that it is equal to the nominal interest rate minus *expected* inflation. This is sometimes called the **ex-ante real interest rate** (ex-ante meaning "before the event"). It is the term involving expected inflation that is the wildcard. In principle, everyone's estimation of the real rate can be different, depending on what their expectations of inflation actually are. In practice, there is probably a rough consensus, at any point in time, so that changes in real interest rates do have definite effects on the economy; but even this fact is not much use in trying to work out what the expectations were in any past period. No attempt is made to resolve these problems here, and the numbers in Table 8.9 represent simply the **ex-post real interest rate** (ex-post meaning "after the event"): that is, the nominal rate minus the *actual* inflation rate, as it turned out to be. This, therefore, only gives an approximate indication of what the "true" real interest was, as it appeared at the time.

In Figure 8.4, the numbers from Table 8.9 are displayed in a graphical format. The important point is that the behavior of real interest rates is not always the same as that of nominal rates, as illustrated in Figure 8.3. As mentioned, it must in fact be the real rate that is of primary significance from the point of view of business decision-making. Therefore Figure 8.4 provides somewhat more meaningful information than the one simply graphing out the nominal rates. For example, the information that the real policy rate was as high as 6.8% in 2017 is more significant than the observation that the nominal rate was 11.6% in the same year. The former really is high for the policy rate, whereas the latter may or may not be high depending on what the inflation rate is. Had inflation been 20% in 2017 instead of 4.7%, the ex-post real interest rate would actually have been negative. Again, note that the period of relatively high real interest rates around 2017 to 2019 coincided with the recession and high unemployment of those years.

The Supply of Money

The most obvious definition of the rate of interest, as discussed above, is the payment for the loan of a sum of money. This in turn, however, raises the question of what is meant by the term **money** in a modern economy. The most restrictive definition would be what is called either **the monetary base** or high-powered money — or, sometimes, M0. This consists of, essentially, the liabilities of the central bank, and as the name implies, is the most basic or core money in the system. Using the symbol **H** (to stand for "high-powered money") the definition of the monetary base is:

$$(8.9) \qquad H = CU + R$$

Where CU is currency held by the non-bank public (that is, cash held by all individuals and businesses outside the banking system), and R is bank reserves. Bank reserves consist in turn of the cash that is held by the banks themselves (e.g., in the vaults and tills, and in the ATMs), plus some deposits held by commercial banks with the central bank, which are regarded as equal to cash. Although the liabilities of the central bank do hold a very important place in the economic system (and will continue to do so even if/when cash itself disappears and everything is done electronically) particularly in enabling central bank control over the base interest rate or policy rate — quantitatively they are very small in relation to the nominal size of the economy, and obviously do not serve as the most important form of money used in making transactions. That role is played by the aggregate deposit liabilities of private sector financial institutions, such as commercial banks. The total **money supply**, in the sense of the volume of dollars that is "out there" in the system waiting to be spent, is therefore not given by equation (8.9) but by:

(8.10)   **M = CU + D**

Where **CU** is once again currency in the hand of the non-bank public and **D** stands for deposits in commercial banks or other financial institutions that also perform banking functions, known as the "near banks". The only remaining issue is precisely which deposits (checking deposits, savings deposits, term deposits?), in which institutions, should be included. In fact, most central banks publish series of a number of different monetary aggregates called M1, M2, M3, M4, etc. (and beyond) that successively include more and more types of deposits and more and more institutions.

The relationship between the monetary base and the money supply itself is discussed in detail in the appendix to Chapter 10. For now, we note that the main interest that economists have in the supply of money relates back to the old **quantity theory of money**. This is the idea that money supply growth is the main cause of inflation, or at least that money supply growth is correlated with inflation. The IMF, for example, publishes data on money supply growth for each country, giving two series: one that is called narrow money (meaning usually M1), and another called broad money (usually either M2 or M3, depending on the country). These can then both be compared to inflation. We carry out a similar exercise for Pecunia (the neighboring economy to "Ecoland" from Chapter 7) in Table 8.10, and the results are then graphed in Figure 8.5.

The graphs in Figure 8.5 are actually similar to what we would find in most countries in the modern period. There seems to be little or no relation between narrow money and inflation (presumably because, in today's electronic world, the M1 definition of the money supply is obsolete). However,

Table 8.10:   Money Supply Growth and Inflation in Pecunia

Year	Narrow Money	Broad Money	Inflation
2019	7.6	4.1	2.3
2020	17.8	2.1	1.7
2021	10.6	−1.3	1.2
2022	8.7	1.4	−0.4
2023	8.9	4.3	1.7
2024	14.4	6.9	4.1
2025	15.3	5.9	1.1
2026	4.6	5.0	1.0
2027	11.1	6.2	3.2
2028	11.5	6.3	3.3

Figure 8.5:   Money Supply Growth and Inflation in Pecunia

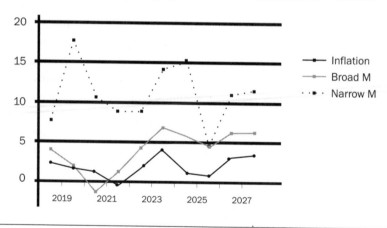

on a more inclusive or up-to-date definition of money, there does seem to be more of a correlation, as the old quantity theorists would have predicted.

Chapter Summary

- Businesspeople are always benchmarking their performance by comparing themselves to the competition. "Yes, we had a 10% increase in our profits last quarter, but our competitors increased profitability by 20%." You can substitute any number of other measures that businesspeople might look at, such as market share, exports, etc.

- It is important also to benchmark the performance of the nation. It is, generally, harder for a businessperson to be successful in a poorly performing economy than it is in an economy that is performing well.

- The Internet is an important tool that can help businesspeople keep up-to-date with statistics. Most national governments have websites providing the latest economic data for their countries. There are also a number of international institutions that provide statistics free of charge on their websites.

- Macroeconomics looks at "big picture" variables, such as: national income, inflation, interest rates, etc.

- It is critical to distinguish between nominal and real values. For most measures of economic activity, we need to analyze real data — that is, after the effects of price changes have been removed. For example, it might be wonderful to earn a 20% return on a government bond; however, if the rate of inflation is 30% we are really losing 10% of our investment every year.

- The macro-economy experiences cyclical activity, moving from periods of expansion to contraction. This is called the business cycle.

- One of the most important issues for a businessperson is to try to understand this cyclical activity and assess the impact it has on the firm. "Is there anything I can do for our business during a downturn?" "Should I try to diversify the business to protect us when economic growth slows, or turns negative?"

- Increasingly, in practice, businesspeople are concerned with the international business cycle. This may, or may not, coincide with the national economic cycle.

Problems

1. What are the components of aggregate expenditure, and what is the relative importance of each of them?

2. Define nominal GDP and real GDP. Is it possible for nominal GDP in a year to be less than real GDP in the same year? Explain.

3. Briefly explain how nominal GDP can increase, yet real GDP decrease, during the same period.

4. What would happen to GDP if large numbers of stay-at-home parents suddenly entered the workplace and hired others to cook, clean, and care for their children? Is this change reflective of an actual change in the physical output of the economy?

5. The Fisher equation says that the nominal interest rate **i** is equal to the real interest rate **r** plus the expected inflation rate **p^e**. Use this concept to complete the following table:

(1) real interest rate (%)	(2) nominal interest rate (%)	(3) expected inflation rate (%)
_____	10	4
_____	10	8
_____	10	12
4	7	_____
–2	12	_____
3	_____	5
–2	_____	9

6. What is the expectations theory of the term structure of interest rates?

7. Explain what the Fisher effect/Fisher hypothesis represents.

Case Study Questions | The Comeback of Caterpillar

Business Cycles

1. Caterpillar produces intermediate goods that are purchased by firms in the heavy construction industry. How might a downturn in the business cycle impact the demand for heavy construction equipment (the 1982–1984 global recession)?

Case Study Questions Continued

2. Why might the impact of a downturn in the business cycle be different in a developing versus developed country?

3. Would the heavy construction equipment industry be a leading or lagging indicator (i.e., does the sector experience sales changes before a general turn in the business cycle or after the cycle has turned, a leading or lagging indicator, respectively)?

4. How did Caterpillar's diversification strategy address the business cycle issue?

Hint: Capital-intensive industries may be more susceptible to economic downturns because expenditures by customers may be postponed until the business cycle improves. The business cycle may be different between developed and developing nations because the economy in developing countries can be more volatile and susceptible to changes in the economy.

Downsizing

1. Between 1990 and 1993 Caterpillar cut 10,000 jobs, yet sales grew from $10 to $15 billion. How is it possible to have such strong sales growth during this period of downsizing?

Developing Nations

1. What is the relationship between population growth and economic development in developing nations and the comeback of Caterpillar?

Hint: Population growth has stagnated in many of the developed nations: some will even experience population declines. Popula-

Case Study Questions Continued

tion growth, accompanied by economic growth, will require expenditures in heavy construction equipment.

Appendix 8.1

The Yield Curve:
A Numerical Example

In the text of this chapter, the concept of the yield curve, describing the term structure of interest rates, was briefly mentioned. A good example of a yield curve would be the range of quotes offered by commercial banks and other financial institutions on residential mortgages for different terms. Table 8A.1 lists the quotes currently offered by the "ACME Trust Company".

From Table 8A.1, it is easy to construct the yield curve for this type of security as in Figure 8A.1, with interest rates on the vertical axis and time on the horizontal axis. This is a so-called "normal" yield. If the curve was negatively sloped instead of positively sloped (that is, with interest rates on

---

Table 8A.1: Residential Mortgage Rate Quotations

Term	Interest Rate
1 year	4.55%
2 years	4.80%
3 years	5.30%
4 years	6.00%
5 years	6.15%
6 years*	6.70%
7 years	7.25%

* interpolated

---

the shorter maturities being higher than those on the longer maturities), it would be called an "inverted" yield curve.

Figure 8A.2 shows a stylized version of an "inverted" yield curve, with short rates higher than long rates.

Figure 8A.1:   A "Normal" Yield Curve

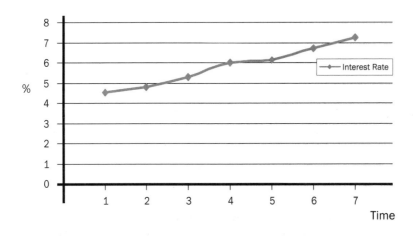

Figure 8A.2:   An Inverted Yield Curve

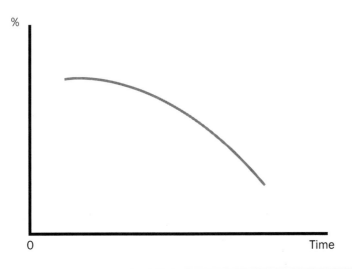

9

The Simple "Keynesian" Model and an Introduction to Fiscal Policy

Introduction

One of the very simplest approaches to macroeconomic policy-making, but one that has certainly been practically important, builds on the **national income identity** discussed in the previous chapter — that is,

$$(9.1) \qquad Y = C + I + G + (X - IM)$$

where the definitions of the symbols remain as previously discussed. This is the premise of the simple Keynesian model, named for J.M. Keynes, the author of the *General Theory*.[1] However, we should be careful to note that the approach to economics described as "Keynesian" in the textbooks is not so much pure Keynes as the interpretation of Keynes's work put forward by influential American economists in the mid-20th century, such as (notably) Paul Samuelson, a Nobel Prize winner and the author of a ubiquitous textbook.[2] The conventional wisdom would have it that this neo-Keynesian model, simple though it is, was actually very influential in practical policy-making in the third quarter of the 20th century. If so, it was apparently very successful in its day as this was generally a period of remarkable economic prosperity, by historical standards, at least for the "advanced industrialized nations". So much so that some authors have dubbed this "the golden age of capitalism".[3] However, critics of the Keynesian approach have argued that this all fell apart in the 1970s, during the era of so-called **stagflation** (i.e., a combination of high unemployment and high inflation), and that Keynesian economics was actually responsible for these conditions. In any event, there was definitely a reaction against Keynesian-style policies over the last two decades of the 20th and into the 21st century, in both academic and policy-making circles all over the world. At least in terms of rhetoric and public pronouncements, policy-makers today usually embrace very different views. On the other hand, however, as a glance at the financial press on any given day will easily confirm, it is very hard to banish Keynesian-type concerns entirely from the world of practical decision-making. Discussions of what to do about the government budget and taxes, for example, remain very much at the center of the public policy debate.

---

[1] John Maynard Keynes, *The General Theory of Employment, Interest and Money* (London: Macmillan, 1936).

[2] Paul A. Samuelson, *Economics* (New York: McGraw-Hill Book Company, 1948).

[3] S.A. Marglin and J.B. Schor (Eds.), *The Golden Age of Capitalism: Reinterpreting the Post-War Experience* (Oxford: Clarendon Press, 1990).

The Theory of Effective Demand and the Investment Multiplier

To illustrate the essence of the Keynesian approach, let us temporarily simplify the argument still further by imagining a very basic economy with no "foreign sector" — that is, an economy that does not trade with the rest of the world — and no "public sector", meaning that (in spite of what was said about the government earlier) there is no government expenditure or taxation, at least to begin with. In this case, the national income identity reduces to:

$$(9.2) \qquad Y = C + I$$

The crucial step now is to argue that aggregate consumption itself depends on income, and to add a "consumption function" of the type:

$$(9.3) \qquad C = cY \qquad\qquad 0 < c < 1$$

We should note that equation (9.3) is the simplest possible version of a consumption function, illustrating the basic idea that consumption will increase with income. Most textbooks would usually add a constant term to this expression, reflecting the idea that even if income were reduced to zero, there would still be some minimum level of consumption (presumably financed out of past savings). However, as this does not add anything important to the argument, we have omitted it to reduce the number of algebraic symbols employed. In any event, the argument is that if c is around 0.8, then 80% of income is spent on consumption goods, and the rest is saved. In (9.3), c is what is known as the **marginal propensity to consume** (MPC), meaning if a consumer were to receive an extra (or marginal) dollar of income, 80 cents of this would be spent, and 20 cents saved. The **marginal propensity to save** (MPS), meanwhile, is evidently 0.2 (or $1 - c$), in this case. As equation (9.3) is a simple proportional relationship, we should note that the MPC coincides with the **average propensity to consume** (APC) in this case. This will not always be true, and for the more general functional form, the usual relationship between marginal and average concepts (as discussed in Chapter 4) would apply.

Now substitute equation (9.3) into equation (9.2), and solve for national income, **Y**. The result is:

$$(9.4) \qquad Y = [1/(1 - c)]I$$

Recall that the meaning of **I** is the demand for investment goods, or the amount spent by firms on new plant and capital equipment. So, equation (9.4) claims that the level of output in the economy (in this very simple economy) is determined by the amount spent on investment goods (the *demand* for investment goods), multiplied by a term involving the MPC (or MPS). For this reason it is sometimes known as the **theory of effective demand**. The expression $[1/(1 - c)]$ itself is known as the **multiplier**. More formally:

(9.5) $\Delta Y/\Delta I = 1/(1 - c)$

Put this way, the multiplier shows by how much GDP will expand if there is an increase in investment spending (and also by how much it will decline if investment spending falls off). In our example, with $c = 0.8$, the multiplier has a value of 5.0 (or 1/0.2). Therefore, if a steady amount of $10 billion, for example, is spent on investment in every period, GDP each period will be $50 billion. If an *additional* $1 billion is spent on investment (for a total now of $11 billion), then GDP will increase by $5 billion (to a total of $55 billion each period).

How does this work? The argument goes something like this. The extra $1 billion spent on plant and machinery represents $1 billion of additional income for entrepreneurs and workers in the capital goods industry. As we have already said, in general around 80% of any additional income will be spent and 20% saved. So, there will now be $800 million of the *new* income spent on consumer goods by the producers in the capital goods industry. This then creates another $800 million worth of income for the producers in the consumer goods industries. Further, out of this $800 million, 80% (or $640 million) will also be spent on some more goods in a third round. And so on. Thus far, we already can account for $1,000 million + $800 million + $640 million + ... + (x million) of additional spending, and we are nowhere near the end of the chain. The expression $[1/(1 - c)]$ simply represents the final amount by which GDP will have increased when the process converges. The initial increase in spending is literally "multiplied" several times over before the effects die out.

The argument can also be illustrated in graphical form in the diagram in Figure 9.1. Figure 9.1 graphs "expenditure" **E** against "income" **Y**. But by definition, expenditure must equal income (or **E = Y**), so this is an illustration of the so-called **circular flow of income**, meaning that what is expenditure to one person is income to another. The identity **E = Y** is therefore represented by the 45° line from the origin. In our simplified model, total expenditure is just equal to consumption spending plus investment spending — that is, **E = C + I** (as **E = Y**, this is obviously the same as equation [9.2]), and the expenditure function slopes upward with respect to income, because consumption increases with income, as discussed. Equilibrium income is determined at the point where the expenditure function crosses the 45° line. When the level of investment is **I1**, the equilibrium level of income will be **Y1**. Now suppose that investment increases to **I2**. This will shift the expenditure function vertically upward by the amount **(I2 − I1)**. In the new

Figure 9.1: Income and Expenditure Analysis

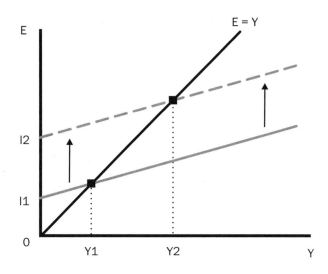

equilibrium, the level of income will increase to **Y2**, and the multiplier effect is shown by the fact that the increase in income (**Y2 – Y1**) turns out to be greater than the initial increase in investment (**I2 – I1**). If investment falls off, the multiplier relationship will obviously work in reverse.

Criticisms of "Keynesian Economics"

If all of the above is true and, moreover, if this idea of a society "spending its way to prosperity" did indeed seem to work in the real world in several jurisdictions during the third quarter of the 20th century (according to many observers), we might well ask why there remains any discussion of economic problems at all? Why not just increase spending by whatever amount necessary to produce full employment? Clearly, critics would say that the whole argument is just "too good to be true". One obvious point is that the argument seems to imply that just by increasing the *demand* for any product or service, the quantities supplied of that product will always be forthcoming. There is no discussion of any supply problems, scarcity, the incentives facing firms and entrepreneurs, etc. It would not be fair to accuse J.M. Keynes himself of this as there actually is a detailed discussion of supply in the *General Theory*. It is, however, an obvious criticism to make of subsequent "Keynesianism". Such concerns have led some observers to conclude that even if the orthodox Keynesian model may be appropriate for an economy in a deep depression (when supply issues are not the problem, and it is just a question of getting things moving), it does not apply more generally. We will begin the discussion of the supply side of macroeconomics in Chapter 10, and it will continue in the chapters that follow.

Another reason the Keynesian model is frowned on, particularly by fiscal conservatives, is for what it seems to imply for the public finances, the **government budget deficit** and the **national debt**. The term **fiscal policy** means basically the national government's policies on issues of government spending and taxation. If, as the Keynesians believed, all that is needed for economic prosperity is more spending, the thought is bound to occur that rather than waiting for the private sector to invest, the government itself can do the spending. All it would need to do is just build more schools, hospitals, roads, public housing, etc. All these are presumably "good things" in themselves, but in addition, according to Keynesians, such spending would actually boost the rest of economy also. It is obvious that conservative critics would then have serious concerns about what such an approach would do to the public finances and, beyond that, to the inflation rate and the value of existing financial assets. We can begin to understand this debate by now reintroducing the public sector once again to our simple model of the economy.

The Public Sector

Allowing for the existence of government spending and taxes means that the national income identity must now include government spending again, and it will become:

(9.6) $Y = C + I + G$

Also, as taxes are now being collected, consumption must depend on "net of tax" income, or disposable income, where T stands for total tax collection:

(9.7) $C = c(Y - T)$

Hence, the solution for GDP is now:

(9.8) $Y = [1/(1 - c)][I + G - cT]$

Just as an increase in private sector investment will cause an increase in GDP, through the multiplier process it seems that an increase in government spending will do the same thing. However, an increase in taxes will do the opposite and reduce the level of output. Therefore, in addition to the investment multiplier, we can derive the **government expenditure multiplier** and the **tax multiplier** as follows:

(9.9) $\Delta Y / \Delta G \; = \; 1/(1 \, - \, c)$

(9.10) $\Delta Y / \Delta T \; = \; -c/(1 \, - \, c)$

An increase in government spending will increase the level of GDP, as will a tax cut. A tax increase will reduce the level of real GDP.

One interesting point to notice is that the tax multiplier is less in absolute value than the government expenditure multiplier. The reason for this is that *all* of any increase in government expenditure will be spent (by definition), whereas any increase in taxes **(1 – c)** of that amount would have been saved anyway. If taxes increase by $1,000, for example, and if the MPC is 0.8 as before, $200 of that amount would have been saved anyway. The net reduction in spending is only $800. Now, imagine a situation in which government spending is increased by $1,000, and this is "financed" by an increase in taxes of exactly the same amount. All of the $1,000 spent by the government will be a stimulus to the economy, but the drag on the economy caused by the taxes is actually only $800. So there is a net stimulus to the economy of $200, even though in budgetary terms the increase in government spending is exactly offset by the increase in taxes. This is sometimes described by saying that the **balanced budget multiplier** is positive. This expression may be somewhat misleading, however, as it is only the *change* in the budget that is balanced. There is no information about the existing state of the budget.

In general, of course, and the balanced budget multiplier concept notwithstanding, the concern of fiscal conservatives is that there is a clear temptation *both* to increase spending and also to reduce taxes, as both will apparently lead to improved economic outcomes. In the conservative view, it is doubtful that such a loose fiscal policy would result in improved economic outcomes, and in any event conservatives believe it will certainly lead to larger budget deficits. Conservatives do, of course, tend to favor tax cuts themselves, and sometimes, like the Keynesians, argue that this would boost the economy. Their reasoning, however, is different — focusing on the incentive effects that lower taxes will have on firms and individuals (encouraging them to work harder). In general, fiscal conservatives believe in "small government" and think that supply-side tax cuts further this goal.

International Aspects

If we now bring back the net exports term in equation (9.1) and define net exports as:

(9.11) $NX = X - IM$

we can see that there must also be a **trade multiplier** or **international multiplier** of the general form:

(9.12) $\Delta Y / \Delta NX = 1/(1 - c)$

As with our discussion of the consumption function earlier, the reader should note that (9.12) is the simplest possible version of the concept. Many textbooks also argue that there is a systematic **marginal propensity to import** (separate from the propensity to consume itself) whereby the demand specifically for foreign goods systematically increases with income. This would reduce the overall value of all the multipliers in equations (9.9), (9.10), and (9.12), due to leakages from the domestic economy. For example, if **m**, a positive fraction, is the propensity to import, the value of the government expenditure multiplier, for instance, is reduced to $\Delta Y / \Delta G = 1/(1 - c + m)$.

For the present purposes, however, we simply note that the existence of the international multiplier (whatever its precise value) provides a mechanism whereby changes in macroeconomic conditions can be transmitted across international borders and become global, as in a **global recession** or a **global boom**. Suppose, for example, that there is a recession in a large economy A, and that this reduces income in A, and hence reduces A's demand for imports from all other countries. The NX term for the small country B will consequently be reduced and, according to equation (9.12), this will also cause a recession in B. In other words, the recession becomes global. An expansion in the larger country, A, would have the opposite effect.

The Government Budget Deficit and the National Debt

Returning now to the question of the public finances, we should note that government spending (as defined above) and taxes are not the only factors that determine the size of the budget deficit and the national debt. The interest payments on the existing debt are also relevant. In what follows, let the symbol **D** stand for the national debt, or the value of government bonds outstanding. Hence ΔD must be new borrowing or the deficit. Then (in real terms) the so-called **government budget constraint** will be given by:

(9.13) $\Delta D = G - T + rD$

where **r** is the real interest rate on government debt. The overall deficit actually consists of two main components, the so-called **primary deficit** (or **G − T**), plus the interest payments on the outstanding debt.

There is much debate and, frequently, much hand-wringing in the public policy arena, whenever the overall deficit gets "too large". However, the expression for the government budget constraint does illustrate that dealing with a deficit may well be a much more complicated matter than just the obvious remedies of cutting spending and increasing taxes. The interest rate, for example, may to a large extent be controlled by the monetary policy of the government's own central bank. Thus, if the deficit increases because interest rates have been increased, the government may have only itself to blame. Also, note that the *totals* of government expenditures and tax collection will actually depend on the state of the economy. If there is a recession, for example, total income will go down. Therefore, even if tax rates remained unchanged, the total amount of income taxes collected must be reduced. Similarly, during a recession government spending may automatically go up (paying more in unemployment benefits, for example). This means that if, as the Keynesians claim, fiscal policy also affects the state of the economy, then there could be a serious problem of a "vicious cycle" in trying to reduce a deficit. For example, one seemingly obvious way to reduce a deficit is to raise tax rates; but if the higher taxes do slow down the economy, actual **tax revenues** may fall. Evidently, there are many pitfalls and much scope for debate about the appropriate fiscal policy.

A great deal of attention is also paid in the public policy debates to the **debt/GDP ratio**, and the levels of this indicator that are supposedly viable or sustainable. We should note, first, that a change in this ratio (i.e., **D/Y**) is given by the following formula:

$$(9.14) \qquad \Delta(D/Y) = (D/Y)[\Delta D/D - \Delta Y/Y]$$

where $\Delta Y/Y$ is the same thing as **y** (the rate of economic growth). Now take equation (9.13) above, and divide through by **Y** itself. The result will be:

$$(9.15) \qquad \Delta D/Y = (G - T)/Y + r(D/Y)$$

Combining the two equations (9.14) and (9.15) then gives the following expression for the evolution of the debt/GDP ratio:

$$(9.16) \qquad \Delta(D/Y) = (G - T)/Y + (® - y)(D/Y)$$

It is clear that if the primary deficit (as a percentage of GDP) increases, the debt/GDP ratio will increase. Beyond this, however (if the primary deficit/GDP ratio is stable), the behavior of the debt/GDP ratio is going to depend on the expression $r - y$, which is the difference between the real interest rate and the economic growth rate. If the real interest rate is high and the growth rate is low, the debt/GDP ratio will just go on increasing. The interest payments keep piling up, increasing the amount of debt, and the growth rate of the denominator of the debt/GDP ratio is not fast enough to offset it. On the other hand, if $r < y$, the interest burden is not so large, and the economy is growing faster than this anyway. The **D/Y** ratio will eventually settle down to some constant value and will not continuously increase.

Once again, as in the case of the annual deficit, we should note that government complaints about how the debt/ratio is getting "out of control" may sometimes be disingenuous. For example, and as mentioned in the discussion of the deficit, if the real rate of interest increases (because the state central bank is pursuing a "tight money" policy to cure inflation, for example), then, of course, this will increase the debt burden of the government, both because of the higher interest rate itself, and also because the tight money policy will reduce the growth rate (reduce **y**). Similarly, if **austerity policies**, such as cutting spending and increasing taxes (designed to make direct inroads into the deficit and the debt), do, in fact, reduce the rate of growth, they may end up indirectly making the **D/Y** ratio worse rather than better.

Chapter Summary

- It is probably fair to say that the Keynesian approach to policy arose out of the Great Depression of the 1930s, which was long, deep, and international. There literally seemed to be no way out. Countries raised tariffs to protect local industries and jobs; but, of course, trading partners retaliated (remember game theory). As a result, world trade collapsed, with a huge international multiplier effect. This trade multiplier obviously works in much the same way as the government expenditure multiplier and investment multiplier in the domestic economy.

- Government expenditures were greater than revenues, so governments contracted spending. This negative multiplier effect made the situation worse.

- Keynes argued that the problem was insufficient aggregate demand. Government spending must be increased and, through the multiplier effect, national income and jobs would be increased.

- The Keynesian model seemed at one time to be a great success. And it is true that there has not been a "great depression" for over 70 years.

- Economists still debate the merits of the Keynesian model. What about the supply side of the equation? What about overspending? What about the government budget deficit and national debt? What about inflation? The reaction against Keynes has lasted now for more than a quarter century.

- While important points have been raised, they obscure the underlying message of Keynes, the view that the level of demand in an economy should be "managed" (presumably by government) to smooth what seemed to be the excessive booms and busts of the capitalist system. Such a notion in itself, of course, was enough to make Keynes anathema to political conservatives and libertarians. The mix of instruments has changed over the past 70 years — tax policy, competition law, monetary policy, international trade agreements, and so on — but the case for macroeconomic management of the economy still seems persuasive to many, and certainly discussions of macroeconomic policy continue to dominate the business pages.

- As the world has become more global and interdependent, then logically this type of approach would imply a need to "manage" demand in the global economy also. This would lead to greater importance for international financial institutions, such as the International Monetary Fund (IMF) and the World Bank.

Problems

1. How would government officials use a knowledge of the marginal propensity to consume when considering a tax cut?

2. Explain why investment is likely more volatile than consumption.

3. The economy is in a recession. To increase income by $1,000, government spending must increase by $100. The consumption function is $C = cY$; investment is $400; government purchases are $300; taxes are $150; and net exports are $(-)$100.
   (a) What is the current level of GDP?
   (b) To double GDP from its current level, what must be the size of the primary deficit?

4. Explain why public policy-makers are so often concerned about:
   (a) The size of the annual budget deficit
   (b) The ratio of the national debt to GDP

5. What are the key components of the simple Keynesian model? What is the role of the multiplier in the Keynesian model?

6. Suppose the Ecoland economy is represented by the following equations:

   $$Y = C + I + G \qquad C = 500 + 0.5YD \qquad T = 600$$
   $$I = 300 \qquad YD = Y - T \qquad G = 2{,}000$$

   (a) Given the above variables, calculate the equilibrium level of output.

   (b) Now, assume that consumer confidence decreases, causing a reduction in the autonomous component of consumption from 500 to 400. What is the new equilibrium level of output? How much does income change as a result of this event? What is the multiplier for this economy?

7. Explain what is meant by automatic stabilizers and how they work to minimize fluctuations in economic activity.

Case Study Question | The Comeback of Caterpillar

Interest Rates

1. What is the basis for the argument that Caterpillar is in an interest rate-sensitive industry?

Hint: Caterpillar requires capital for investment purpose (a $1.8 billion plant modernization in 1986). Heavy construction equipment can be an expensive expenditure for Caterpillar's customers, which may require debt financing.

Appendix 9.1

IS/LM and Aggregate Demand

Many economists have argued that the basic Keynesian model best provides a description of an economy experiencing depression. Keynes published the *General Theory* in 1936, during the Great Depression. In effect, the model holds the general price level constant. An increase in demand leads to an increase in consumption, income, and employment through the multiplier effect. For the purposes of exposition, Sir John Hicks famously "fit" Keynesian economics into a two-dimensional analysis.[1] This allowed the construction of a simple graphical framework to better understand the argument. Hicks's **IS/LM model** has two main purposes. First, it is an equilibrium model of the economy in its own right when prices are held constant. It relates real economic activity (GDP) to fiscal policy and monetary policy and, specifically, the real rate of interest. Second, when prices are allowed to change, it facilitates a more detailed discussion of the determinants of **aggregate demand** than the simpler **MV = PY** approach (to be discussed in Chapter 10).

The **IS curve** indicates the relationship between **investment** and **savings** (or, more broadly, total **injections** and **leakages** from the circular flow of income) at different levels of **national income** (real GDP). That is, there are alternative levels of GDP at which aggregate investment equals aggregate savings. To derive the IS schedule, we begin with savings and investment schedules in Figure 9A.1. The investment schedule is negatively sloped with respect to the interest rate. The saving schedule is positively sloped with respect to interest, and the level of income, **Y**, is a shift variable (more income means more savings).

At an interest rate of **r1** and national income of **Y1**, national savings equals national investment at point "**A**". What happens if national income increases to **Y2**? Savings will increase, the interest rate will fall to **r2**, and

---

[1] John Hicks, "Mr. Keynes and the Classics", *Econometrica* (April 1937) 5: 144–59.

Figure 9A.1: Investment and Savings

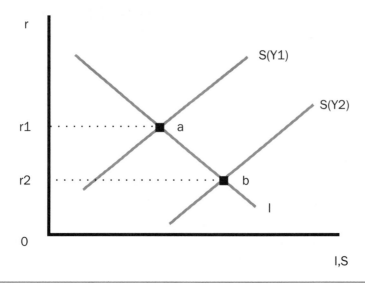

Figure 9A.2: The IS Curve

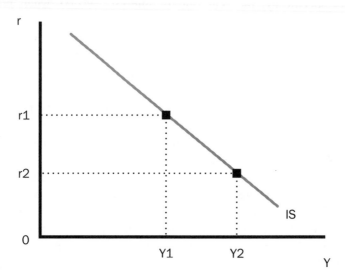

investment will increase to **I2**. Savings and investments are now equal at point **"B"**. Repeating this exercise several times to obtain a series of equilibrium relationships between savings and investment, it is possible to derive the IS schedule, a relationship between real interest rates and real GDP, as in Figure 9A.2.

The IS curve slopes downward and to the right. As we have already seen, a decrease in the rate of interest causes an increase in business investment. This increase in investment then causes an increase in national income, **Y**, via the multiplier relationship.

The purpose of the **LM curve**, meanwhile, is to capture another relationship between the real rate of interest and real income, which is consistent with equilibrium in the **money market**. We start with the money supply and money demand schedules. Figure 9A.3 shows the relationship between **money supply** and **demand**. The demand schedule to hold real money balances (**M/P**) is basically like any other demand curve: that is, it slopes downward and to the right. What is the logic behind this? At lower interest rates, investors hold more of their financial assets as liquid balances (that is, "money") for "speculative" reasons. They hope interest rates will go up in the future, and they do not want to be locked into long-term, poorly paying investments. The diagram also depicts a vertical money supply function, reflecting the assumption that the money supply is fully controlled by the monetary authorities (the central bank). If national income is **Y1**, the

Figure 9A.3: Money Demand and Supply

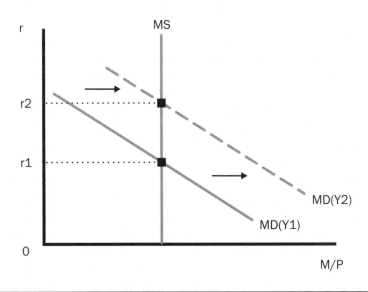

Figure 9A.4: The LM Curve

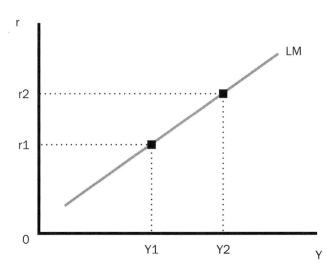

equilibrium rate of interest must be **r1**, where money demand equals money supply. An increase in national income to **Y2** shifts the money demand curve out and raises the interest rate to **r2**. With no change in the money supply, the new, higher equilibrium rate of interest must now be **r2**. Repeating the exercise a number of times, we can then derive the LM schedule, showing the relationship between interest rates and income for a given money supply, as in Figure 9A.4.

The LM schedule slopes upward and to the right. Higher levels of national income increase money demand. With a fixed money supply, interest rates increase with increased income and, therefore, money demand for transactions purposes goes up. That is, we must hold more money balances to conduct transactions at the higher national income.

In Figure 9A.5, we then combine the IS and LM schedules to obtain the equilibrium levels of the interest rate and national income. (Remember, we are holding the price level constant in this analysis.) At point **"A"**, there is equilibrium in both the goods market and the money market, with a real rate of interest (**r1**) and real national income (**Y1**). The IS/LM model can then help to explain some economic results that most businesspeople seem to learn intuitively. For example, what happens when the government decides to spend additional amounts of money through fiscal policy? In this case (as shown in Figure 9A.6), economic activity increases, but according to the IS/LM model the real rate of interest is also driven up. The increase

Figure 9A.5: Equilibrium Income and Interest Rate

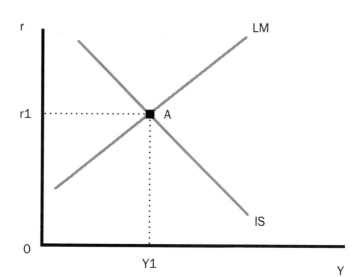

Figure 9A.6: An Expansionary Fiscal Policy

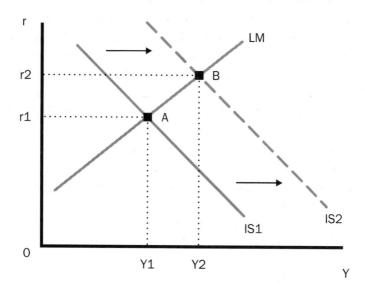

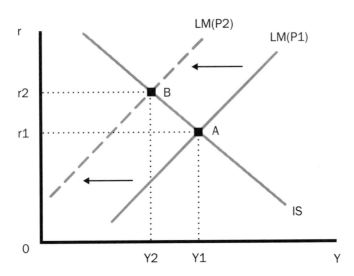

Figure 9A.7: A Price Rise

in public sector spending partially "crowds out" private sector investment, as a result of this rise in interest rates. The reader may also wish to work the effects of other types of change into this framework, such as that of an increase or a reduction in the money supply.

We can also use the IS/LM framework to derive a construct known as the **aggregate demand curve**. Figure 9A.7 shows the IS/LM relationship for each given price level in the economy. Now, what happens when there is an increase in the aggregate price level, **P**? The LM curve shifts back to the left. Why? This is the equivalent of a decrease in the **real money supply**. The existing nominal supply of money has less purchasing power. Figure 9A.7 actually contains all the information necessary to derive the aggregate demand curve. If we repeat the exercise of increasing the price level several times we can trace out a relationship between **P** and **Y**. The AD schedule shows the relationship between the aggregate price level and national income on the demand side.

There is an inverse relationship between the price level and the demand for real GDP, as shown in Figure 9A.8. An increase in the price level causes a decrease in aggregate demand *along* the AD curve. What happens is that an increase in the price level causes a decrease in the real money supply, which in turn causes an increase in the rate of interest. The increase in the rate of interest decreases the demand for private sector

Figure 9A.8:   The Aggregate Demand Curve

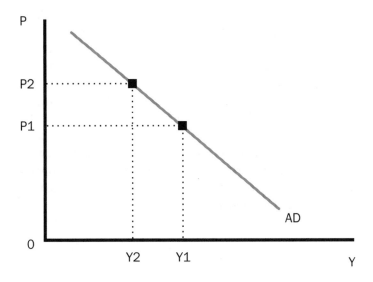

Figure 9A.9:   A Shift in the Aggregate Demand Curve

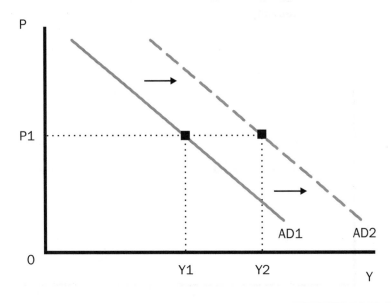

investment spending, resulting in an overall decrease in demand from **Y1** to **Y2**.

Recall that expansionary fiscal policy shifts the IS curve outward and to the right, and that expansionary monetary policy shifts the LM curve outward and to the right. *Either* of these actions will shift the aggregate demand curve itself outward and to the right, at each price level in the economy. Figure 9A.9 captures these effects. In order to then determine the impact of these demand changes on the price level itself, it would also be necessary to assess the productive capacity of the economy, as reflected in the complementary notion of the **aggregate supply curve**. This will be discussed in more detail in Chapter . In effect, as previously suggested, "Keynesian" economists basically assumed there would be few supply-side/capacity difficulties, particularly if the economy was initially operating below full employment. The AS curve in this case would be a horizontal line at a given price level, as illustrated in Figure 9A.10.

Figure 9A.10: Aggregate Demand and Supply with Excess Capacity

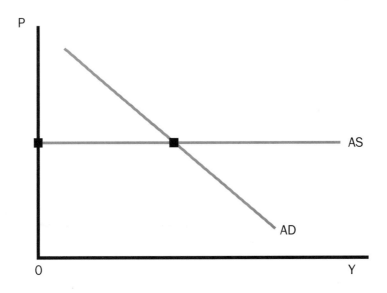

10

Money and
Inflation

Introduction

At the opposite end of the ideological spectrum from the simple Keynesian model, an even more traditional view of macroeconomic processes is represented by the **quantity theory of money**. This is actually a much older set of ideas even than those of Keynes, going back more than 250 years. Remarkably, however, these ancient doctrines underwent a major revival both in academia, and in the political arena, in the last half of the 20th century under the name of **monetarism**. These developments are often associated with the name of the late Professor Milton Friedman, of the University of Chicago.[1] There are some obvious difficulties in applying these ideas in a modern "credit economy" and, in particular, in defining what the money supply actually consists of at any point in time. Therefore, by the time of writing in the early 21st century, there are probably very few leading economists who would still claim to be monetarists as such. However, the apparent distancing of the contemporary economics profession from "pure" monetarist thought is largely illusory. Another term for the same general set of ideas is **classical economics**,[2] and it would also be fair to say that to this day the *basic* notions of classical economics remain the basis of orthodox or mainstream economic thought. These include the general idea that there is a relationship between money and inflation and, perhaps even more so, the fundamental belief that the growth rate of the economy is determined on the supply side of the economy, rather than on the demand side (as the Keynesians would have had it). There are some contemporary nuances in modern policy-making that differ from monetarism in its heyday, particularly having to do with the role of interest rates in the way monetary policy is conducted. In fact, we mentioned in Chapter 8 that the main **monetary policy instrument** is now an interest rate set by the central bank. Hence, in what follows, when we speak about an increase in the money supply, in reality this is typically brought about by a cut in the policy-related interest rate, designed to stimulate lending by the commercial banks. Similarly, a decrease in the money supply would involve an interest rate hike. With this caveat, however, the present chapter focuses on the basic principles of the quantity theory.

---

[1] Milton Friedman, "The role of monetary policy", *American Economic Review* (March 1968) 58(1): 1–17.

[2] Recall that, earlier, in the context of microeconomics, we also used the term "neoclassical". In practice, both expressions refer to very much the same sort of mindset on economic issues.

The Equation of Exchange

The simplest version of the quantity theory, which Friedman once called a "caricature",[3] can be illustrated by the so-called **equation of exchange**:

$$(10.1) \qquad MV = PY$$

In equation (10.1), **PY** is just nominal GDP, as defined in previous chapters. Meanwhile, **M** is one definition or another of the total money supply. In a modern economy it mostly consists of the deposit liabilities of financial institutions, such as banks (rather than notes or coins), and its physical existence is probably just magnetic traces on a computer disk. In spite of this, however, the social power of money is, nonetheless, obviously as real today as it ever was. Today's money really differs only in form rather than substance from previous incarnations. As mentioned, central banks publish statistics on a number of different versions of **M**, giving them labels such as M0, M1, M2, M2+, M2++, etc. These differ according to which liabilities of which financial institutions are included. There now seems to be a general consensus that a somewhat "broad" definition of the money supply, such as the M2++ definition or something similar, would represent the most accurate definition in a modern economy. Meanwhile, the velocity term, **V**, has the connotation of how rapidly money changes hands. To conduct, for example, $100,000 worth of business over a given time period does not literally require 100,000 actual dollars (because the money changes hands). It may be possible to undertake $100,000 worth of transactions with, for example, only $20,000 or $40,000 in existence, depending on how sophisticated the banking system is.

As it stands above, the equation of exchange **MV = PY** is simply a tautology (something that is true by definition). Nominal GDP, **PY**, which is a **flow variable**, is a sum of money per period of time, and the money supply, **M**, a **stock variable**, is also a sum of money, the average money holding during that period. There is, therefore, always some number, **V**, that will arithmetically relate these two sums. If **PY** = 100,000, and **M** = 20,000, then **V** = 5; but if **PY** = 100,000 and **M** = 40,000, then **V** = 2.5, and so on. What would convert **MV = PY** from a tautology into a theory about how the economy operates are certain behavioral assumptions made about each of its components. In fact, to get to the simplest and most straightforward version of the quantity theory (the caricature version), the following assumptions must be made:

---

[3] Milton Friedman, "The quantity theory of money: a restatement", in M. Friedman (ed.), *Studies in the Quantity Theory of Money* (Chicago: University of Chicago Press, 1956).

- Change in the money supply, M, will not affect the level of real GDP (i.e., money is *neutral*).

- The money supply is "exogenous" (this means that, for example, its level is completely determined by policy decisions made by the central bank).

- For the purposes of monetary analysis, the velocity of circulation, **V**, can be treated as a behavioral constant, determined by the current technological state of development of the banking system.

If all these assumptions are made, then changes in the quantity of money (which must be initiated by the central bank as, by assumption, it controls the money supply) can only change prices. As **M** goes up, **P** must go up, and by the same proportion. For example, a doubling of the money supply will lead to a doubling of the price level, a tripling of the money supply will lead to tripling of the price level, and so on (and vice versa). A more "dynamic" version of this result follows in equation (10.2) below:

$$(10.2) \qquad \Delta P/P = \Delta M/M - \Delta Y/Y$$

This equation simply expresses the quantity theory in terms of proportional changes. In this notation, $\Delta P/P$ is the inflation rate (the same as lower case **p** as defined earlier), $\Delta M/M$ is the proportional rate of change of the money supply (**m**), and $\Delta Y/Y$ is the rate of change of real GDP (**y**). Equation (10.2) says that if velocity is constant, the inflation rate will be equal to the difference between the rate of monetary growth and the rate of growth of the real economy. This was really the fundamental policy insight of the monetarists. The idea that, basically, the cause of inflation is a rate of growth of the money supply in excess of the rate of growth of the real economy. Suppose, for example, that real GDP is growing at around 3%, and the money supply is growing faster than this, at around 9% per year. According to a monetarist, this will explain why the inflation rate will be around 6% at the same time. The theory also suggests a very simple method of reducing the inflation rate, and even of achieving "zero inflation" (or stable prices). To get to a zero inflation rate, for example, all that seems necessary is to reduce money supply growth from 9% to 3%, and stable prices will automatically ensue. Since stable prices or zero inflation (or at least "low" inflation) is the professed goal of most policy-makers to-day,[4] the formula seems to provide an obvious "rule" for monetary policy. However, it becomes somewhat more controversial when we remember that the money supply is actually the sum of the deposit liabilities of the banking system. Hence, reducing the rate of growth of the money supply by six

---

[4] John Crow, *Making Money: An Insider's Perpsective on Finance, Politics, and Canada's Central Bank* (Toronto: John Wiley & Sons Canada, 2002).

Case Study 15

"The End of the Spanish Empire"
Madrid; December 31, 1492

The discovery of the Americas will ruin the Spanish empire. This, of course, sounds paradoxical. It would seem that this huge discovery should secure Spain's role as the leading world power. However, Prof. Sanchez of the University of Madrid views the discovery as a disaster. Prof. Sanchez states, "We have found gold, which gives us more money, but we have not created any new wealth. The result will be a massive inflation that will ruin Spain."

percentage points will also require reducing the rate of growth of bank lending (including lending to business to finance production) by a similar amount. This idea that there could be trade-off between inflation objectives and the performance of the real economy will be discussed in a later chapter. In the simple quantity theory, however, no problem arises, as it is assumed that output (or its rate of growth) is determined entirely by other forces anyway, and will not fall when the growth rate of the money supply is reduced.

Aggregate Demand and Supply

The theory can also be illustrated in graphical form with the device of **aggregate demand and supply curves.** This strategy means that, at least to some extent, it is possible to employ the familiar tools of demand and supply analysis, first discussed in Chapter 2, to macroeconomic as well as microeconomic issues. There are, however, some important differences between the macroeconomic and microeconomic concepts of demand and supply, which will merit attention as we proceed. To get to the **aggregate demand curve**, first note that the equation of exchange can be re-written as:

(10.3) $P = MV/Y$

This gives a downward-sloping relationship between price and output, as in a typical demand function, except that output here is the output of the economy as whole (real GDP), and price is the aggregate price index (not a relative price, as it would be in microeconomics). In shape, the aggregate demand curve is a rectangular hyperbola because of the symmetrical form of the function. The main **shift variable** of the demand curve is the money supply itself, **M**. An increase in the money supply — that is, an **expansionary monetary policy** — shifts the aggregate demand curve out and to the right. In common-sense terms, there is more money to spend on goods and services at each price level. A reduction in the money supply, a **contractionary monetary policy**, shifts the demand curve back and to the left. How, though, would a change in fiscal policy (as discussed in the previous chapter) affect aggregate demand? By definition, in the closed economy with a government sector, it must be true that:

(10.4) $MV = \$C + \$I + \$G$

But, if **M** is fixed (by the central bank), and **V** is also fixed, **MV** cannot change, no matter what happens to nominal government spending (**$G**), so it would now seem that fiscal policy will not "work" in increasing AD. In the logic of algebra, what must happen is that if there is, say, an increase in **$G**, one of the other terms on the right-hand side of the equation will have to fall by the same amount. So, in this case, and contrary to the Keynesian way of looking at things, a change in government spending would not even affect aggregate demand (let alone supply). If this happens it is known as the phenomenon of **crowding out**. For example, it might be argued that an increase in government spending of, say, $100,000 will simply displace or "crowd out" private investment spending of the same amount. Pointing out the possibility of this case does not necessarily mean that it is true in reality, of course. It all depends on the assumption that **V** is a constant. However, this simple algebra does explain the logic behind a popular argument that is often made in public policy debates.

On the other hand, it should also be noticed that an increase in government spending that is financed by literally "printing money" (i.e., letting **M** increase) *will* increase aggregate demand in exactly same way as an arbitrary increase in **M**. Therefore, changes in fiscal policy in the aggregate demand and supply framework might easily be allowed for by this route. Moreover (as was shown in the appendix to Chapter 9), it would also be possible to construct an aggregate demand curve *not* based on constant velocity, and in that case an increase in government spending or a cut in taxes would shift the demand curve out even without an injection of new money. In that case the effective amount of money *actually available to be spent* could be increased (by increasing velocity).

Figure 10.1: An Increase in Aggregate Demand Affects Only Prices

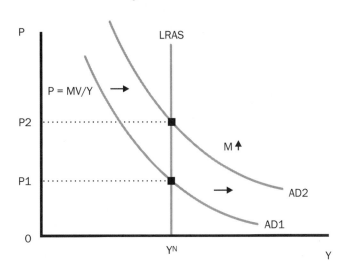

In Figure 10.1, the aggregate demand curve based on MV = PY is juxtaposed with an aggregate supply curve, which is, in fact, vertical at the so-called **natural rate of output**, Y^N (sometimes also called, perhaps misleadingly, the **full employment level of output**). This vertical aggregate supply curve simply reflects the presumption that changes in the nominal money supply will not affect the level of output. The natural rate of output supposedly reflects the equilibrium level of output or real GDP, which would emerge "naturally" from the interplay of market forces, when entrepreneurs, firms, and workers all respond rationally to the various profit and wage incentives that they face. The main question is whether or not this equilibrium, once achieved, is likely to be upset by any rise or fall in the aggregate price index. The vertical aggregate supply curve states, in essence, that it will not. Supposing that **P** rises, what profit incentives do firms/entrepreneurs have to change what they are doing in terms of output and employment offers? The key here is to remember that **P** is supposedly the average level of all prices. Therefore, when **P** rises, *in principle* all prices are going up by the same amount. For the individual entrepreneur, this means not only that the prices of that entrepreneur's output are going up, but also that the prices of all competitors and suppliers are going up by the same proportion. Therefore, on the assumption of **perfect wage and price flexibility**, nominal wage costs are going up by the same proportion

217

also. In real terms, there should really be no incentive for any firm or entrepreneur to make changes, as profit margins will not change. That is what the vertical aggregate supply curve is supposed to show. It says that when aggregate nominal prices rise (or alternatively, when they fall) there is really no incentive for firms to make any changes to their output plans.

Putting the AD and AS curves together, it can therefore be seen that an increase in **M** (whether this is to finance an increase in **$G**, or just as the result of an arbitrary decision by the central bank) will only cause an increase in prices, **P**, in the same proportion. Similarly, a decrease in aggregate demand will only cause a fall in prices. This is exactly what the quantity theory predicts. It is worth noting, once again, the contrast to the simple Keynesian model discussed in the previous chapter. In that world, an increase in demand caused an increase in actual output, with no effect on prices. According to the simplest version of the quantity theory, however, the opposite is true. All the effect is on prices, and none on output. This type of disagreement is the essence of economic controversy in the policy-making arena.

We should note that the device of a vertical aggregate supply curve is not intended to mean that the level of output in the economy is really "fixed", or a constant for all time. It means only that *changes in aggregate*

Figure 10.2: Over Time, Growth Shifts the Long Run Supply Curve Outward

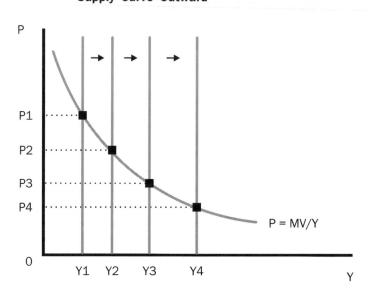

---

demand do not affect output. That is its principal ideological message or purpose (in opposition to the Keynesian assertion). Even if demand does not affect output, it can still be assumed that the economy is growing over time. The implication is only that this growth must be the result of the supposedly more fundamental supply side factors, such as technological change, the accumulation of physical capital, the acquisition of skills by the labor force, the growth of the labor force, etc. This can be shown by an outward shift over time of the vertical AS curve itself (in effect, an increase in the full employment level of output over time), as shown in Figure 10.2. Note that if aggregate demand does not change as the growth process continues (in this specific context, if the money supply is fixed), economic growth would actually be accompanied by a steady fall in prices as time passes. This might be a vision of the "best of all possible worlds" from the point of view of the classical or neoclassical economist. Growth is proceeding "as it should" (due, for example, to technical progress) and, not only is there no inflation, but prices are actually falling. There must be some doubt, however, as to how realistic this vision is. Most episodes of deflation (falling prices) that have occurred in the real world have been associated not with increasing prosperity, but more frequently with tough economic times.

Potential Criticisms of the Quantity Theory

It was mentioned earlier that the simplest quantity theory of money rests on three particular assumptions: the neutrality of money, the constancy of the velocity of circulation, and the control of the money supply by the central bank. Evidently, these are strong assumptions, and it would be easy to challenge that version of the theory just by denying any one or all of them. That is to say, it would be possible to argue:

- Changes in money (**M**) *do* affect output (money is *non-neutral*).

- Velocity (**V**) may not be stable (it may be completely unstable, or changes in **M** may always be offset by changes in **V**).

- In a "credit economy", in which most of the "money supply" consists of the liabilities of private financial institutions, **M** may not be an *exogenous* variable, but an *endogenous* variable, not fully controlled by the central bank.

So the theory would not be very robust if it could be fatally damaged by any of the above. In fact, it might be argued that the real contribution of the 20th century monetarists (from their own point of view) was that they were able to develop a more realistic and flexible version of the quantity theory that preserved the main intuitions about the relationship between money and inflation, and also about output being mainly determined on the supply side, but was able to handle these potential criticisms in a more convincing manner. That is to say, the monetarists did believe that the basic ideas of the quantity theory were true and also of practical importance, and set about developing a theory to show that at least this need not depend on unrealistic assumptions.[5]

The Velocity of Circulation and the Demand for Money

First, it will obviously *not* be the case that velocity is a strict constant in practice. However, for changes in velocity to do much to upset the quantity theory, they would either have to be totally unpredictable in behavior, or (the opposite case) they would have to change in *exactly* the reverse direction from any changes in **M**. On the other hand, if velocity can change, but always does so in a predictable manner (and never enough to totally offset changes in **M**), then this can easily be allowed for in working out the precise quantitative relationship between **M** and **P**. It would not affect the basic causal chain. One of the main preoccupations of the monetarist economists in their earliest studies was, in fact, the issue of whether or not the **demand for money** was a stable and predictable relationship empirically. If so, this would imply that velocity itself would also behave in a stable and predictable manner. The point is that the velocity of circulation is really the reciprocal of the demand for money: that is, there is an inverse relationship between velocity and money demand. If money is in circulation, then, by definition, we cannot be holding it as idle balances, and vice versa.

The typical money demand function from the macroeconomic textbooks, actually common to both monetarists and Keynesians in the 20th century, was:

$$(10.5) \qquad M/P = L(\overset{+}{Y}, \overset{-}{i})$$

This suggests that the demand for real money balance depends positively on GDP, and negatively on the nominal rate of interest. If income increases, more money is required to carry out the increased volume of transactions. On the other hand, if interest increases wealth holders will be

---

[5] John Smithin, *Controversies in Monetary Economics*, Revised Edition (Cheltenham: Edward Elgar, 2003).

more likely to move out of "cash" and invest in some higher-earning asset. The point of most of the academic studies that were carried out on the demand for money was indeed to show that this demand function was stable and predictable (even if they did not always necessarily succeed, depending on the precise definition of money used). If the function was reasonably predictable changes in velocity would also be more or less predictable. The quantity theory of money could then be written as:

$$(10.6) \qquad MV(\overset{+}{i}) = PY$$

Velocity in this case would not be absolutely constant, it would change when interest rates change. However, as long as the changes are predictable they can be allowed for in inflation calculations, and this would not damage the main proposition — that the inflation rate depends on the rate of monetary growth. The relation between the velocity of circulation and the demand for money is more easily seen if we rewrite equation (10.6) as follows:

$$(10.7) \qquad M/P = Y/V(i)$$

Clearly, equation (10.7) is just a specific functional form of (10.5)

As discussed earlier, these days the monetary policy of most central banks focuses on the interest rate itself in the first instance. The money supply then adjusts to achieve these interest rate targets. The central bank assumes that money demand/velocity and ultimately the price level will then adjust accordingly.

The Money Multiplier and the Supply of Money

The second issue, of whether or not money is endogenous in a system with a developed banking system, can be addressed within the quantity theory framework by the concept of the **money multiplier**, discussed in detail in the appendix to this chapter. It must be recognized, of course, that in a credit economy money is "created" whenever the commercial banks extend loans, and "destroyed" when the loans are repaid. However, the argument made by monetarists and others is that in order to exercise this money-creating power, the commercial banks must always hold **reserves** of the base money of the system, in order to satisfy any of their depositors who happen to ask for payment in "cash". As base money consists essentially of the liabilities of the central bank, the authorities can at least control the quantity of base money, and via this route control the overall money supply also. The use of the term multiplier in this context implies that the final change in the over money supply M will be some multiple of the initial change in the monetary base H. It may, nonetheless, be predictable/controllable. As already mentioned, in the contemporary world the most prominent **monetary policy instrument** designed to exercise this control (certainly in terms of coverage in the news media) is changes in the policy-related interest rate, such as the federal funds rate in the USA, or the main refinancing rate in the Euro zone. These are typically overnight financing rates between the main commercial banks and other financial institutions participating in the official clearing house run by the central bank. With differing institutional arrangements in each jurisdiction, such rates are effectively under the control of the central bank. In terms of the money multiplier process, an increase in this rate increases the penalty for the commercial banks for *not* having sufficient reserves on hand to meet obligations, and hence tends to restrain commercial bank lending and the ultimate growth of the money supply (and vice versa). Refer to the appendix at the end of the chapter for further discussion of the mechanism of the process.

The Non-Neutrality of Money in the "Short Run"

If it is possible to solve the problem of how the central bank can exert control over the total of bank lending (and hence over the money supply) by appealing to the institutional arrangements, the final problem that monetarists and other quantity theorists had to solve is the issue of whether these monetary policy changes might affect actual output (real GDP) itself, rather than just prices. This was a problem from the point of view of the basic theory because there have obviously been many historical episodes (including very recent episodes) in which it seems obvious to market participants that the activities of the central bank have indeed had a decisive impact on the course of the real economy, either positively or negatively. Certainly it is true in modern times that whenever the central bank raises interest rates (recall that high interest rates mean "tight money"), both players in the stock market and genuine entrepreneurs all become nervous. They are more cheerful when there is an interest rate cut (or an "easy money" policy).

The solution of contemporary classical economists to the problem of the effect of money on real income is, in fact, exactly the same as that of the earliest writers on the quantity theory centuries before. Essentially, the impact of money on output is conceded for the "short run" but not the "long run". Monetary changes are thought to be non-neutral in the short run, but neutral in the long run. In this way, it is possible to retain the basic proposition about the long-run relationship between monetary changes

Case Study 16

"A Race to the Bottom"
London; April 23, 2019

The Bank of England has raised the base lending rate once again. The base rate has now been increased for the fifth consecutive time. A Bank of England spokesperson said that this increase was necessary to restrain inflationary pressures as the rate of inflation has now risen to 2.9%. However, much of this increase can be attributed to one-time events, such as the poor weather conditions in Europe. The core or structural rate of inflation remains unchanged at 1.4%. Some skeptical economists have therefore argued that this rate hike has less to do with the actual rate of inflation in the UK than an attempt to establish the Bank's anti-inflationary credentials among the international central banking community. That is, who can achieve the lowest national rate of inflation? It may not be a coincidence that the Federal Reserve Board in the USA also raised the federal funds rate after the two most recent meetings of the Federal Open Market Committee. In both cases, the increases were by relatively large jumps of 50 basis points.

and inflation while at the same time providing a coherent explanation for major business cycle fluctuations. The blame for both types of problems (inflation *and* the business cycle) can be laid firmly at the door of the central bank.

Recall that the explanation for the aggregate supply curve being vertical in the context of the quantity theory was "perfect wage and price flexibility". That was why a change in aggregate demand would not affect prices. It was assumed that all prices and costs would rise together, and there would be no incentive for entrepreneurs to make any changes. A simple explanation for the short-run non-neutrality of money, therefore, is that in practice all prices and wages do not adjust as smoothly as this. There are either temporary **nominal rigidities** in some prices or costs (such as wages), or **mistaken expectations** of future inflation, which means that at least some economic actors will have made explicit or implicit contracts (such as accepting a given wage rate via a union contract, or agreeing to supply raw materials or intermediate goods at certain prices), which turn out to be too low or too high. Then, for example, if prices rise but wages lag behind for some time, that will provide a profit incentive for firms to expand output and employment, at least until wages catch up. We can write a generic short-run aggregate supply curve (SRAS) to capture these ideas as follows:

$$(10.8) \qquad Y = Y^N(P/P^e)$$

This equation suggests that when actual prices turn out to be the same as expected prices $(P = P^e),$ output will be at the so-called natural rate, and the supply curve will be vertical. If actual prices turn out to be greater than expected prices, output supplied will be above the natural rate. If actual prices fall below expectations, output supplied will be less than the natural rate. The reason for this formulation is that, for given expectations, P^e, economic actors will obviously have made decisions and agreed to contracts on exactly that basis. Therefore, if prices actually rise higher than expected, some players will be making windfall profits because their workers or suppliers have guessed too low. These firms or entrepreneurs will therefore have an incentive to expand output. Similarly, if actual selling prices turn out to be less than expected, some firms will be making losses because their costs are too high. They will therefore reduce output and employment. The point is that at each level of price expectations, an increase (decrease) in actual prices will cause an increase (decrease) in output along the SRAS. In the short run, therefore, an increase in aggregate demand caused, for example, by an increase in **M** will tend to stimulate an increase in output and employment (an upturn in the business cycle), and vice versa, as shown in Figure .3.

In the nature of things, however (the argument continues), such a stimulative or depressing effect cannot last forever. Expectations will adjust, contracts will be re-written, and the boom or slump must eventually fade away as everyone adjusts to the new situation. In other words, it is explicitly argued that the stimulative effect of, for example, an expansionary money policy will be temporary, and the final impact will only be on prices

Figure 10.3: The Short-Run Non-Neutrality of Money

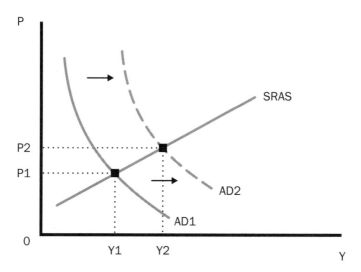

(just as in the quantity theory). Similarly, if a tight money policy causes a recession or depression, the argument is also that this will not go on forever, and the only *lasting* impact will be lower prices. Figure 10.4 illustrates the case of an increase in the money supply and Figure 10.5, a decrease in the money supply.

Suppose the economy in Figure 10.4 starts in "equilibrium" at point "**A**". Then there is increase in the money supply, shifting the aggregate demand curve out and to the right. For as long as **Pe**, the expectation of prices, does not change, the original short-run supply curve will continue to be relevant, and there will be boom conditions in the economy (a higher level of output, and a somewhat higher price level), as at point "**B**". However, presumably the experience of the boom itself must, sooner or later, cause expectations to change. Economic actors will start to "up the *ante*", ask for higher wages, build higher prices into contracts, and so on. As this occurs, short-run supply will begin to fall, and the SRAS will start shifting back and to the left. Eventually, the boom will fade away completely, and the final position will be at point "**C**". Here there is no difference in output from what it was initially, just higher prices. If we compare only the situations at the starting point "**A**" and the final outcome "**C**", all that has happened is that the increase in the money supply has caused an increase in prices. The quantity theory therefore holds in the long run. In the short run, however, there is a stimulus to output and employment. The

Figure 10.4: An Expansionary Monetary Policy

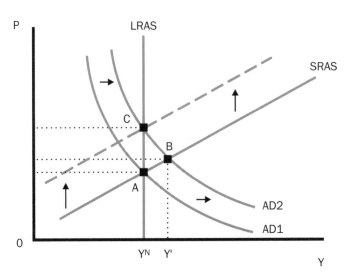

Figure 10.5: A Contractionary Monetary Policy

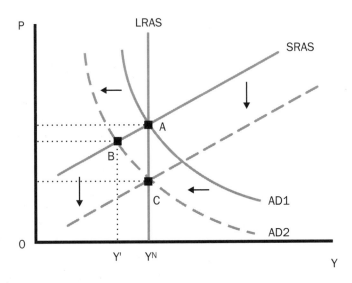

time horizon over which this is all supposed to happen is presumably of the order of magnitude of the typical business cycle: maybe a year, 18 months, or two years for the expansionary phase.

Figure 10.5 shows the opposite case of a contractionary monetary policy. For some reason, the central bank feels that the average level of prices at the initial starting point "A" is too high, and decides to reduce it by permanently reducing the supply of money. Aggregate demand is, therefore, reduced, but the initial impact of this is as much on real GDP as on prices. There is a recession as the economy slides backward along the SRAS curve. Expectations have been falsified in a downward direction. Contracts will have been signed and agreements reached, including wage agreements, on the assumption that prices were going to be higher than they actually turned out to be. Profits get squeezed and hence there must be an economic downturn. But, or so the argument continues, once a recession has been experienced at point "B" for at least some period of time, the very experience of these tough economic times and unemployment will cause economic actors to begin to revise their expectations downward, to ask for lower wages, set lower prices, and so on. Then, the short-run aggregate supply curve will begin to shift down and to the right. Supply will increase as workers and others price themselves back into the market. Eventually, the recession will be over, the initial level of output will be restored, and there will be lower prices all round, as at point "C". One way of looking at this is that, in effect, the central bank is deliberately creating a recession and unemployment, in order to force the various economic actors to ratchet back their expectations. This could be quite a sensitive issue politically if the process is generally understood this way, so central banks are usually at great pains to stress how (in their view) the sacrifice is worth it. The slogan "short-term pain for long-term gain" expresses exactly this point of view, even if there may be some doubts as to how short the pain and how long the gain will be. (Also, whether those who suffer the pain, i.e., those who lose their jobs or go bankrupt, are the same group as those who gain. The latter will, presumably, consist mainly of those who already have substantial financial holdings, the real value of which increases with lower prices.)

Finally, note that the model of economic activity implicit in Figures 10.4 and 10.5 might be seen as a compromise between the extremes of the simple Keynesian model, on the one hand, and the crude version of quantity theory on the other. In the simple Keynesian model, it was suggested that an increase in aggregate demand would permanently increase output and employment; but, meanwhile, nothing much was said about the impact on prices. In the basic version of the quantity theory, on the other hand, all the effect of an increase in demand was on prices, and none on the level of output. Now, in the model distinguishing between short-run and long-run effects, there is still an argument that a demand increase will boost economic activity *for a while* (together with some upward pressure on prices), just as the Keynesians claimed; but it is also believed that this will disappear eventually and leave the final impact only on prices, as in the monetarist/classical view. This compromise, however, obviously does add more weight to the classical side of the scales that to the Keynesian, and this intellectual stance continues to have a definite impact on the way policy is conducted in the real world.

Chapter Summary

- Monetarist theory was based on the ancient quantity theory of money.

- In its most simplified version, the quantity theory argues that inflation is a purely monetary phenomenon. If we grow the money supply too fast, we will experience inflation.

- By "too fast", we mean an increase in the money supply that is larger than the growth in real economic output (GDP).

- In classical economic models, including monetarist models, all economic growth occurs from the "supply side". Changes in technology, research and development, innovation, and the discovery of new resources are supposed to be the main factors that lead to real economic growth.

- As a result, monetarist or classical economic thinking leaves no room for interventionist government policy: at least, not on the demand side. The only policy option that might exist is to assist businesspeople on the supply side (e.g., to minimize regulations, keep taxes low, re-train workers, etc.).

- Obviously, the simplistic assumptions of the strict quantity theory are unrealistic, but it is possible to resurrect the theory to make it fit better with a modern credit economy, and preserve the main ideas.

- We now have two "simplistic" models of how a market system works: Keynesian and classical. In the latter, there is no role for an active government to co-ordinate economic activity. In the Keynesian model, government can play an important role in the stabilizing of the economy.

- On grounds of common sense, the practical businessperson might be inclined to argue that the "truth" lies someplace in between these two extremes, but this is not usually the position taken by participants in economic controversy, who tend to be partisans for one view or the other.

- Why do these ideas matter to you as a businessperson? Because they are associated with different political philosophies and public policies, all of which have a definite impact on business. Classical- or monetarist-type theories are normally associated with "conservative" political parties (think of the obvious example of Prime Minister Margaret Thatcher in England in the 1980s), while Keynesian theories are more "liberal", in the American sense of this term (think of activist governments with high spending and taxation, for example, Sweden in the second half of the 20th century).

Problems

1. The simplest version of the quantity theory of money assumes that velocity is relatively constant, and that real GDP increases at its long-run rate of growth. Suppose that over the past few decades, the long-run growth rate of real GDP has been about 3% per year. This figure is supposed to be the result of changes in population, resources, and technological change, which are all typically viewed as exogenous.

   (a) Substituting these values into the percentage change version of the quantity equation yields (fill in the blanks):

   % change in M + _____ = % change in P + _____

   or, rearranging:

   % change in P = % change in M − _____%.

   (b) Given the assumptions above concerning velocity and real GDP growth, complete the following table for four *successive* periods (the values for V and Y in period 2 are already entered). Calculate the price level P by using the quantity equation MV = PY.

Table 1

(1) period	(2) M	(3) % change in M	(4) V	(5) % change in V	(6) P	(7) % change in P	(8) Y	(9) % change in Y
1	100		2.0		1.0		200	
		3		0		_____		**3**
2	103		2.0		____		206	
3	97	_____	____	_____	____	_____	____	_____
4	107	_____	____	_____	____	_____	____	_____

(c) Use a calculator to verify that the percentage change version of the quantity equation is a good approximation to the percentage changes in Table 1.

2. Recall that the Fisher equation says that the nominal interest rate is equal to the real interest rate plus expected inflation. Thus, the Fisher equation is (fill in the blanks using the notation of Chapter 8):

$$\underline{\hspace{2cm}} = \underline{\hspace{2cm}} + \underline{\hspace{2cm}}$$

(a) Recall from Question 1 that if the long-run annual growth of real output is 3%, and velocity is constant, then the quantity equation implies that (fill in the blanks):

% Change in P = % Change in M − _____%.

(b) Since the percentage change in P is the same thing as the rate of inflation, the above equation suggests that an increase in the rate of money growth of 1% causes a 1% increase in inflation. Assume "perfect foresight", meaning that the expected rate of inflation turns out to be the actual rate. Then, according to the Fisher equation, a 1% increase in inflation causes a 1% increase in the nominal interest rate **i** (the real interest rate **r** is presumed to be affected only by real variables). Now use all of this information to complete Table 2 below.

Table 2

(1)	(2)	(3)	(4)	(5)
% change in P	% change in M	expected inflation rate (%)	real interest rate (%)	nominal interest rate (%)
0	3	0	3	3
_____	4	_____	3	_____
_____	5	_____	3	_____
_____	2	_____	3	_____
_____	8	_____	3	_____

3. Compare and contrast the ways monetary policy and fiscal policy influence the economy.

4. Do you think that an improvement in banking technology would lead to an increase or decrease in the aggregate price level?

5. What policies would a "classical" or "monetarist" economist suggest to reduce persistent unemployment?

6. Suppose that statistical information tells us that the aggregate demand curve for a particular economy can be approximated by the equation $P = 15000/Y$:
   (a) Construct a graph for the aggregate demand curve over a range for the aggregate price index of $P = 120$ to $P = 50$.
   (b) What is total nominal aggregate demand at $Y = 200$, $Y = 160$, and $Y = 130$, respectively?
   (c) What does the above information tell you about the elasticity of the aggregate demand curve? (Recall Chapter 2.)
   (d) Suppose $V = 3$, and the money supply doubles. Redraw the new aggregate demand curve. Is the elasticity of the aggregate demand curve affected?

7. What is the money multiplier, and what factors determine its size?

Appendix 10.1

Money and Banking

In this appendix we provide some more detail about the relationship between commercial bank lending and the money supply, and the involvement of the state **central bank** in this process.

We illustrate first with a simple example of a **deposit multiplier**. This explains how banks create money when they make loans. Then we will discuss the concept of the money multiplier itself, which purports to explain how the central bank can control the process. For the exposition of the deposit multiplier, make the following assumptions:

- There is only one type of bank deposit **D** (or, alternatively, define **D** as widely as possible).

- There is no "cash drain" from the system (once a deposit is made it will not be withdrawn, and all future transactions will be made by check or electronic transfer).

- The banks always wish to be "fully loaned up".

- The required reserve ratio is 10% (or 0.1).

These assumptions are made just for the sake of simplicity and will be relaxed later. Note, however, that as there will be no actual withdrawals from the banking system, we must think of the required reserve ratio in this case being imposed by legislation (which is, in fact, the case in several jurisdictions). Otherwise, there would be no incentive for the banks to keep reserves. In reality, of course, even if there was no legislation regarding reserve requirements, the banks would have to keep *some* reserves to guard against the eventuality of withdrawals. Also, note that the 10% reserve ratio is obviously far too large to be realistic in the modern world. It is chosen just to make the numbers easy.

Now suppose that a bank (Bank "A") starts up in business, and has no initial assets or liabilities (it just hangs out a sign saying, "We Will Now Accept Deposits"), and someone does deposit $100 in cash. The bank's balance sheet immediately after this transaction will look like the following:

Bank "A" Initial Balance Sheet

Assets		Liabilities	
Reserves	100	Deposits	100
	100		100

Notice that the actual reserve to deposits (**R/D**) ratio is 100/100 or 1.0, whereas the required reserve ratio is only 0.1. The implication is that the bank has **excess reserves** equal to $90. This means that they can make loans up to this amount and, even if all of that cash passes to another bank *via* the clearing house, they would still have $10 left to satisfy the reserve requirement. As the business of banking is to make loans, they will therefore lend out the $90; and even if they do lose the cash in a **"clearing drain"**, the balance sheet will look just fine from their point of view. It will be as follows:

Bank "A" 2nd Balance Sheet
(after making $90 loan)

Assets		Liabilities	
Reserves	10	Deposits	100
Loans	90		
	100		100

On the asset side, they now have cash reserves equal to $10 and loans equal to $90. They would, in fact, prefer this split to the initial balance sheet, as the loans (hopefully) will yield an interest income in the future, whereas cash reserves yield nothing. There are now no excess reserves (the bank is fully loaned up) and the actual **R/D** ratio is down to the required level of 10%. But, notice that there must be some other bank, Bank "B", that has received the $90 in cash. Their balance sheet in the first instance will be:

Bank "B" Initial Balance Sheet

Assets		Liabilities	
Cash	90	Deposits	90
	90		90

Bank B is now in the position that Bank A was to start with. The **R/D** ratio is at 100%, and they are holding excess reserves. The total of excess reserves must be $81 in this case. To maintain a **R/D** ratio of 10% with deposits of $90, Bank B would need to keep $9 of cash. In other words, this bank can make loans of $81; and even if they lose all the cash as their customers write cheques to people banking with other institutions, they can still adhere to the legal R/D ratio. The second balance sheet will be:

Bank "B" 2nd Balance Sheet
(after making $81 Loan)

Assets		Liabilities	
Cash	9	Deposits	90
Loans	81		
	90		90

Once again, this would be a preferred position for Bank B. The point to notice now, however, is that, as asserted above, the money supply is growing all the time as this process of bank lending is going on. The basic definition of the money supply **M**, is:

(10A.1) $M = CU + D$

where **CU** is currency held outside the banking system by individuals and (non-bank) business firms, and **D** is bank deposits. At the start of the current exercise, **CU** was $100 and **D** was zero, so the total money supply was $100. At the point reached by the time of Bank B's second balance sheet, **CU** was down to zero (all the cash was inside the banking system), but the total of **D** was $190, made up of $100 in Bank A and $90 in Bank B. The total money supply was thus also equal to $190 at this stage. The money supply, **M**, had already almost doubled. Moreover, the process of money creation is nowhere near finished yet. There is, presumably, now some Bank "C" with $81 of cash reserves and deposits and, therefore, excess reserves equal to $72.90. If they make loans equal to that amount, the money will increase by a further $72.90, and so on.

This is obviously a process that can continue through many more iterations. We can say more concisely that the eventual change in the money supply must be the sum of the total change in deposits in all the banks. In other words:

(10A.2) $\Delta D =$ Δ in deposits in Bank "A"
               $+ \Delta$ in deposits in Bank "B"
               $+ \Delta$ in deposits in Bank "C"
               $+ \Delta$ in deposits in Bank "D"
               $+$ .... (etc.)

There does not have to be a literally infinite number of banks. Instead of postulating the existence of banks "D", "E", or "F", maybe there are only three banks, and (say) the $72.90 from Bank C is recycled back into

Bank A. In any event, the **infinite series** in equation (10A.2) can be expressed numerically as:

(10A.3) $\Delta D = 100 + 90 + 81 + 72.90 + ...$

and, in symbols:

(10A.4) $\Delta D = \Delta R + (1 - 0.1)\Delta R + (1 - 0.1)^2\Delta R$
$+ (1 - 0.1)^3\Delta R + ...$

Mathematically, the infinite series will converge to:

(10A.5) $\Delta D/\Delta R = 1/0.1 = 10$

where 0.1 is the required reserve ratio. In other words, the deposit multiplier is 10, given the original assumptions. An initial injection of cash reserves of $100 will cause the money supply (via the process of bank lending) to increase by $1,000. (This makes sense, as the required reserve ratio is 10%, and that is really the only restriction on the system.)

The purpose of this discussion of the deposit multiplier was to drive home the point about how the money supply increases as the banking system extends loans, given an initial injection of reserves. Now, we will move on from the simple deposit multiplier to the money multiplier itself. This discussion will take account of:

• the role of the central bank, and the argument that the central bank can control the process, as it is the ultimate source of reserves

• the possibility of "cash drain" from the banking system (not allowed for in the discussion of the deposit multiplier)

The main point is that, as previously mentioned in Chapter 8, the base money of the system in any modern economy consists simply of the liabilities of the central bank. The various monetary policy techniques that the central bank can use to attempt to control the final total of bank lending revolve around this fact. We can see this by now looking at a stylized version of the central bank's balance sheet, as in Table 10A.1. On the asset side, the main items that a central bank will acquire in its financial market dealings are the bonds of its own government, and also foreign exchange: that is, foreign currency assets denominated in yen, Euros, US dollars, etc. (assuming that the domestic currency is not one of those). On the liabilities side, the first two items break down as follows:

(10A.6)   **notes outstanding = CU + vault & till cash**

(10A.7)   **deposits with central bank = total bank reserves**
– vault & till cash

Table 10A.1: The Central Bank Balance Sheet

Assets	Liabilities
Government bonds	Total currency notes outstanding
Foreign exchange	Deposits of the commercial banking system in the central bank
	Government deposits
Total	Total

Vault & till cash is that part of the total of currency outstanding held by the banks as part of their **reserves** (literally in vaults and tills, and ABM machines), and total reserves, **R**, consist of vault & till cash plus the deposits held by commercial banks with the central bank as part of the clearing house system. Meanwhile recall that the definition of the **monetary base**, **H**, of the system is simply currency held by the non-bank public, **cu**, plus bank reserves (**H** because the monetary base is sometimes also called **"high-powered money"**). In short:

(10A.8) $H = CU + R$

From equations (10A.6), (10A.7), and (10A.8), it can therefore be seen that the first two items on the liabilities side of the central bank balance sheet simply represent the sum of the base money in the system, **H**. This constitutes the "cash" that the banking system and the public need to acquire in order to carry on their financial activities. For instance, the cash that was injected into the banking system to "get the ball rolling" in the deposit multiplier example above must originally have come from the central bank. The argument can then be made that just by re-arranging its balance sheet, by buying and selling assets, the central bank can exert control over the whole lending activity of the system. This is, in fact, the goal of monetary policy, from this point of view.

Taking the two definitions, that of the monetary supply (**M = CU + D**), and the monetary base (**H = CU + R**), and with a bit of algebraic manipulation, the relationship between the monetary base and the money supply can be expressed as follows:

(10A.9) $M = [(1 + CU/D)/(CU/D + R/D)]H$

According to this, the relationship between the monetary base (the liabilities of the central bank) and the money supply (the liabilities of the commercial banking system) depends on the **banking ratios**, namely, the **cash/ deposits ratio (C/D)** and the **reserves/deposits ratio (R/D)**. The first of these sums up the behavior of the general public (how much of their total monetary assets will be held in cash rather than deposits), and the second sums up the behavior of the banks (what is the lowest **R/D** ratio they can "get away with"?). From equation (10A.9) we can then derive the money multiplier, which is supposed to predict by how much the total supply will expand for a given injection of base money by the central bank. The money multiplier is given by the expression:

$$(10A.10) \qquad \Delta M/\Delta H \ = \ (1 + CU/D)/(CU/D + R/D)$$

Note that this differs from the simple deposit multiplier formula simply by allowing for the fact that the **CU/D** ratio is non-zero (that is, in practice, some people will always be coming into the bank and asking for cash). To illustrate, suppose that in a particular economy the total cash in the hands of the non-bank public is **CU** = $39.9 billion, bank deposits are **D** = $665.0 billion, and bank reserves are **R** = $4.7 billion. Therefore, **CU/D** = 0.06 and **R/D** = 0.007 (less than 1%, actually quite a realistic number for an advanced modern economy). Therefore, the numerical value of the money multiplier will be:

$$(10A.11) \qquad \frac{\Delta M}{\Delta H} \ = \ \frac{1.00 + 0.06}{0.06 + 0.007} \ = \ 15.82$$

Hence, an injection of, for example, $100 of base money into the system will lead to an increase of $1582 in the overall money supply. The mechanism by which this occurs is simply the same bank lending process as discussed above. If $100 of base money is *withdrawn* from the system, bank loans will be called in, and the money supply will shrink by $1582.

Looking at the conduct of monetary policy through the lens of the money multiplier concept, the various tools and techniques used by central banks in pursuing monetary policy may then be seen as simply different devices for either injecting more base money into the system or withdrawing it. In terms of the theoretical concerns discussed in Chapter 10, this provides an explanation of how the money could continue to be treated as exogenous (i.e., under the control of the central bank), even though in reality is it actually created and destroyed in the course of the lending activities of the commercial banks. Table 10A.2 lists some of the main financial techniques employed by central banks to achieve these goals.

As already mentioned in Chapter 8, the most prominent of the monetary policy instruments in the contemporary world, certainly from the standpoint of the news media, are changes in the policy-related interest rate,

---

Table 10A.2: The Main Central Bank Policy Instruments

- changes in the "policy-related" interest rate

- open market operations

- deposit switching (drawdowns and re-deposits)

---

such as the federal funds rate in the USA, the main refinancing rate in the Euro-zone, or the overnight rate in Canada. These are, typically, overnight financing rates between the main commercial banks/financial institutions participating in the official clearing house run by the central bank, and (*via* differing institutional arrangements) are effectively under the control of the central bank. In terms of he money multiplier, an increase in this rate increases the penalty to the commercial bank for *not* having sufficient reserves on hand to meet obligations (it would then need to borrow in the overnight market) and, hence, tends to restrain commercial bank lending to avoid getting into this situation.

The term **open market operations** refers to purchases and sales of the debt of the central bank's own government in the secondary market. An open market purchase of government bonds by the central bank (paid for by the creation of additional central bank liabilities to serve as reserves for the commercial banks) will inject new base money into the system and is, therefore, an expansionary monetary policy. An open market sale has the opposite effect. In effect, an addition to the asset side of the central bank's balance sheet (buying a bond) must cause an increase on the liabilities side also (and hence an increase in the monetary base), and vice versa.

The possibility of **deposit switching** arises for those central banks that accept deposits from their own government (this may not be true in every jurisdiction). The government, in the sense of the **Ministry of Finance** or the **Treasury**, will also have bank accounts in the commercial banking system. Therefore, an easy way of injecting cash into the private economy is just to switch government deposits from the central bank to the commercial banks. Often the government will delegate to the central bank the authority to do this, as monetary conditions dictate. A so-called **redeposit** transfers government funds from the central bank to the commercial banks, and tends to expand the monetary base and money supply. A **drawdown** is the opposite transaction and has the opposite effect.

It is perhaps somewhat misleading, given the way monetary policy is actually conducted in the modern world, to treat these different monetary policy techniques (and others that could be mentioned) as if they are separate choices to be made by its monetary authorities. Although this type of treatment does fit the exposition of the money multiplier analysis, in reality, at the time of writing, most central banks do focus on a target for the overnight rate (or similar) as the main monetary policy instrument. The other techniques come in to assist or reinforce the attainment of the target. Practically speaking, they will all be used *together* to greater or lesser degree, and in the same direction, to achieve the target. When interest rates are raised, the implication is that the central bank wishes to pursue a "tighter" monetary policy; when they are lowered, monetary policy is more "accommodative".

In this presentation of issues in money and banking we have focused primarily on the behavior of the monetary base and the overall money supply, defined as deposits in banks and other similar financial institutions (the **"near banks"**). Of course, the financial sector as a whole involves much more than this. As the world economy has become more complex, the financial services sector has created a wide variety of financial instruments to match the **risk profiles** of savers and investors, including many different categories of stocks and bonds, and a huge variety of **financial derivatives** literally derived from (based on) these. **Financial innovation** allows investors and savers the opportunity to acquire new financial products with the desired risk profile. Business students will, of course, learn much more about the wider financial system in their finance courses. Note, however, that in the end all financial products are ultimately claims on sums of money, and the concept of risk in this context essentially refers to the problems that arise when obligations and **promises to pay** are *not* met. This is why the behavior of the banking system in the process of money and credit creation is fundamental.

11

Is There a Trade-Off between Inflation and Economic Growth?

Introduction

The previous two chapters have given an overview of some different approaches to macroeconomic policy-making, but in one respect they fail to completely capture the macroeconomic environment faced by the business decision-maker. Typically, research reports on the economy prepared by financial institutions and brokerage houses will not refer to the behavior of the price *level* or the level of output, but rather to the inflation *rate* and the rate of economic growth. A forecast will say something like, "Growth will pick up in the next quarter (or year)", or "Inflationary pressures are rising", and so on. Therefore, one objective of the present chapter is simply to recast the discussion in these terms — that is, in language more familiar to "market watchers" in the real world.

Another objective is to address the perennial question of whether there is a "trade-off" between these different objectives of macro policy. As mentioned earlier, in the modern world a great deal of attention is paid by policy-makers to the objective of achieving a low rate of inflation. However, if it was always true that in order to reduce inflation it is also necessary to reduce the growth of the real economy, such a policy stance would not be good news from the point of view either of economic prosperity or the profitability of business enterprises. The usual response to such criticism by the policy-makers is that such a trade-off may indeed exist in the "short run" but that from a longer-term perspective, either there is no trade-off or (even) that low inflation is actually a prerequisite for more permanent economic prosperity.

The Phillips Curve

The idea that there may be a trade-off between inflation and real economic performance was encapsulated in the so-called **Phillips curve**. The original Phillips curve was an empirical relationship, named after its discoverer, between the rate of change of money wages and unemployment in Britain from 1861–1957.[1] Given the close association between wage inflation and price inflation, the idea of a trade-off between price inflation and unemployment seemed to follow. The concept was then taken up and propagated by economists in other countries all over the world, including the USA. So, through the 1960s and early 1970s, and contrary to the historical tendency of "classical" economic ideas, it was widely believed that there existed a permanent and stable negative trade-off between inflation and unemployment, which could be exploited for policy purposes. If so,

---

[1] A.W. Phillips, "The relation between unemployment and the rate of change of money wages in the United Kingdom, 1861–1957", *Economica* (1958) 25: 283–69.

it would be possible for either monetary or fiscal policy to permanently reduce unemployment, but only at the cost of a permanently higher inflation rates, or vice versa. In this view, each society would have to assess the relative costs of inflation and unemployment and choose some optimal mix of the two. A (linear version of) the price-inflation Phillips curve would be:

$$(11.1) \qquad p = a[u^N - u] \qquad\qquad a > 0$$

where u^N has the connotation of the so-called **"natural rate"** of unemployment. This is the level of unemployment (primarily frictional unemployment) that would exist when the economy is also growing at its "natural rate". The idea is that an economy can experience a maximum rate of growth in any period of time based on technology, the skill of the labor force, resources, etc. This determines the "natural rate" of economic growth. Associated with this natural rate of growth is a natural rate of unemployment, which constitutes "full employment". This is not literally zero unemployment but the minimum unemployment rate attainable, given the current state of technology and development, without putting "pressure" on the labor market. The Phillips curve in (11.1) is illustrated diagrammatically in Figure 11.1. The implication of this analysis would be that the unemployment rate can be held down permanently, even below the natural rate (e.g., at **u1**), as long as the inflation rate is high enough.

Figure 11.1: A Linear Phillips "Curve"

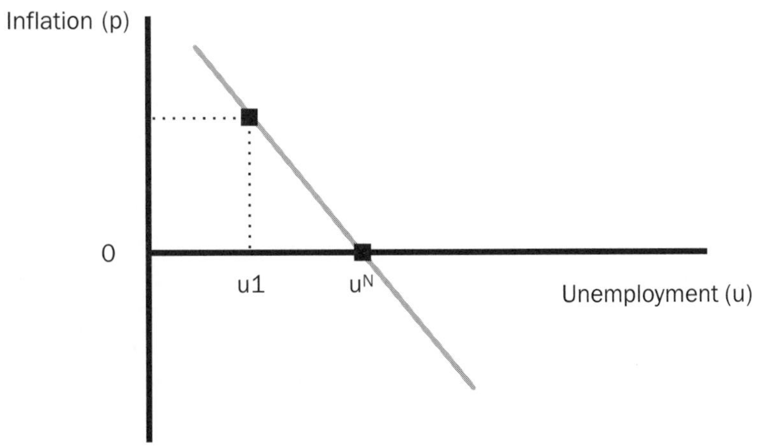

Historically, however, the Phillips curve, in this sense of a potential policy choice, was soon in trouble both in academia and among policy-makers. There were two main problems. The first was simply that these ideas are in basic conflict with what we have described as the main presumptions of classical and neoclassical economics: that is, the economic decisions should be based on real (inflation adjusted) magnitudes rather than on nominal magnitudes. Second, during the 1970s, in particular, the idea of a Phillips curve trade-off seemed to be actively misleading due to the occurrence of "stagflation" in the real world data during that decade. There were episodes in which *both* inflation and unemployment increased in various jurisdictions. It is perhaps worth pointing out that the apparent empirical failures came well *after* the basic theoretical challenge. They were decisive only in the sense that they gave credence to the latter. In any event, belief in a permanent trade-off between inflation and unemployment very quickly declined. It was argued that the short-run or **"expectations-augmented" Phillips curve** could shift bodily whenever there was a change in inflationary expectations. Therefore, in the mainstream macroeconomic models of the later 20th century and up to the present day, any postulated trade-off between inflation and unemployment was held explicitly to be short-term. In the long run, any rate of inflation at all was thought compatible with the natural rate of unemployment, which later came to be called (more neutrally) the **NAIRU** (**non-accelerating inflation rate of unemployment**). The long-run Phillips curve was assumed to be vertical. To illustrate, the expectations-augmented version of the Phillips curve would be:

$$(11.2) \qquad p = a[u^N - u] + p^e$$

This says that, although it is true that inflation will increase whenever unemployment falls below the natural rate, there is also another reason for inflation to increase (even when the labor market is in equilibrium). Inflation will also increase just because inflation expectations increase. The key point is that now, according to equation (11.2), whenever actual and expected inflation are equal, unemployment will be at the natural rate. We then have $p = p^e$ and $u^N = u$. Therefore, there is no long-run trade-off between actual inflation and unemployment, only a temporary, or short-run, trade-off that only exists when actual and expected inflation are not equal. The logic here is simple. In the short run, we may be fooled into thinking that an increase in inflation will lead to a lasting reduction in unemployment. This is shown by a movement along the SRPC. But, over time, we see that the economy cannot, in fact, sustain this level of economic activity. This is then reflected in a shift of the SRPC. In the longer term, output goes back to its natural level, but with a higher rate of inflation. The set of expectations-augmented Phillips curves, and the way they shift over time, is shown in Figure 11.2.

Figure 11.2: Expectations-Augmented Phillips Curves

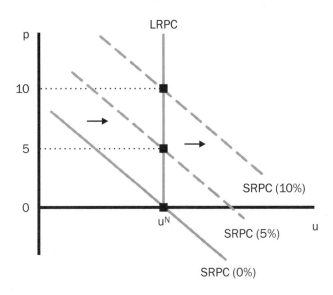

To see the connection between the Phillips curve and the more general aggregate supply formulation discussed in previous chapters, note that there must be some relationship between growth relative to trend and the **unemployment gap**, along the lines of the so-called Okun's Law.[2] Okun's law states that there must be some quantitative relationship between changes in the growth rate of the economy and the unemployment rate. For example, one figure that has often been put forward (for the advanced industrialized countries) is that for the unemployment rate to fall by 1 percentage point, the growth rate would have to increase by about 2.5 percentage points. Whatever the exact number is, there will be a relationship of the form:

$$(11.3) \qquad u - u^N = (b/a)(y^N - y) \qquad\qquad b > 0$$

where **a** in the term **b/a** is, by construction, exactly the same coefficient as in equation (11.1) above, u^N is again the natural rate of unemployment and y^N is the natural rate of GDP growth.. From equations (11.2) and (11.3),

---

[2] Arthur Okun, "Potential GNP: its measurement and significance", *Proceedings of the American Statistical Association* (1962): 98–111.

we can then easily derive a dynamic version of the aggregate supply function:

$$(11.4) \qquad y = y^N + (1/b)(p - p^e)$$

This is basically the same type of supply function as shown in Chapter 10, but now translated into rates of change. There is assumed to be some natural rate of growth, y^N, determined purely by supply-side factors. In addition, the growth rate will temporarily be higher (lower) than the national rate if the actual inflation rate turns out to be greater (less) than expected.

Adaptive Expectations and "Rational" Expectations

We can now develop a complete macroeconomic model, derived from the above, to give a summary account of conventional views on the overall relationship between inflation and economic growth. The relevant equations of the model are:

$$(11.5) \qquad p = m - y$$

$$(11.6) \qquad p = b[y - y^N] + p^e$$

$$(11.7) \qquad m = x\%$$

In the above, equation (11.5) is simply a dynamic version of $MV = PY$ (again assuming that velocity is constant). The inflation rate, p, is then equal to the rate of monetary growth, m, minus the rate of growth of the real economy, y (as in Chapter 10). This serves as a basic version of dynamic aggregate demand. Equation (11.6) is the dynamic short-run aggregate supply curve once again, and equation (11.7) is the simplest possible "monetary policy rule" to determine the rate of growth of the money supply. The rate of monetary growth is just set at some constant level, $x\%$.

There remains the key question of exactly how expectations of inflation are determined. One (more or less) plausible assumption is that expected inflation may depend on the inflation rate that was experienced most recently (in the previous period). In that case:

$$(11.8) \qquad p^e = p_{-1}$$

This is a simple version of the so-called **adaptive expectations** hypothesis, which says that expectations of future economic variables will depend on (i.e., adapt to) actual experience. Obviously more complicated versions of this might be devised, such as making expected inflation a weighted average

Figure 11.3: Response to an Increase in Demand Growth

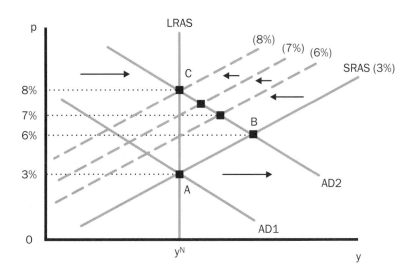

of several past lags of inflation, but the expression in equation (11.8) will suffice to illustrate the basic idea. The way the model works, in the case of an expansionary policy (meaning, in this context, an increase in the rate of growth of the money supply), is shown in Figure 11.3.

Suppose the economy is initially in "equilibrium" at point **"A"**. The inflation rate is 3%, and the GDP growth rate is equal to the natural rate. Then, there is a permanent increase in the rate of monetary growth, and the dynamic aggregate demand curve shifts out from AD1 to AD2. As most economic actors are still expecting the inflation rate to be 3%, when it actually goes up to 6%, there will be an economic boom, at point **"B"** in the diagram. Once a higher inflation rate has been experienced, however, the economic actors will come to expect this rate to continue, and it will be built into contracts. The short-run supply function will shift up, and the next inflation rate actually experienced will be 7%. The rate of growth of the economy also starts to slow down, although it is still higher than the natural rate. Once again, however, expectations will have been falsified, and there will be further adjustments. The process will continue until the inflation rate has risen as high as 8% at point **"C"**. At that stage, the boom in the economy has died out. The economy is only growing at its natural rate once again, and, in the end, demand expansion has just left the economy with a higher inflation rate. Once again, we see that the main idea is that the demand expansion will cause only a temporary boom (a higher than normal growth rate), but it will eventually just lead to inflation. The story is basically the same as that discussed in the previous chapter, but now expressed in terms of inflation rates and growth rates (the way it is usually presented in the financial press) rather than in terms of the level of prices and the level of output. It goes without saying that a policy of demand reduction to reduce the inflation rate will have the reverse set of effects, and we leave it to the reader to work out this case.

The above discussion has actually been a very standard way of thinking about the macroeconomy for generations, albeit expressed here in more "modern" mathematical language. Note, however, that as presented, it depends heavily on the assumption of adaptive expectations. Hence, part of the reason for the furor raised by the concept of **rational expectations**, when first introduced to macroeconomics in the 1970s and 1980s, was that it seemed to disturb this tidy solution to the distinction between the long run and short run, while at the same time *claiming* to be more consistent (than the adaptive version) with respect to approved economic theory and methodology.

The complaint would be that (according to the approved economic methodology) the various actors taking part in the economy are supposed to be **rational agents**, who always make economic decisions in what they perceive to be their own best interests. From this point of view, the problem with the adaptive expectations hypothesis is that people forming expectations in this way do not seem to do so rationally. They just form expectations via a simple "rule of thumb" and hence consistently make mistakes, which cannot be in their best interest. The rational agent, it is believed, should think more carefully about the situation, arrive at a *rational expectation* of the inflation rate, and then act accordingly. Note, however, that in our simple model, with no uncertainty, and if the change in government policy is announced, this rational agent should really have no difficulty in working out the implications of the simple quantity theory of money. They should, in fact, be able to form a completely accurate estimate of what the inflation rate will be. In short, the rational expectation of inflation in our simple world is:

$$(11.9) \qquad \mathbf{p^e = p}$$

And, in that case, obviously:

$$(11.10) \qquad \mathbf{y = y^N}$$

The conclusion would then be that under rational expectations, real GDP growth is *always* at its natural rate, except for any random policy disturbances, which by definition cannot be foreseen. This result, when first articulated, was certainly appealing for those economists who believe in *laissez*

Case Study 17

"Quebec's Monetary Policy"
Quebec City; June 20, 2028

The recently independent country of Quebec is involved in intense discussions with respect to its optimal monetary policy. Professor Yves Bertrand argues that a sovereign Quebec requires an independent currency and its own monetary policy. According to Prof. Bertrand, "This will allow Quebec to establish a monetary policy that best reflects its individuality, and its unique economic, social, and political requirements. We need to be able to determine our own inflation rate and the overall rate of economic expansion, and to set our own rate of interest." However, Marc-Andre Levine, President of the new Republic of Quebec, argues that the only viable option is for the Republic to adopt the American currency. The President has stated, "We are too small to establish our own monetary policy. All important decisions are made by the Federal Reserve Board in Washington. We are a small, open economy. It is not possible for us to have a separate monetary policy. Even if it were possible, what difference would this make to the real economic opportunities of the citizens of our Republic"? In response, Professor Bertrand has asked, "Why, then, did we bother to have an independent country at all, if we cannot even set our own monetary policy?"

faire and therefore are suspicious of any government involvement in the economy. The systematic or deliberate use of monetary policy (or of fiscal policy, in a more complete model) apparently has no effect whatsoever except on the inflation rate. Policy does not affect the growth rate of real GDP or the unemployment rate at all, even in the short-run. Therefore, from the perspective of political economy, this so-called **policy irrelevance** result had a powerful ideological charge. It implies that government can only make things worse; it cannot make things any better. At the same time, however, and in a sense unfortunately for the more traditional economist, policy irrelevance also seemed to wreck the plausible argument that allows for *some* short-run real impact of monetary/demand changes (for the sake of realism), while nonetheless insisting on the quantity theory for the long run. As mentioned in the earlier discussion of monetarism, the point is that, in practice, changes in policy *do* seem to most observers to have some effect on output and employment. Businesspeople would probably be most unwise in their planning, for example, if they acted on the assumption that a concerted policy to bring down the inflation rate would not have some negative impact on their bottom line, at least in the short term. The original point of distinguishing between short- and long-run effects was precisely to allow for this element of realism, while reassuring the business community that a downturn would not last forever. From a *traditionally* classical point of view, therefore, complete policy irrelevance would seem to be too much of a good thing. It presented a view of the economy that may accord with certain ideological preconceptions, but was not really credible from the practical point of view.

This defect in the theory could be repaired in a number of obvious ways; for example, by allowing nominal wages to be set in advance for more than one period (as in theories of overlapping contracts, and staggered wage setting — think of unionized wage contracts here), so that even if inflation expectations are perfect, it is not possible for everyone to act on them. Another way to repair the defect in the theory would be by recognizing that information itself is costly, and that, therefore, the use of some simple rule of thumb in forming expectations might be "rational" after all. In fact, there is an entire school of modern economists (misleadingly) named the **New Keynesian** school, which is devoted to repairing the model in these and other ways.[3] In the end, however, debates of this kind are open-ended and can go on forever. Looking at the matter from first principles, it seems clear that *if* the basic premise is an economy that always eventually reverts to some natural state (including natural rates of economic

---

[3] Misleading, because the views expressed by New Keynesians are really just a variant on the more traditional "classical" themes, whereas the rival **"New Classicals"** insist on the relatively more extreme position that the economy is always in "long-run equilibrium".

growth, unemployment, and real interest), then the "monetary disequilibrium theorists"[4] must have common sense on their side in their attempts to explain the actual deviations from, or fluctuations around, these natural levels. Rigidities, misperceptions, and imperfections of various kinds can be the only explanation.

It can also be argued, however, that a far more significant debate would be whether or not this particular way of looking at the economy — as if it behaves rather like a pendulum that always swings back to some pre-determined position — is in itself either an accurate or useful way of thinking about socioeconomic issues. In a purely classical or **"New Classical"** world (see footnote 3 on the page 250), there can be no such thing as involuntary unemployment. Workers would simply lower their wage offer until everyone was fully employed and the economy would be at the natural rate of unemployment. The term "natural" rate of unemployment, can be a very unfortunate and misleading concept as, from the human point of view, there is nothing "natural" about unemployment. Unemployment causes a great deal of social disruption. At the macroeconomic level, unemployment represents a loss of potential output (the nation is below the production possibility frontier); and at the individual level, unemployment causes great personal and family stress. In many respects the "natural rate" is a social construct. We even observe different natural rates from nation to nation based on their economic and social policies. It should be noted that the United States, for example, went from a double-digit natural rate of unemployment to zero unemployment (actually labor shortages) with the declaration of war during World War II, more than 60 years ago.

Modern Monetary Economics: The "New Consensus" on Macroeconomic Policy

In this section, we discuss what some have called the "new consensus" model of macroeconomic policy, although to call it a consensus may be somewhat exaggerated. Essentially, it refers to the approach to macroeconomic policy-making that was widely accepted, and in use, in central banks, finance ministries, research institutes, etc., for policy-making purposes at the beginning of the 21st century.[5] It should go without saying, also, that to call something a consensus does not necessarily imply that is it "true", or scientifically accurate. It just means that is widely accepted at a

---

[4] Leland B. Yeager, *The Fluttering Veil: Essays on Monetary Disequilibrium*, edited by G. Selgin (Indianapolis: Liberty Fund, 1997).
[5] John B. Taylor, "Teaching modern macroeconomics at the principles level", *American Economic Review* (May 2000) 90(2): 90–94.

particular point in time. From the point of view of a business executive, who is in some way playing a strategic game against the policy authorities (trying to figure out what they will do next, and what the impact will be on business conditions), the value of studying it is mainly to get some idea of the thought process that is currently going on in policy-making circles.

Philosophically speaking, the current consensus is really not much different from the tradition of monetarism described in the previous chapter or, for that matter, from the whole lineage of classical/neoclassical economic thinking. It is simply the latest development of this current of thought. Such things as low inflation, "sound money", fiscal prudence, and so on are given pride of place. Economic growth is thought to depend entirely on supply side factors, which will determine a "natural" growth rate for each economy. This growth rate is admittedly not immutable. It may be changed or improved upon, but only by technological change or improvements in productivity. Changes on the demand side, caused for example by changes in monetary or fiscal policy, may be allowed to have temporary effects on growth, but are confidently believed to have no lasting impact. All this is, of course, very familiar. The main difference from traditional ideas that emerges in the new consensus model is, as already discussed, simply a recognition that in reality central banks conduct monetary policy *via* changes in interest rates rather than by directly fixing the level or the rate of growth of the monetary base. The central bank sets the "policy-related" interest rate, and the money supply adjusts endogenously as a result of the subsequent lending and borrowing activities of the commercial banks and the public. This idea may not actually have been that much of a revelation to long-time "Fed watchers" in the financial markets and to certain groups of heterodox economists, such as the **Post Keynesians**, but it did require some adjustments to what had become conventional academic economic thinking, as set out earlier. In particular, it required the construction of an economic model making no reference to some traditional concepts such as **money demand and supply,** the **LM curve** (discussed in the appendix to Chapter 9), **velocity**, etc.[6]

One problem with the idea that the interest rate can be a *policy* variable, at least from the point of view of conventional economics, is that, according to the usual way of looking at things, interest rates should also be determined in a "market" like any other price. In this case, the market is the market for **"loanable funds"** as discussed in Chapter 3. This idea is illustrated in Figure 11.4. The variables in this figure are all expressed in nominal terms, and the demand curve for loanable funds (the supply of securities) is shown as downward sloping with respect to the nominal rate of interest. That is, bor-

---

[6] David Romer, "Keynesian macroeconomics without the LM curve", *Journal of Economic Perspectives* (Spring 2000) 14(2): 149–70.

Figure 11.4: **The "Loanable Funds" Theory of Interest Rates and a Modification in the Case of Bank Lending**

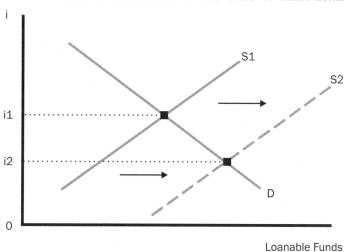

rowing will increase as the nominal interest rate falls. The supply curve of loanable funds (the demand for securities) is shown as upward sloping. These funds are presumed to come from "savers", and the idea is that nominal saving will increase as the nominal interest rises. The standard economic argument, then, would be that the interest rate is determined by the intersection of the demand and supply curves as at **i1**, for example. However, if, on the contrary, the idea is that the central bank is setting the interest rate, presumably its "target" will be some other level, such as **i2**. If **i2** is lower than the theoretical market equilibrium, then what must be happening is that the central bank is directly or indirectly making available the additional funds to satisfy the demand at that level, regardless of the amount of current saving. This is shown by a rational outward shift of the supply curve of loanable funds (caused by money creation by the central bank and the banking system), as illustrated by the broken line. In the microeconomic context of a single securities market we argued that there may be credit rationing if the interest was set "too low", but the difference here at the macro level is that the funds are now being made available via endogenous credit creation, even though the interest is "low", and hence it is possible for the central bank to keep the interest rate down at the lower lever, **i2**.

Of course, there are a number of possible caveats to the idea that the central bank rather than the "market" determines the interest rates and, as mentioned, a traditional plank of orthodox economics was to strongly deny that possibility. In the first place, it is true that the central bank only controls one specific interest rate, and a very short-dated one at that. For monetary policy to be the decisive factor, it must therefore be assumed, and argued, that there is some well-defined **transmissions mechanism** whereby changes in the policy rate eventually feed through to the other rates in the system. Second, it can always be claimed (and is sometimes claimed by central banks themselves) that, rather than lead, the central bank always follows the market in interest rate changes. On the other hand, contrary to both these arguments, in the modern world a brief glance at the financial pages or Internet sites dealing with financial matters will soon reveal headlines such as:

> *"Central Bank Hikes Rates"*

> *"Interest Rate Cut Takes Markets by Surprise"*

> *"No Change in Key Interest Rates Foreseen"*

The authors of such articles are seemingly quite sure that such pronouncements are meaningful.

The basic framework for policy analysis in the new consensus model consists of just three macroeconomic relationships. First, there is a demand function resembling the IS curve from the appendix in Chapter 9:

$$(11.11) \qquad y = d - hr \qquad\qquad h > 0$$

This equation simply says that demand growth depends positively on some autonomous component **d** (which we may take to include fiscal policy actions) and, negatively, on the real rate of interest. The latter arises because a lower interest rate will presumably cause an increase in investment expenditure as a percentage of GDP. Second, there is a short-run supply function (SRAS), resembling a short-run Phillips curve (SRPC) or an "accelerationist" aggregate supply/inflation equation:

$$(11.12) \qquad p - p_{-1} = b[y_{-1} - y^N] \qquad\qquad b > 0$$

This says that the rate of inflation will be greater in the current period than in the previous period if GDP growth was above its "natural rate" in the previous period. When a Phillips Curve is drawn against the growth rate rather than the unemployment rate, it is of course, in principle, a positively-sloped rather than a negatively-sloped relationship as was seen in the previous section. In this case, however, the SRAS will come out as a flat line, as the inflation rate depends only on what occurred in the previous period. Finally, there will be a **central bank reaction function** of some kind, such as:

$$(11.13) \qquad r = r_0 + e[p - p^*] \qquad\qquad e > 0$$

Equation (11.13) is a simplified version of the much-discussed **Taylor rule** for monetary policy,[7] and says that the central bank will increase the *real* policy rate if the inflation rate is higher than some arbitrary target level **p*** (and vice versa). In effect, the monetary policy is one of **inflation targeting**. Note that the actual policy instrument of the central bank must be a nominal interest rate (again, usually a nominal overnight rate of some kind), so that, in practice, "increasing the real rate" usually means increasing the policy instrument by more than one-for-one with any increase in observed inflation.[8]

Now, by substituting equation (11.13) into equation (11.14), and re-arranging equation (11.12), we can construct a simple aggregate demand and supply model resembling those discussed previously. This is given by the following two equations:

(11.14) $p = [(1/eh)d + p^* - (1/e)r_0] - (1/eh)y$ (demand)

(11.15) $p = p_{-1} + b[y_{-1} - y^N]$ (supply)

The supply relationship in equation (11.15) is just the SRPC, and the demand relationship in equation (11.14) shows a familiar downward sloping demand-side relationship in **(p,y)** space. Note, however, that this is now due solely to the assumed response of monetary policy. That is, whenever inflation increases, the central bank will raise interest rates (and, hence, reduce demand). Also, we should continue to be aware of the implicit assumption that changes in the interest rate under the control of the central bank do feed through into those interest rates relevant to the firms making investment decisions. There are three "shift variables" for the constructed demand function. First is autonomous demand growth, **d**, including such things as fiscal policy (changes in the government budget). An increase in the demand parameter **d** increases overall demand growth. Second, there is the inflation target itself, **p***. A lower inflation target will reduce demand because the central bank will raise interest rates in the attempt to achieve it. A more relaxed (higher) target for inflation, however, will tend to increase demand. Effectively, the inflation target represents the "stance of monetary policy" in this context. Finally, the intercept term in the monetary rule (or **r₀**) can also be a shift variable. Note, however, that this has a rather ambiguous status. Most textbooks refer to this as the **natural rate of interest**, or the "equilibrium" interest rate, meaning something like the real rate of interest that would exist in a barter capital market *if* there was no

---

[7] John B. Taylor, "Discretion versus policy rules in practice", *Carnegie-Rochester Conference Series on Public Policy* (1993) 39: 195–214.

[8] N. Gregory Mankiw, "US monetary policy during the 1990s", NBER Working Paper 8471, September 2001.

such thing as money and no interference from central banks.[9] If this were true, it could not be changed because it would just be a given number. In practice, however, there seems to be no way for central banks to actually know what the natural rate might be if, indeed, it is even a meaningful concept. So, in reality, the r_0 term can also only be some number chosen by the central bank on the basis of experience, "rules of thumb", or something similar. If, therefore, the implicit target for r_0 is lowered, this also represents something like an expansionary monetary policy. Actual real interest rates must be cut to accommodate this change in views, and vice versa.

As one example of how demand changes work out in this framework, the graph in Figure 11.6 shows the impact of an expansionary fiscal policy. This figure obviously looks very similar to those shown in the previous section, which is not surprising since the basic economic philosophy is unchanged. One difference, as mentioned, is that the short-run supply curve (SRAS) now comes out flat, which occurs because changes in inflation only happen with a lag, according to equation (11.15). The initial impact of a demand change will simply be a boom (as the economy moves to point

Figure 11.5: The Effects of a Demand Expansion

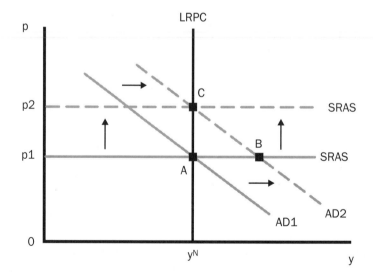

---

[9] This is the classic definition from K. Wicksell, *Interest or Prices*. New York: Augustus M. Kelley (1965).

"B"), and changes in inflation will only come later. This presentation of the SRAS or supply curve is consistent with that in many contemporary textbooks, and it does not alter the basic interpretation of the model. The main conceptual difference from the model of the previous section is in the interpretation of what is occurring behind the scenes, as far as monetary policy responses are concerned. The essential idea is again that a demand expansion will cause an initial boom in the economy, but then will start to put upward pressure on the inflation rate, and the boom will eventually fade away. However, note that now some part of this response is *deliberately* caused by the monetary policy reaction. In other words, in response to the incipient increase in inflation, the central bank explicitly takes action to hike interest rates and move the economy back along the AD function. The final equilibrium of the economy is at point **"C"**, where the growth rate of the economy is back to its supposedly "natural" rate, and all that has happened is that inflation is (after all) higher and interest rates are higher. It can be argued, though, that the final rise in inflation is less than it otherwise would have been because of the monetary policy response, which dampens inflationary pressures overall.

Figure 11.6 shows what will occur when the inflation target itself is revised downward. Suppose the central bank has been working with an inflation target of, for example, 3%, but then it decides that only zero inflation (stable prices) will do. The target therefore becomes 0%. Evidently, the central bank will need to pursue a "tight money" policy (raise interest

Figure 11.6: A Lower Inflation Target

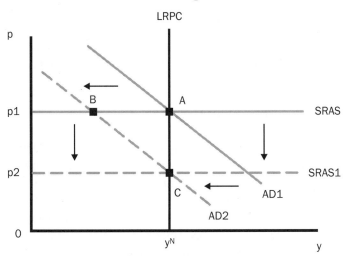

rates) in the attempt to hit the new target. The demand schedule will move back and to the left. There will be a monetary policy-induced reduction in demand. Once again, as a result of this hard-line stance taken by the central bank, there will initially be a recession, at point **"B"**. Then, so the argument goes, the usual downward adjustments of expectations must eventually take place. The end result of having a lower inflation target will therefore be a lower *actual* rate of inflation, but fortunately (according to those who advocate this model) no permanent reduction in the rate of economic growth. One interesting point is that the target itself is never actually achieved. A lower target will reduce the actual inflation rate to some lower level; but unless the r_0 term is adjusted upward as well, the target itself will be elusive, as can be seen from equation (11.17) below.

We can summarize the basic results of the new consensus as follows. In the long run, the growth rate of output will conform to the natural rate. That is:

$$(11.16) \qquad y = y^N$$

Meanwhile, the ongoing inflation rate will be determined by:

$$(11.17) \qquad p = (1/eh)d - (1/e)r_0 + p^* - (1/eh)y^N$$

In other words, a demand expansion, such as an increase in the budget deficit, will ultimately only lead to inflation. This result, of course, is a key element in the rejection of anything like a "Keynesian" approach to policy. Meanwhile, a "tougher" (lower) inflation target will always lead to a one-to-one decrease in the actual inflation rate, even if the target itself is not actually achieved. Similarly, a tighter monetary policy, as a result of an upward re-evaluation of the intercept term in the monetary policy rule, r_0, will also reduce the inflation rate. Finally, as indeed was suggested by the original quantity theory of money, an increase in the natural rate of growth (e.g., as a result of technical progress) will reduce the inflation rate.

The actual real interest rate that prevails in equilibrium will be given by:

$$(11.18) \qquad r = (1/h)(d - y^N)$$

This is consistent with some traditional arguments that a demand increase (such as an increase in government spending or a reduction in taxation) will tend to raise interest rates. An increase in the demand parameter, **d**, will indeed cause an increase in the real rate of interest. The mechanism by which this occurs, however, is not so much a question of "market forces" as of the monetary policy response of the central bank. The demand increase causes an increase in inflation, and interest rates are raised by the central bank in response to this. Similarly, according to equation

(11.17) an increase in the natural growth rate will tend to *reduce* the real rate of interest. This is because an increase in supply-led growth will reduce inflation, and allow the central bank to reduce interest rates. Note that, interestingly enough, the setting of r_0 itself does not seem to affect the level of real interest rates that eventually emerges. The reason is that if r_0 is lowered (raised) this will then cause a rise (fall) in inflation, and there will always be an offsetting policy response via the central bank reaction function.

Finally, we can ask what would need to happen to achieve, for argument's sake, a zero inflation rate (often regarded as the desired objective of orthodox economic policy). It is clear from equations (11.17) and (11.18) that not only must p^* (the target) be zero and the interest rate raised whenever actual inflation goes higher, but also that the intercept term in the monetary policy rule, r_0, must be adjusted, so that in the end:

$$(11.19) \qquad r_0 = (1/h)(d - y^N)$$

In this sense *only* could the r_0 term be called a "natural rate". It is a natural rate in the sense that, if and when r_0 and r coincide (and if the target is zero), the inflation rate will also be zero. However, as mentioned, if r_0 is also the intercept term in a "rule", it would be difficult to know what it should be beforehand.

Chapter Summary

- The concept of the Phillips curve seemed at one time to be a natural complement to "Keynesian economics". It suggested a trade-off between inflation and unemployment, which could be deliberately chosen by the society concerned. An interventionist government could literally "fine tune" the economy through the use of active macroeconomic management (monetary and fiscal policy).

- Historically, the period of stagflation in the 1970s cast doubt on this. It showed that an economy can have the double misery of high unemployment and high inflation.

- However, the new theory of rational expectations proved equally difficult to assimilate. With sufficient information, businesspeople and consumers will "see the game", form sets of rational expectations, and behave accordingly.

- The logical conclusion seems to be policy irrelevance. People can see the game, so why bother? Also implied is the perhaps somewhat counterintuitive notion that *all* macro policies should be abandoned because they are "irrelevant." This would, however, fit in with the basic ideas of economic and fiscal conservatives in the political arena.

- In themselves, on the other hand, the mere existence of national central banks and the international financial institutions (such as the IMF), the sheer size of the public sector generally, and the vigor of the continued debate about government spending and taxes make it seem hardly credible that policy has no effect at all. Policy-makers certainly still talk and act as if it makes a difference.

- A centerpiece of orthodox economic thinking is the idea of the "natural rate" of unemployment, about which nothing can be done. From the human point of view, however, there is nothing "natural" about unemployment and this would still lead to demands for government policies to provide meaningful work for all of its citizens, consistent with stable prices.

Problems

1. At one time, policy makers interpreted the Phillips curve as offering a viable menu of inflation-unemployment choices. Today, the curve is no longer viewed this way. Why has the interpretation changed?

2. Suppose that inflation is 3%, unemployment 7%, and the budget deficit is 3 billion Rand. Make the cases for and against expansionary and contractionary monetary and fiscal policies. Explain which policy you favor.

3. Suppose the Okun's law coefficient has increased for a number of countries. Does this increase cause unemployment to be more or less sensitive to deviations of output growth from normal? Briefly explain.

4. Explain why you agree or disagree with the following statement:

   The acceptance of rational expectations totally discredits the notion that policy activism should be pursued if output lies below its natural rate.

5. What is the natural rate of unemployment? What would explain the differences in the natural rate between developed countries?

6. Explain how the original Phillips curve differs from the expectations-augmented Phillips curve (the modified, or accelerationist, Phillips curve).

Appendix 11.1

Interest Rates and Aggregate Demand Growth

One difference between the modern monetary model, known as the **new consensus**, and that employed during the heyday of monetarism — in addition to the different role of the central bank reaction function — is that the demand side is once again derived from the familiar $Y = C + I + G + (X - IM)$ breakdown of GDP from the national accounts (that is, rather than the $MV = PY$ of the quantity theory). Of course, it is also true $MV = PY = \$C + \$I + \$G + \$(X - IM)$, so it is possible to get at a description of aggregate demand either way. To illustrate, first use the simplified version of the GDP breakdown (by eliminating government and the private sector) and we have:

(11A.1) $\qquad Y = C + I$

Now, modify the consumption function slightly by making this depend on last period's income — which the consumers must know and have observed — rather than current income (which might not be fully known at the time when purchasing decisions are made). This gives:

(11A.2) $\qquad C = {}_cY_{-1}$

Next, substitute 11A.2 into 11A.1:

(11A.3) $\qquad Y = {}_cY_{-1} + I$

then divide through by Y_{-1}:

(11A.4) $\qquad Y/Y_{-1} = c + (Y/Y_{-1})(I/Y)$

At this point, we can introduce the notation that $x = I/Y$. Also, recall that $c = 1 - s$, and that the growth rate, y, is defined as $y = (Y - Y_{-1})/Y_{-1}$. Therefore:

(11A.5) $(1+y)(1-x) = 1 - s$

which is approximately the same as:

(11A.6) $y = x - s$

Finally, we can argue that investment as a percentage of GDP will depend on the real interest rate. That is, it will tend to increase when interest rates are low, and fall when interest rates are high, making the cost of borrowing prohibitive. (Recall the IS curve of Appendix 9). For example, this might be shown by the equation:

(11A.7) $x = \chi_0 - hr$

Then substituting (11A.7) into (11A.6) we arrive at:

(11A.8) $y = d - hr$

where the demand parameter, **d**, is given by $\mathbf{d} = \boldsymbol{\chi_0} - \mathbf{s}$. Equation (11A.8) is, therefore, obviously the same as (11.11) in the new consensus model.

12

The Global Economy II: The Balance of Payments and Exchange Rates

Introduction

In the discussion of economic indicators in Chapter 8, the importance of the balance of payments numbers and of the foreign exchange rate was mentioned, but no details given. This therefore is the task of the present chapter. The balance of payments is essentially the record of the domestic economy's dealings with the rest of the world during a specific accounting period, such as a quarter or a year. The foreign exchange rate, as we will define it here, is the foreign currency price of one unit of the domestic currency. If Switzerland is the domestic economy, for example, then (at the time of writing) the exchange rate of the Swiss franc with the Euro is 0.66 (that is, it takes €0.66 to buy a Swiss franc). Similarly, if Australia is the domestic economy, the exchange rate of the Australian dollar with the US dollar is 0.73 (it takes 73 US cents to buy an Australian dollar).

The Balance of Payments and International Flows of Funds

The **overall balance of payments** of the domestic economy may be defined as the balance across the **current account** and the **capital account**. The latter reflects net new international borrowing and lending and equity investment, and the former comprises the balance of trade in goods and services, plus net interest and dividend payments on past capital transactions (**foreign investment income**). In symbolic terms, this can be written as:

$$(12.1) \qquad BP = CA + KA$$

BP stands for "balance of payments", **CA** for "current account", and **KA** for "capital account".

In a **fixed exchange rate** system, it is possible for an overall surplus or deficit on the balance of payments to occur, and this will be reflected in changes in the level of **foreign exchange reserves** held by the domestic central bank. This can be termed **"official financing"** (or **OF**). Official holdings of foreign exchange reserves will increase when there is a balance of payments surplus, and they will decrease if there is a balance of payments deficit, as shown in equation (12.2):

$$(12.2) \qquad OF = BP = CA + KA$$

Table 12.1 gives some illustrative numbers for the current account, the capital account, and official financing for Ecoland in a particular year. The reader should note that in actual published statistics, the balance of payments data will likely be presented in considerably more detail than in

---

Table 12.1:   Balance of Payments for Ecoland, 2028

(billions of Ecodollars)

Current Account	+ 31,864
Capital Account	− 19,435
Statistical Discrepancy	− 8,076
Overall Balance	+ 4,353
Δ in International Reserves	+ 4,353

---

the stylized form shown in Table 12.1. For example, what is described above as the "capital account" (for short) may appear as the **capital and financial accounts** (reflecting a distinction between **foreign direct investment** and purely financial transactions). Similarly, the current account may be subdivided into entries such as the **merchandise trade balance**, **net foreign investment income**, etc. The purpose of the more streamlined presentation here is simply to focus on basic principles. Another point to notice is that in published statistics the **"OF"** term may be entered with the "wrong" sign (e.g., negative 4,353 rather than positive 4,353) so as to conform to the principles of **double entry bookkeeping** and make the bottom line come out to zero. The purpose of Table 12.1, however, is to show what is *actually happening* to foreign exchange reserves. The numbers are all net figures, and a positive number implies a flow of funds into Ecoland, and vice versa.

In this particular year, 2028, the current account for Ecoland was positive, meaning either that exports were greater than imports or that foreign investment income was high (or both). The capital account was negative, meaning that Ecolanders were lending more to foreigners than the other way around. In principle, the "statistical discrepancy" term should not exist, but we include one because such discrepancies frequently do appear in published accounts (for obvious reasons). The discrepancy in this particular year, however, does not affect the basic picture. In short, the current account is greater than the capital account and the overall balance of payments is in surplus. This is reflected in an increase in central bank holdings of foreign exchange reserves of the same amount. The reason that the foreign exchange reserves have increased is that the central bank will have intervened in the foreign exchange markets to prevent the domestic currency from appreciating. In other words, they have sold their own currency and bought foreign exchange.

In a pure **floating exchange rate system**, however, the domestic authorities will not intervene in the foreign exchange markets, and overall deficits or surpluses in the balance of payments will not emerge. They are always eliminated by exchange rate changes. Hence, in this case there will be no change in the official holdings of foreign exchange reserves:

$$(12.3) \qquad \mathbf{OF \ = \ BP \ = \ 0}$$

This situation rarely occurs in practice because there is almost never a completely pure float. Actual floating rate regimes are usually "managed floats" or "dirty floats", at least to some degree. However, the theoretical case of the pure float, in which equation (12.3) holds, does unambiguously establish the general principle embodied in the following expression, which is obtained from equations (12.2) and (12.3) combined:

$$(12.4) \qquad \mathbf{CA \ = \ -KA}$$

The general principle is simply that the current account usually moves in the opposite direction to the capital account. This will also be true in most cases even outside the case of the pure float, up to a correction for changes in the volume of official financing. Moreover, the latter will typically not be large enough to upset the basic relationship. One reason for noting the inverse relationship between the current account and the capital account is that in the past many economists seem to have implicitly visualized the direction of causality in the balance of payments flowing from the former to the latter. An improvement in "competitiveness" would supposedly lead to a current account surplus. Roughly speaking, exports would be greater than imports, and the nation as a whole would be earning more than it was spending. It would then be natural to find outlets to invest these surplus funds abroad, causing capital outflow. A nation "living beyond its means", on the other hand, with a negative current account, would, from this perspective, be forced to borrow abroad to make up the difference, thus causing capital inflow. This was the standard way of looking at the process. One of the results of globalization and the increased international mobility of capital in recent years, however, has been to make it seem that, if anything, the causality is now apparently the other way round. Capital account developments dominate the current account, and the trade performance of the nation seems to emerge almost as a side effect of what is happening on the capital account. This can be of crucial importance for some developing countries, in particular.

Increased volume and volatility of capital flows may be undesirable and uncomfortable developments for all sorts of reasons. However, it is still not clear that, as some economists on both the left and the right of the political spectrum seem to think, they necessarily point to the conclusion that the national economies should respond by giving up whatever policy options they still possess — that is, by either fixing the exchange rate or joining a common currency area, or similar.

The balance of payments numbers discussed above can be linked to the standard macroeconomic national accounts framework by recalling the following definition of gross domestic product (GDP):

(12.5) $\qquad$ **GDP = Y = C + I + G + (X − IM)**

C stands for consumption, **I** for investment spending, **G** for government spending, and **(X − IM)** for net exports. But GDP, as the name implies, is simply the value-added output produced *domestically*. For an open economy, there is another potential source of income — namely, foreign investment income. Therefore, it is important to distinguish between **gross national product** (GNP) and GDP as follows:

(12.6) $\qquad$ **GNP = Y + FII**

FII is foreign investment income (identified above as one of the two main components of the current account). This can be either positive or negative, depending on whether the domestic economy is a net creditor or a net debtor nation. The point is that in the open economy, national income can be either greater or less than what is produced domestically, depending on the foreign credit position. Finally, by definition:

(12.7) $\qquad$ **GNP = C + S + T**

where **S** is total domestic saving and **T** is total tax collection. Now, using equations (12.5), (12.6), and (12.7), cancelling the **C**s and re-arranging, we can arrive at the following expression:

(12.8) $\qquad$ **(G − T) + (I − S) = (IM − X) − FII**

This can also be stated as:

(12.9) $\qquad$ **(G − T) + (I − S) = −CA**

In this expression, **(G − T)** is the government budget deficit, **(I − S)** is the domestic investment/savings balance, and **CA** is the current account. This identity became quite well known in the 1980s and 1990s, as it was then the basis for the so-called "twin deficits" argument. This suggests that a government budget deficit must *inevitably* lead to a current account deficit on the balance of payments. If **(G − T)** stands for the government budget deficit, and it is a positive number (government expenditures greater than taxation), and if we can also assume that **I = S**, or close to it, then there must also be a positive number on the right-hand side of the equa-

Case Study 18

"China Car Absorbs American Auto"
Detroit; 2012

The American Auto Co. has officially been taken over by its strategic business partner, China Car. The American brand will continue to be used on a selected number of models produced for the US market. Automotive analyst, Sebastian Cole, argues that the demise of American Auto can be directly attributed to the collapse of its Panther brand at the turn of the century. Dr. Cole stated, "When American Auto discontinued production of the Panther, it lost its high-end brand image." However, Panther could not have survived. Production was physically located in the UK, and the rise of the British pound relative to the US dollar at the beginning of the century was the blow that finally knocked out the formerly prestigious product line. As a result of the demise of Panther, American was positioned in direct competition with Japanese, Korean, and Chinese manufacturers. Without a flagship product, such as Panther, American Auto was unable to differentiate itself in the marketplace and became a takeover target.

tion. But this is the *negative* of the current account, so the current account itself must be in deficit. Hence, it might seem, or could be argued, that a government budget deficit actually leads to a current account deficit. There is an obvious flaw in the argument, however (which did not stop it from being highly influential toward the end of 20th century), as there is no real warrant for the **I = S** assumption on which it depends. Evidently, a government budget deficit can be associated with any of a current account deficit, a current account surplus, or a neutral position on current account, depending on the sign and magnitude of the term **I − S**. In other words, if the national government spends more than it takes in through taxation, this *might* imply an imbalance in the current account, such as imports greater than exports. However, this does not have to be the case if, for example, the citizens of the country are "savers". Possibly, therefore, a more meaningful version of equation (12.9) would be:

$$(12.10) \qquad [(G - T) + I] - S = KA - OF$$

This now says, reasonably enough (as far as the algebra is concerned), that if domestic saving is not enough to finance *both* the budget deficit and domestic investment, the funds must either be borrowed from abroad (positive capital inflow) or obtained from sales of foreign exchange reserves, with the latter, again, necessarily small in magnitude. These relationships are sometimes expressed by saying that **"net national dissaving"** must be financed either by capital inflow or sales of foreign exchange reserves. Note that, once again, this way of describing things puts the emphasis on the capital account as the active element in balance of payments developments. Net national dissaving will lead to capital inflow, which in turn leads to a current account deficit (presumably via exchange rate changes), and vice versa.

Exchange Rates

In what follows we use the symbol **E** to stand for the **nominal exchange rate**, defined earlier as the foreign currency price of one unit of domestic currency. For example, the Swiss franc/Euro exchange mentioned earlier can be expressed as **E** = 0.66. When **E** goes up, the domestic currency is **appreciating** (getting stronger), and when **E** goes down, the domestic currency is **depreciating** (getting weaker).[1]

Perhaps a more useful concept, certainly from the point of view of those making business decisions on the ground, is that of the **real**

---

[1] It would, of course, be equally possible to define the exchange rate the other way around (that is, as the domestic currency price of one unit of foreign exchange), and some textbooks and financial articles do just this. To deal with this issue, students simply need always to be careful about exactly how the exchange rate is defined in any particular context.

exchange rate, which we will define here as the relative price of domestic and foreign goods.[2] That is:

(12.11) $Q = EP/P*$

Here, the symbol **Q** will stand for the real exchange rate, with **E** the nominal exchange rate, **P*** the foreign price level, and **P** the domestic price level. If we want to work out an *aggregate* real exchange rate, the **P** terms would involve aggregate price indices of some kind. Also, a similar concept can be applied at the microeconomic level for any individual good or service that is traded. Suppose, for example, that an identical automobile is manufactured in plants on both sides of the Canada/US border in, for example, Windsor, Ontario and Detroit, Michigan. The price of the American car is US$25,000, and the price of the Canadian car is C$29,000. But which is actually cheaper? Suppose that the Canadian/US dollar exchange rate is **E** = 0.76 (i.e., one Canadian dollar is worth 76 US cents). The price of the Canadian vehicle in US dollars is then (0.76 × 29,000) or US$22,040. The Canadian car is actually more competitively priced, and we can work out **Q** as (22,040/25,000) or **Q** = 0.88. The Canadians (or rather, in practice, the Canadian subsidiaries of the US parent firms) are obviously likely to sell more cars in these circumstances. In general, then, when **Q** falls, implying a **real depreciation**, foreign goods will be more expensive and domestic goods more "competitive", whereas if **Q** rises, that is a **real appreciation**, foreign goods become relatively cheaper and domestic goods less competitive.

Alternative Exchange Rate Regimes

The policy debate about the relationship between different currencies has often revolved around the issue of whether rates of exchange between alternative standards of value should be **floating** or **fixed**. In the case of floating or **flexible** exchange rates, the exchange rate between any two currencies is determined proximately by relative supplies and demand on the international financial markets. In the fixed exchange rate case, the relationship between national currencies is kept within narrow limits according to some international agreement or convention, and domestic central banks must stand ready to take whatever action is needed to force the value of the currency to remain within the pre-set bounds. This would include intervention in the foreign exchange markets to buy or sell as large a volume of the currency as is required, and would also include changes in interest rates.

---

[2] As with the nominal exchange rate, it would be possible to define the real exchange rate the opposite way around, and caution is needed here also.

As well as the extremes of fixed and floating rates, some compromise between the two in the form of a **managed float** is advocated by some. This is a situation in which exchange rates are floating in principle, but the monetary authorities do take a view about what the appropriate value of the exchange rate should be (against any or all of its competitors at any point in time), and periodically take action to achieve this. Frequently, too, some view would be taken as to the speed of the appreciation or depreciation of the currency, if not its absolute level. Another point of view would be to push the concept of fixed exchange rates to its logical conclusion, and question whether there is any merit in the different political jurisdictions having a separate currency at all. In other words, there are many who advocate a single currency, or a **currency union**, among several states. Even if there are probably very few advocates of a single world currency at this point in time, these sorts of arrangements are in place, for example, in the narrower (regional) context of the European Union (EU), where a single currency, the Euro, was established in the 1999–2002 period. There are also a few other examples of currency unions on a smaller scale in other parts of the world. "Dollarization", for example, is not quite the same thing as currency as currency union. This is where a smaller country literally uses the currency of a foreign nation in its own domestic transactions; it is not a question of all the players giving up their individual currencies for a new common currency. In this case, of course, all monetary policy is effectively decided by the larger country. The different options are summarized in Table 12.2.

One of the main motivations for fixing the exchange rate, or a fortiori moving toward a single currency, would presumably be to create a more stable environment for business decision-making and to reduce transaction costs, uncertainty, etc. Also, if the currency to which the domestic currency is pegged has a low inflation regime, this may be seen as a way of importing "discipline" to the domestic economy. However, there is a downside to

---

Table 12.2:   Alternative Exchange Rate Regimes

- Fixed Exchange Rates

- Flexible (Floating) Exchange Rates

- "Managed" or "Dirty" Float

- Currency Union

- "Dollarization"

---

fixed exchange rates because if the exchange rate is fixed, the monetary policy options available to the domestic economy become severely limited. In effect, the only policy to be pursued is to fix the exchange rate, and everything else (including the results for domestic output and employment) must be subordinated to this. The domestic country loses economic sovereignty in that sense. This is even more obvious in the case of a currency union, where the individual member states, by definition, will have no monetary policy options. As shown in the appendix to this chapter, at one time there was a lively debate as to the different types of policy option that would still be available under different exchange rate regimes. It was sometimes suggested, for example, that under flexible exchange rates monetary policy would "work", but fiscal policy would not; whereas under fixed exchange rates, the opposite was true. That is, monetary policy would be ruled out, but fiscal policy would still "work", at least in the short run. However, this latter argument about how a fixed exchange rate system might still allow some scope for activist fiscal policy was never very convincing in practice. Consider the case of the currency union in the contemporary EU, for example. As a matter of fact, *fiscal* policy options in the EU are very limited also, as it is not feasible for the different states to have very different tax rates, deficit/GDP ratios, etc., without destabilizing the system. In practical terms, as opposed to short-run theory, a commitment to fix the exchange rate must essentially restrict the domestic policy options across the board. (And, according to some advocates, it is more or less explicitly designed to do just that.) Another point that can be made about the downside of a fixed rate regime is that it is the real exchange rate that really matters for economic decision-making, not the nominal rate. A fixed nominal rate may make the necessary real exchange rate adjustments more difficult to achieve, rather than less.

Table 12.3:   The Evolution of the International Monetary System

1873–1914:	The international gold standard
1918–1939:	Monetary "disorder"
1944–1973:	Bretton Woods system
1973–?:	Floating exchange rates (sometimes "managed") among the major currencies; other alternatives have been explored, both bilaterally and regionally

---

In any event, Table 12.3 provides a broad overview of the different exchange rate regimes that have existed in the world economy for the past century and a half. The 50 years or so before WWI were the heyday of the **international gold standard**. This was a de facto fixed exchange rate regime, as each national currency was convertible to a given quantity of gold, implying a fixed ratio between the currencies themselves. Effectively, there was already, in a manner of speaking, a "single currency", and to a large extent, a globalized economy (albeit at a lower level of technology), a century ago. The gold standard broke down, however, with the advent of WWI, and the interwar period was one of "monetary disorder". Attempts to restore the gold standard failed, and many currencies began to float against one another in circumstances that hardly gave the idea of flexible exchange rates a "good name". In particular, this was the era of so-called "beggar thy neighbor" policies, including competitive depreciations of one currency against another, and the world economic trading system essentially broke down. After WWII, there was, therefore, a conscious effort to restore some order to the international monetary system, and the result was a new regime of fixed exchange rates, known as the **Bretton Woods system**, named after a place in New Hampshire, USA, at which the decisive conference took place in 1944. It was dubbed a "gold exchange standard". Only one currency, the US dollar, was convertible to gold; the rest were defined in terms of the US dollar itself. Exchange rates were "fixed but adjustable", and this last provision did lead to a number of high-profile exchange crises during the years the Bretton Woods system was in place. The system did, however, provide the framework for the international monetary system for around 30 years until the financial crisis of 1971, when the USA announced it would no longer redeem US dollars in gold. Then the system collapsed, in spite of all efforts to repair it, in the 1971–1973 period. The only remnant of the Bretton Woods system today is the continued existence of some of the international financial institutions that were set up at that time, including the **International Monetary Fund** (IMF) and the **World Bank**.

From the early 1970s to the present there has been no question of money being convertible to precious metals, and the major currencies have been floating against one another. This has been the main characteristic of the international monetary system. There have been other features, though, on a bilateral and regional basis, that have tended to go in the opposite direction. Some countries, for example, have tried to unilaterally "peg" their own national currency against that of one of the major players, often the US dollar. Many such attempts, however, have ended in financial crisis when the peg proved unsustainable. There was also a regional regime of fixed exchange rates in place in Europe from 1979–1999: the European Monetary System (EMS). As mentioned, this morphed into a full currency union after 1999, and there are other examples of currency union, usually between smaller states — for example, in the Eastern Caribbean and in West Africa. Another option that has been on the table, and much discussed in South America in particular, is so-called **"dollarization"**, either by directly adopting the US dollar for use in the domestic economy, or via **currency board** arrangements. As is well known, however, the currency board arrangement in Argentina collapsed with disastrous consequences in 2001. The only real conclusion that can be drawn from this history is that international currency arrangements have been in a state of flux as long as anyone can remember, and the debate over what is likely to be the "best" or "optimal" exchange rate regime is likely to continue. The main issues in the evolution of the international monetary system can, therefore, be summed up as follows:

Case Study 19

"Finally, A Floating Currency"
Beijing; October 17, 2011

China has finally made the decision to float its currency. The choice was clear. In order to join the ranks of the most powerful economic nations, a floating currency seemed to be a basic requirement. Previously, China had systematically undervalued its currency in order to be competitive in international markets. Foreign exchange was also required to support the domestic commercial banking system. As a result, some banks consistently issued questionable loans, and the system was in constant danger of default. Now, as a result of sweeping reform, the banking system is solvent, and the need for foreign exchange has been reduced. China is able to float the currency, and the authorities will be able to "manage" the economy in a manner similar to that of their major competitors.

- There has been an ongoing search for an appropriate currency/exchange rate regime at both regional and global levels, and this continues.

- The downside of a solution involving a fixed exchange rate regime or a currency union is that when exchange rates are fixed, "monetary sovereignty" is lost.

In the following section we discuss some of the more technical aspects of the operation of flexible exchange rates and fixed exchange rates, respectively.

Exchange Rate Determination: Flexible Exchange Rates

In a floating exchange rate system, the foreign currency price of a unit of domestic currency is determined by "market forces", which can be illustrated by a typical demand and supply diagram, as in Figure 12.1.

The quantity on the horizontal axis of this diagram is that part of the domestic money supply outstanding that is offered for sale in the foreign

Figure 12.1: The Market for Domestic Currency as Foreign Exchange

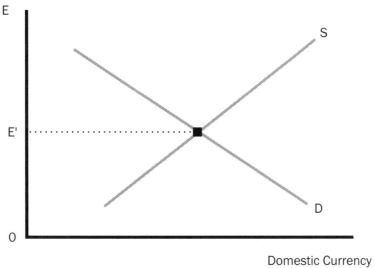

exchange market. The supply of domestic currency (for this purpose) basically arises from anything that is a *negative* item in the balance of payments. For example, if a domestic resident wants to purchase foreign goods (imports), they must first acquire the foreign currency needed to pay for them; hence, domestic currency must be offered to the market to accomplish this. Similarly, if a domestic resident wants to make an investment in another country (capital outflow), they must also acquire foreign currency, and will offer domestic currency for sale. The demand for domestic currency, meanwhile, arises from anything that appears as a *positive* item in the balance of payments. If a foreigner wishes to buy domestic exports, that person also has a demand for the domestic currency to pay for these items. Similarly, if foreigners wish to purchase domestic securities, they must first acquire domestic currency. Putting the demand and supply curves together, the argument is, as usual, that the exchange rate will be determined by "market forces" at the intersection of demand and supply.

We can explore this idea a bit further by now considering some examples of how changes in certain economic variables are likely to affect the exchange rate. Suppose, for example, that the domestic central bank raises the domestic nominal interest rate, while interest rates in the rest of the world remain unchanged. The result is illustrated in Figure 12.2. There will be an impact on both sides of the foreign exchange market. The higher interest rates in the domestic economy will encourage some foreign resi-

Figure 12.2: An Increase in Domestic Nominal Interest Rates

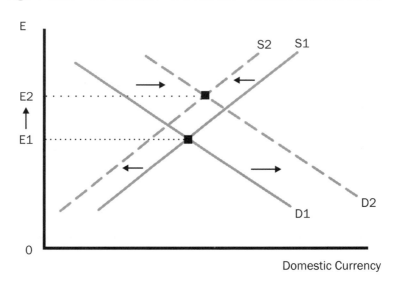

Domestic Currency

Figure 12.3: An Increase in Prices in the Domestic Economy

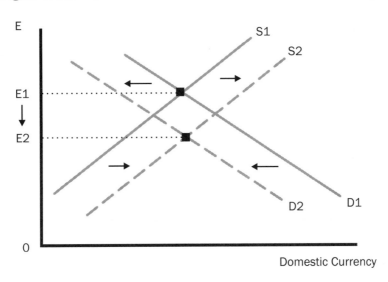

dents to invest in domestic securities, thus increasing the demand for the domestic currency. At the same time, some domestic residents will now decide not to invest in foreign securities (because domestic interest rates have increased). Therefore, the supply of domestic currency to the foreign exchange market will also be reduced. Putting the two effects together, the result is an increase in the price of the domestic currency, or in other words, an appreciation of the exchange rate, from E1 to E2.

The impact of an increase in the domestic price level is shown in Figure 12.3. Obviously, if prices rise in the domestic economy, and there is no change elsewhere, domestic goods will lose competitiveness on world markets. Fewer foreigners will buy domestic goods, and the demand for the domestic currency will be reduced. At the same time, some domestic consumers will switch to buying foreign goods, and the supply of domestic currency (in exchange for foreign currency) will be increased. The impact of the increase in prices in the domestic economy is therefore to depreciate the foreign exchange rate. Essentially, the exchange rate has to depreciate (E falls) to offset the effect of higher nominal prices in the domestic economy.

In Figure 12.4, finally, we consider an example of change that affects only one side of the foreign exchange market. Suppose, for example, that there is an economic boom in the economy of one of the major trading

Figure 12.4: An Increase in Income in a Foreign Country

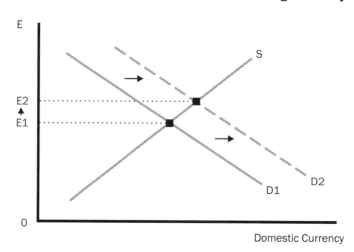

partners of the domestic economy, but that economic growth remains slug-
gish at home. The economic prosperity in the foreign country will increase
incomes abroad, and at least some of that increase in foreign income will
be spent on imports (from their point of view). The exports of the domestic economy will increase, and the demand for the domestic currency by
foreigners (to pay for the domestic exports) will also increase. Therefore,
the exchange rate will tend to increase (E rises). In short, the impact of
economic prosperity abroad will tend to lead to an appreciation of the exchange rate. At this point, we leave it to the reader to work out some further examples of economic changes that are likely to affect the exchange
rate in one direction or another.

Exchange Rate Determination:
Fixed Exchange Rates

In the case of fixed exchange rates, the idea is to *prevent* the various
economic changes from having any effect on the exchange rate in the manner just discussed, and the question naturally arises: how this can be
achieved? It will not happen just as a result of the different countries
coming to an agreement or signing a treaty. Specific actions have to be
taken, usually by the central bank, to ensure that the exchange rate "peg"

Figure 12.5: The Central Bank Sells Foreign Exchange

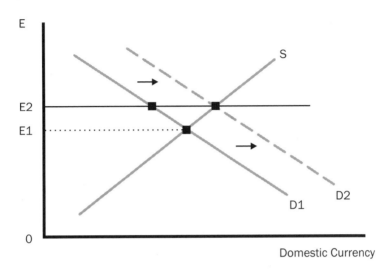

remains in place. Typically, the domestic authorities will be trying to fix the exchange rate at some level other than the one that market forces dictate, and there are obviously two possible scenarios. In some cases, the desired value of the exchange rate will be **overvalued** by comparison with what market outcomes would dictate. In other cases it will be **undervalued**. Figure 12.5 looks at the case of an overvaluation.

In Figure 12.5, the central bank is trying to keep the exchange rate at E2, whereas according to the "market", the equilibrium level is really E1. No one would actually be willing to sell foreign exchange (buy the domestic currency) at E2, so in effect the central bank itself must be willing to offer that deal. As we have seen earlier, it will typically have some foreign exchange reserves on hand from previous foreign exchange dealings. Now, in order to keep the exchange rate at an artificially high level, it must be willing to sell these reserves (buy its own currency) at the high level E2. By this means the central bank can keep the market price at the higher level, at least as long as it has any foreign exchange reserves left. The process is shown in the diagram by a temporary shift of the demand curve for domestic currency over to the right. The central bank is artificially adding its "demand" for its own currency to the demand that originally existed in the market.

Two observations are in order. First, we can now see explicitly why it is that an overall deficit in the balance of payments leads to an outflow of foreign exchange reserves. By definition, when the currency is overvalued, the balance of payments will be in deficit (this is what it means for a currency to be overvalued). One way of handling this would be simply to let the currency depreciate. However, if the exchange rate is fixed, this avenue is ruled out. To keep the currency at the higher level, the central bank must sell foreign exchange reserves. Therefore, a balance of payment deficit leads directly to a fall in holdings of foreign exchange reserves. Second, it is now quite clear what a **"foreign exchange crisis"** consists of. The attempt to maintain an overvalued foreign exchange rate leads to an outflow of foreign exchange reserves. This can only go on as long as the reserves hold out. When the reserves have all been used up, there is nothing left but to let the currency go, and find its (usually much lower) market level. This is the crisis. The problem may be postponed for a while by borrowing foreign exchange from other central banks or the IMF, but there is obviously a limit to this also. There are basically three options when the central bank runs out of foreign exchange reserves:

- Borrow reserves from another country or an international institution (e.g., the IMF).

- Adjust the pegged exchange rate. The government moves the peg closer to the market value. (The crisis will do this anyhow if they don't take action.)

- Undertake domestic "adjustments" to bring the supply and demand of the currency into balance. A change in fiscal policy by raising taxes and lowering expenditures may be required.

For some developing countries, the "choice" is all three. Devalue the currency, and borrow from the IMF with loan provisions, *both* of which require domestic adjustments (cutting spending and raising taxes).

The reasons for maintaining an overvalued currency most likely have to do with questions of national prestige, attempts to maintain "confidence", etc. An alternative possibility is to deliberately *undervalue* the currency. The motive here, presumably, would be to improve price competitiveness in international markets and to increase exports. This case is illustrated in Figure 12.6. In this case, the equilibrium exchange rate is E1, but the domestic authorities want to keep the rate down to E2 to gain some advantage in the global marketplace. Other players in the foreign exchange market, however, are not willing to sell the domestic currency at the rate E2, so the domestic central bank must step in and offer to do so. This is relatively easy, of course, for it can create ("print") as much domestic currency as it likes. From this point of view, it does not matter how many domestic currency units are offered in exchange for a unit of foreign currency. In the diagram, the supply of domestic currency is artificially pushed over to the right, as the central bank creates the money and then buys up foreign exchange. This situation of an undervalued currency will

Figure 12.6: The Central Bank Buys Foreign Exchange

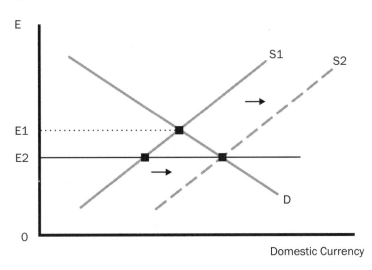

evidently be associated with a surplus on the overall balance of payments, and therefore it is now easily seen why, under fixed exchange rates, a persistent balance of payments surplus leads to an increase in central bank holdings of foreign exchange reserves. Also, on the face of it, this seems to be a situation that might be sustainable for a longer time period than the opposite case of the overvalued exchange rate.

The problem in the case of an overvalued exchange rate was that the central bank would soon run out of foreign exchange reserves, and it would have no means of acquiring any more. In the case of an undervaluation, however, there is no problem for the central bank in creating as much domestic currency as it would like. There will eventually be a downside, nonetheless, because, as was stressed in earlier chapters, an increase in the domestic money supply will be likely to cause inflation. In the long run, therefore, in terms of the real exchange rate ($Q = EP/P^*$), whatever advantage is gained by having a low E to start with may eventually be completely offset by a higher P. Also, at some point the trading partners of the country with an undervalued exchange rate are likely to lose patience. The complaint is that the undervalued currency allows the country concerned to obtain the benefit of trade while using the system to create greater economic activity and jobs for themselves. For example, this situation formed the basis of a long-running dispute between the USA and Japan in the last decades of the 20th century. In more recent years, the USA has expressed similar concerns with respect to China.

"Classical" Adjustment Mechanisms in the Global Economy

In this section, we will discuss stylized versions of the adjustment mechanisms that classical and neoclassical economists believe to exist in the global economy, in the cases of flexible exchange and fixed exchange rates,

---

Case Study 20

"Outsourcing Created Two Million New Jobs Last Year"
Washington, DC; June 25, 2014

It was just a few years ago that people were complaining about the outsourcing of jobs from the United States. It was argued that jobs were being moved abroad, and that this was creating unemployment and excessive dislocation in the US labor market. A recent study by the General Accounting Office (GAO) has that shown that this has not been the case. In fact, outsourcing has created 2 million net new jobs in the past year. A spokesperson for the GAO indicated that there were two reasons for this job creation. On the one hand, US business has become more productive as a result of outsourcing and has, therefore, been able to create new wealth. This has led to the creation of a large number of new jobs in areas such as health care and tourism. Second, the fall in the exchange rate of the US dollar relative to those countries who were the recipients of outsourced jobs has resulted in a surge of exports from the United States to these countries.

respectively. The emphasis must be on the word "stylized" because, in reality (perhaps needless to say), things are unlikely to work as smoothly as they can be made to seem in textbook discussions. For example, when, under fixed exchange rates, it is suggested below that changes in foreign exchange reserves are meant to have one impact or another on the domestic economy, remember that if there are not enough foreign exchanges reserves to begin with, the domestic central bank can soon run out, and there will be a financial crisis. Similarly, when we argue that domestic prices are supposed to adjust in response to balance of payments developments, we should likewise remember that they are only likely to do so after a long struggle. If prices are supposed to fall, for instance, it may actually take a long recession and heavy unemployment to achieve this result. With these caveats, there is nonetheless some value in setting out in detail the sequence of events thought likely to occur.

In what follows, we assume for the sake of argument that the exogenous policy event is simply an increase in the domestic money supply, **M**. The reader will no doubt be interested to work through some other cases in the same way. We set out the sequence of events by which the economy is supposed to adjust to this change, first under flexible exchange rates, then under fixed rates.

Flexible Exchange Rates
- **M** rises.
- According to the quantity theory, domestic prices (**P**) will rise.
- The real exchange rate (**Q** = **EP/P***) will rise because there is a real appreciation.
- The balance of payments (**BP**) moves toward a deficit because foreign goods are cheaper, and domestic goods are less "competitive".
- The nominal exchange rate (**E**) will therefore fall (depreciate); this offsets the rise in prices, restores **Q**, and the **BP** gets back into equilibrium.
- The net effect is that the original "inflationary" monetary policy is offset by a depreciation of the nominal exchange rate.

Fixed Exchange Rates
- **M** rises.
- Domestic prices (**P**) will rise.
- The real exchange rate (**Q** = **EP/P***) will rise because there is a real appreciation.

- The balance of payments (**BP**) moves toward a deficit because foreign goods are cheaper, and domestic goods are less "competitive".
- The nominal exchange rate (**E**) should fall (depreciate), but now it is *fixed* and cannot.
- The central bank will buy its own currency (sell foreign exchange) to prevent **E** from falling (to prevent depreciation).
- Foreign exchange reserves decline; as a result, high-powered money (**H**) and the domestic money supply (**M**) fall.
- The original monetary expansion is offset, and prices (**P**) fall again.
- The original value of the real exchange rate (**Q**) is restored, and the **BP** moves back to equilibrium.
- The net effect shows that it is ultimately *not possible* for the domestic economy to expand the money supply, **M**, under fixed exchange rates. If it tries to do so, it will be forced to reverse the policy because of its obligation to a fixed exchange rate. This example illustrates how the domestic economy cannot control monetary policy under fixed exchange rates.

So, in general, the basic conclusion is that under flexible exchange rates, it is the exchange rate itself that does the adjusting. Under a fixed exchange rate regime, however, it is government policy that must be adjusted to make sure that the exchange rate peg is maintained. The latter circumstance is one of the reasons why fixed exchange rate regimes tend to commend themselves to political conservatives. They are frequently seen as a method of "tying the hands" of the domestic government. This is very obviously so in the case of a common currency, as then there is literally nothing for the national government to manipulate. Against this, of course, there are also political conservatives who believe in the rule of "the market" at all costs, which would tend to militate in favor of flexible exchange rates.

Chapter Summary

- Exports and imports, a country's current account, are a critical measure of the health of an economy.

- Chronic current account difficulties are a serious concern and may be (but are not invariably) associated with fiscal imbalance when government expenditures exceed tax revenues.

- The world economy has tried a number of alternative exchange rate regimes. The current system (for the major players) is a floating rate regime, which generally lets the market decide the value of a currency. Occasionally, this becomes a "managed float" with periodic intervention by governments to manage abrupt changes. Some other countries still try to fix or "peg" their exchange rate against one of the major currencies on a united basis. In the European Union, a number of countries have adopted a common currency, the Euro. However, this still floats against all the others.

- Until recently, the balance of payments was dominated by the trade in goods and services. Today, financial capital flows account for the largest component in most country's BOP account.

- International institutions, such as the IMF, have gained importance in helping to manage the international trading system. On the other hand, globalization and capital mobility have made the world trading systems more interdependent. As a result, a financial crisis, for example in Asia, can impact other countries, such as Mexico and Russia, through a process called "contagion".

- There can be individual benefits if one country "cheats the system" by artificially maintaining an undervalued rate of exchange. But, as we discussed in the chapter on game theory, it may be difficult to perpetuate a win/lose game if the game is repetitive. Sooner or later, the trading partners will call "foul."

Problems

1. Economists are divided on whether a country should join a system in which members agree to limit fluctuations in the exchange rates among their currencies. Describe the advantages and disadvantages of such a move.

2. An American tourist wants to buy a Mercedes while traveling in Germany, but she is currently carrying nothing but British pounds. The Mercedes costs €200,000. The identical car costs $40,000 in the USA. The exchange rate for dollars and British pounds is $2 = £1, while £1 exchanges for €10. Should she buy the Mercedes in Germany or the USA?

3. Explain the international gold standard of the late 19th and early 20th centuries, and the reasons for its demise.

4. Distinguish between the devaluation and revaluation of a currency.

5. Explain why an increase in the supply of dollar-denominated assets leads to a depreciation of the currency under flexible exchange rates.

Case Study Questions | # The Comeback of Caterpillar

Exchange Rates

1. The crisis of 1982–1984 stemmed from "unfavorable currency exchange rates." How could exchange rates cause a "crisis" for Caterpillar?
2. What are the exchange rate issues associated with global outsourcing?

Foreign Direct Investment (FDI)

1. By 1965 Caterpillar had established foreign manufacturing facilities in Britain, Canada, Australia, Brazil, France, Mexico, Belgium, India, and Japan. Why was foreign direct investment an important component of Caterpillar's strategy?
2. What are the pros and cons of FDI versus joint ventures?

Hint: Exports are a critical component of Caterpillar's strategy. Fluctuating exchange rates impact a firm's pricing policy. One approach to mitigating exchange rate fluctuations is to establish production centers in consuming nations.

Appendix 12.1

The Mundell-Fleming Model

The well-known and widely cited **Mundell-Fleming model** claims to describe the impact of alternative exchange rate regimes, such as those discussed above, on the appropriate policy choice, monetary or fiscal, for a small open economy. However, it is important to stress that this is a short-run model only. In the longer term, under fixed exchange rates, small open economies will surely encounter difficulties if *either* their monetary or fiscal policy is inconsistent with those of their major trading partners. The model employs an international version of the IS/LM framework as developed in the appendix to Chapter 9. A new factor is the balance of payments (BP) schedule. This indicates all combinations of interest rates and GDP at which the balance of payments can be in equilibrium. In Figure 12A.1, a combination of **"internal balance"** and **"external balance"** is achieved at equilibrium **"A"**, at an interest rate of **r*** (the world interest rate), and income level of **Y1**. Basically, in order to maintain external balance, the argument is that the interest rate in the small open economy must be at the "world level".

Under fixed exchange rates, the argument (similar to what was suggested earlier in the chapter) is that monetary policy becomes completely ineffective. The focus of the central bank is to maintain a fixed rate of exchange. Therefore, monetary policy cannot be used to target other policy variables, such as national income and the price level. Figure 12A.2 indicates the effect of a contractionary monetary policy, for example. The LM function (from the appendix to Chapter 9) shifts backward and to the left, from LM1 to LM2. This *temporarily* increases the domestic rate of interest, which then causes an inflow of capital into the country in search of the higher rates of return. To maintain the fixed exchange rate, however, the central bank is forced to sell the local currency. As a result, the LM function must shift back to the starting point, bringing interest rates back to global levels.

Figure 12A.1: Internal and External Balance

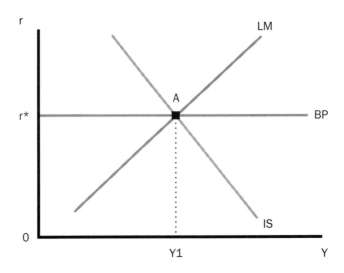

**Figure 12A.2: A Contractionary Monetary Policy Under
Fixed Exchange Rates**

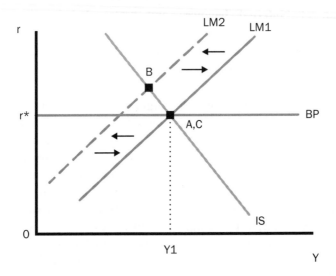

Figure 12A.3: A Contractionary Fiscal Policy Under Fixed Exchange Rates

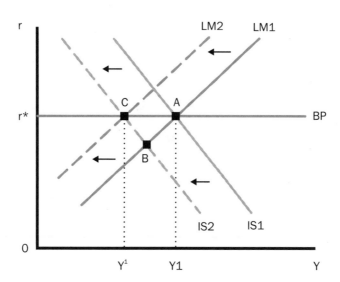

Fiscal policy, however, is thought to be "effective", at least in the short run under fixed exchange rates, as in Figure 12A.3. A decrease in government expenditures shifts the IS function (again, from the appendix to Chapter 9) backward and to the left, from IS1 to IS2, and temporarily makes the local rate of interest fall below the world rate. The result is capItal outflow, as local investors move funds abroad in search of greater returns. To keep the exchange rate fixed, the central bank is forced to buy the local currency in the foreign exchange market. The money supply is reduced, causing the LM function to shift backward and to the left. The interest rate returns to **r***, but the level of income falls still further.

Under flexible exchange rates, the above results are reversed: monetary policy supposedly becomes *more* effective in the short run than it would in a closed economy. For example, in Figure 12A.4 a fall in the rate of inTerest as a result of the expansionary monetary policy not only stimulates investment *but also* causes a currency depreciation, which will lead to an increase in exports. *Both* the increase in investment and the increase in exports will contribute to an increase in income.

The final prediction of the analysis is to the effect that the small open economy will find it difficult to use fiscal policy to manage the economy under a flexible exchange rate system. Consider an increase in govern-

Figure 12A.4: An Expansionary Monetary Policy Under Flexible Exchange Rates

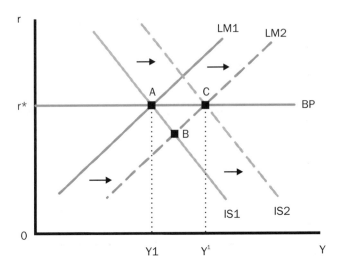

Figure 12A.5: An Expansionary Fiscal Policy Under Flexible Exchange Rates

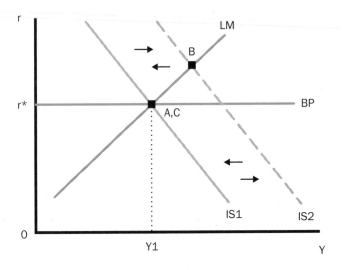

ment spending. In Figure 12A.5, the increased spending shifts the IS curve outward and to the right. The IS curve shifts from IS1 to IS2, forcing the domestic interest rate temporarily above the world rate. Capital will flow into the country, causing an increase in the value of the currency, an appreciation. Exports will become less competitive, and the IS curve (representing the total demand for the nation's products) will shift back because of this. Eventually it will shift all the way back to IS1, restoring the initial interest rate and level of income.

The thinking behind the Mundell-Fleming model may help to explain some of the choices about exchange rate systems made in the past by Canada (in some ways, the textbook case of the "small open economy"). During the 1950s, most of the developed world adopted a system of fixed exchange rates under the Bretton Woods post-war international economic framework. However, Canada felt it needed to maintain an effective monetary policy to influence domestic economic activity, and it adopted a flexible exchange rate system. (Remember, monetary policy is thought to be "effective" under flexible exchange rates.) Canada did join the fixed exchange rate system briefly from 1962 until 1970, at which point the Canadian dollar floated once again. Then, all the developed nations followed Canada by moving to a more flexible system within the next few years. Given the economic turbulence of the 1970s, most countries now preferred to use monetary policy to manage the domestic economy, and this required a shift from fixed to flexible exchange rates.

13

The Global Economy III: Some Topics in International Finance

Introduction

This short (but quite difficult) chapter follows up on some of the issues around exchange rates and international capital flows in the modern global economy introduced in Chapter 12. In particular, we discuss some key financial arbitrage conditions (business students may be familiar with these from their courses in finance), and how they impinge on economic conditions in a world in which the free flow of financial capital is very much a fact of life.

Covered Interest Parity

The usual starting point for a more detailed discussion of the relationship between monetary policy, the exchange rate regime, and international capital flows is the so-called **covered interest parity** (CIP) condition:

$$(13.1) \qquad i - i^* = (E - F)/F$$

E is the current **nominal spot exchange rate**, defined in Chapter 12 as the foreign currency price of one unit of domestic currency; **i** is the **domestic nominal interest rate**; and **i*** is the **foreign** or **"world" nominal interest rate** currently prevailing. The symbol **F** represents the **forward exchange rate**, which is the price of domestic currency quoted for forward delivery at some specified time in the future (e.g., three months, six months, or one year forward). It goes without saying that these interest rates refer to domestic and foreign securities with similar terms to maturity and risk characteristics, and that the terms to maturity match the length of the forward contracts.

What does the CIP condition mean? It says that domestic interest rates can be higher than foreign interest rates only if the forward exchange rate is less than the spot exchange rate (i.e., if there is a **forward discount**). If, for example, the domestic interest rate is 5%, the foreign interest rate is 3%, and the spot exchange rate is $E = 0.75$, then the forward rate **F** must be around 0.735, which is *less* than the spot rate. At first sight, this seems to imply quite severe restrictions on the behavior of the domestic interest rate. Whether or not this is true, however, will be discussed in more detail below.

The CIP condition will hold in situations of so-called **"perfect capital mobility"**. The reason the CIP concept attracts attention today is that with the increasing globalization and liberalization of capital markets, it becomes increasingly reasonable to argue that perfect capital mobility does hold, at least between the major financial centers. To see how perfect capital mobility would work, imagine a domestic resident who has a choice between investing a dollar in a domestic security for say a year and, alternatively, investing that same dollar in a foreign security for the same period. The return, **R(h)**, on the first alternative is:

(13.2) $R(h) = 1 + i$

For the second alternative, on the other hand, the return **R(f)** will be:

(13.3) $R(f) = E(1 + i^*)(1/F)$

The initial dollar can be converted into **E** units of the foreign currency, and then invested at the foreign interest rate **i***. At the same time, the total proceeds can be sold forward at the rate (**1/F**) to lock in the return (from the domestic residents' point of view). Note that this is a completely risk-free transaction. Therefore, if there is perfect capital mobility, **arbitrage** in the financial markets will equalize these two rates of return. That is:

(13.4) $1 + i = E(1 + i^*)(1/F)$

From equation (13.4) we can then solve for the interest differential:

(13.5) $i - i^* = (E - F)/F + [(E - F)/F]i^*$

The second term on the right-hand side of equation (13.5) can be ignored (as it will be close to zero); hence, we arrive at the same formula as in equation (13.1) above. In short, we can sum up the concept of CIP by saying that under perfect capital mobility, rates of return in the different financial centers must be equalized when covered by a forward contract.

Uncovered Interest Parity, Purchasing Power Parity, and Real Interest Parity

A rather stronger condition than CIP would be **"uncovered interest parity"** (UIP), or:

(13.6) $i - i^* = (E - E')/E'$

This says that expected rates of return in different financial centers will be equalized even when *not* covered by a forward contract. In other words, in the case of purchasing a foreign security, the investor does not bother to sell the foreign currency proceeds forward and hence remains exposed to foreign exchange risk. The symbol **E'** now stands for the **expected future spot rate**. This is *not* in principle the *same* thing as the forward rate. It is the consensus expectation, at the current time, of what the future exchange rate will actually turn out to be, and this is a different thing than if the price changed *now* for forward delivery. However, note that *if* CIP and UIP are both supposed to hold, then by definition, it must be true that:

(13.7) $F = E'$

This result would be consistent with *rational expectations* or **efficient markets** theory in finance, and would indicate that in the above circumstances the forward exchange rate corresponds exactly to the market's "best guess" of what the future spot rate will be.

Another key element in what might be described as the orthodox or neoclassical approach to the foreign exchanges is the concept of **"purchasing power parity"** (PPP), which dates back at least to the work of Marshall and Cassel more than a century ago.[1] This has to do with the real exchange rate between any two different currencies, defined in the previous chapter as:

(13.8) $Q = EP/P*$

where **P** and **P*** are the aggregate price levels prevailing in the domestic economy and in the rest of the world, respectively. The purchasing power parity doctrine asserts (symmetrically with other elements of orthodox monetary theory) that the relative price of foreign and domestic goods should be thought of as a "real" variable, corresponding to the terms of trade derived from a barter-oriented international trade model, such as that discussed in Chapter 7. The assumption, therefore, is that it cannot permanently be changed purely by factors having to do with money and macroeconomic policy. Two versions of PPP are usually mentioned in the textbooks: **absolute PPP** and **relative PPP**. In absolute PPP, which is also known as the **"law of one price"**, the equilibrium value of the real exchange rate is taken to be **Q = 1**. This implies that prices should literally be equal in the different jurisdictions when adjusted for exchange rates. The concept of relative PPP is (somewhat) more realistic, in the sense that it simply asserts that **Q** is a constant rather than that it is equal to one. This, then, supposedly allows for any "genuine" reasons why the real price of goods may differ in one jurisdiction versus another, including transportation costs, the presence of non-traded goods, and so forth. Prices should not be expected to be literally the same all over the world just because there are transportation costs for goods and resources, and also because much modern economic activity is in the form of non-traded services (restaurants, hotels, hair stylists, etc.). But, again, the point is that monetary policy per se is not supposed to affect these underlying relative

---

[1] Steven Pressman, *Fifty Major Economists* (London: Routledge, 1999).

Case Study 21

"The Deal Is Done! One Currency for North America"
Toronto; April 23, 2023

Well, it finally happened. Almost 30 years after the North American Free Trade Agreement (NAFTA) was ratified, there is now a common currency among Mexico, the United States, and Canada. After a century and a half, the Canadian "loonie" has disappeared, to be incorporated into the new "northo", which will be the name of the single currency. The head of the Canadian Chamber of Commerce expressed great pleasure with the final agreement, and said that he believes that the common currency will be a great benefit for Canadian business. He expressed the view that real gross domestic product will increase by an additional one to two percent each year for the next 10 years. However, this view is not universally shared by the business community. The chairperson of the Furniture Manufacturers' Association of Ontario expressed great concern. In her view, furniture manufacturers will no longer be competitive in the North American marketplace, and future production will move to such countries as China or India. Similar concerns were expressed by the leader of the Canadian Auto Workers (CAW). As many as 500,000 direct and indirect manufacturing jobs may be lost because of the agreement. The Premier of the Province of Quebec expressed support

Case Study 21 continued

for the new northo. As a separatist, in her opinion this will ensure success in the next referendum for Quebec independence. There is every possibility that the common North American currency will be adopted by an independent Quebec.

prices, whatever they are. In what follows, it will be the most convenient strategy to identify the orthodox model with the basic case of **Q = 1**, but note that this makes no real difference to the underlying argument. In this specific case, there would be a very simple theory indeed of exchange rate determination.

$$(13.9) \qquad E = P*/P$$

This claims that the exchange rate must eventually conform to the ratio of foreign and domestic prices.

Finally, by combining the UIP and PPP conditions (implying that the expected change in the exchange rate in equation (13.6) would then be equal to the inflation differential), it can also be asserted that *if* CIP, UIP, and PPP all hold, then:

$$(13.10) \qquad r = r*$$

This is the condition of **real interest rate parity** (RIP), which in effect says that domestic *real* interest rates must conform to those established in "world markets".

Some Problems with Interest Parity and Purchasing Power Parity Assumptions

If the condition of real interest parity does hold, it would seem to preclude the domestic central bank from having any influence over the real rate of interest in its own jurisdiction, and hence render useless any analysis of monetary policy worked out in the closed economy context. However, and as has been seen elsewhere in our discussions of the various alternative visions of the way the economy operates, such a conclusion is based, in an essential way, on the sequence of progressively stronger assumptions that are needed to derive it. If any of those assumptions can be challenged and are questionable, then the final conclusion may be questionable also.

In the present case, it seems to be generally conceded on all sides that the CIP assumption embodied in equation (13.1) is accurate. One argument often made is that this is simply the logical consequence of perfect capital mobility in the contemporary global economy. If there are now few political or technological barriers to the movement of financial capital around the world, then a simple arbitrage argument suffices to establish that rates of return on assets with similar risk characteristics and maturities should be equal when covered by a forward contract. Where the orthodox model is on weaker ground, however, is not so much the assumption that CIP always holds, but the additional assumption that UIP always holds also. This implies that rates of return in different centers can be equal even when *not* covered by a forward contract, or, equivalently, that the forward exchange rate and the consensus expectation of the future spot rate are always the same. However, there seems little basis in reality for this latter argument. In practice, even in conditions in which financial capital is completely mobile in a technical sense, UIP only holds up to the inclusion of what is usually called a **"currency risk premium"**,[2] which is required by foreign investors if they are to hold assets denominated in the domestic currency. The point is that even if financial capital can cross borders electronically at the "push of a button", it must still be the case that assets denominated in different currencies and whose exchange rates are liable to change are still not **perfect substitutes**. That is, even given perfect capital mobility, there need not be **"perfect asset substitutability"**. In other words, it continues to matter precisely which "promises to pay" (US dollars, Euros, Canadian dollars, Mexican pesos, or Japanese yen) the investor holds at any given moment. Following this line of thought, if **z** is the currency risk premium, we therefore have:

$$(13.11) \qquad i - i^* = [(E - E')/E'] + z$$

What is now being said is that the forward exchange rate is *not* equal to the expected future spot rate, or, equivalently, that the currency risk premium must be included in the pricing of the forward contract. In other words:

---

[2] J.A. Frankel, "International capital mobility: a review", *American Economic Review* (1992) 82(2): 197–202.

(13.12) $F \neq E'$

Another dubious assumption in arriving at the RIP result above was the concept of purchasing power parity itself. Empirically, it is well known that exchange rates more often deviate from the supposed PPP levels (absolute or relative) than not.[3] One plausible way of explaining this is to argue that in a *monetary* international economy, the real exchange rate may itself be an endogenous variable and may, therefore, in principle be subject to manipulation by public policy, rather than being completely determined by the barter terms of trade. In this case — that is, if the equilibrium Q is not a constant — t hen there would be no real meaning in the PPP theorem in its usual sense.

Finally, if neither UIP nor PPP holds, then real interest parity does not hold either. In fact, the real interest differential would be given by:

(13.13) $r - r^* = [(Q - Q')/Q'] + z$

The conclusion is that in an environment with separate monetary systems and in which exchange rates are free to move, then (even in a world in which there is perfect capital mobility) real interest rates in the domestic economy can deviate from those elsewhere by an amount equal to the expected *real* appreciation or depreciation of the currency, and the risk premium.

Fixed Exchange Rates and the Domestic Rate of Interest

On the other hand, in a "credible" fixed exchange rate regime, it is true that the domestic monetary authorities lose control of the domestic rate of interest. In such an environment, the nominal exchange rate is not expected to change, so that $E - E' = 0$, by definition. Also, if the regime really is "credible", in the sense that it is confidently expected to hold without reservation, then there is no risk and $z = 0$ also. Therefore, it must be the case that:

(13.14) $i = i^*$

In this situation the domestic nominal interest cannot deviate from the "world" interest rate (or, in the case of a currency union, the rate set by the supranational central bank), and there is no domestic control over

---

[3] Marc Lavoie, "A Post Keynesian view of interest parity theorems", *Journal of Post Keynesian Economics* (Fall 2000) 23(1): 163–79.

monetary policy. Recall that this is actually a traditional conclusion of the literature on fixed exchange rates. The definition of a "credible" fixed exchange rate regime used here is, of course, very strong, and in the case where there is some doubt about the permanence of the regime, or if periodic adjustments are allowed, the conclusion is softened. There would now be some scope for a forward market and a currency risk premium. Suppose, for example, that the exchange rate is not actually expected to change, but there is still some residual doubt about this. In such a case:

$$(13.15) \qquad i - i^* = z$$

It is important to realize, however, that to achieve this degree of policy independence under fixed exchange rates implies that the regime itself is less than perfect in some sense. There must be an "escape clause", or some doubt about the authorities' willingness to make a permanent commitment. On the other hand, in either an irrevocable fixed exchange rate regime or (to take the relevant modern cases) a currency union or a currency board, nominal interest rates will indeed be the same in all jurisdictions. Real interest rates could still fortuitously differ if there were any residual inflation differentials, but (by definition again) in that case there would still be no scope for domestic monetary policy to influence either the inflation rate or domestic real rates. In general, in the absence of such residual inflation differentials, we would also have $Q' = Q$, and hence:

$$(13.16) \qquad r = r^*$$

This is the real interest parity condition once again, which is now being *imposed* by the nature of the exchange rate regime. What is being demonstrated here is really the same point made in Chapter 12. This is how a fixed rate regime, and therefore a fortiori a common currency solution, tends to close off whatever policy options remain available to the domestic policy-makers in the modern globalized economy. The counter-argument from proponents of fixed exchange rates, or a single currency, would be that the supposed benefits to real living standards arising from such arrangements more than offset any such losses.

Chapter Summary

• Some important concepts in international finance are the three interest parity conditions: covered interest parity (CIP), uncovered interest parity (UIP), and real interest parity (RIP). There is also another "parity" condition: the purchasing power parity theory of exchange rates (PPP).

- The concept of PPP is critical to an understanding of relative living standards around the world. If we read that citizens of a nation with a per capita income of U.S.$5,000 have a life expectancy of almost 70 years, one of the reasons is simply that their money "goes further". It has greater purchasing power in the domestic market than would the case if per capita income was only a few hundred U.S. dollars.

- It is crucial to distinguish between perfect capital mobility and perfect asset substitutability. Perfect capital mobility is just the consequence of increasing "globalization" and the liberalization of capital flows. However, perfect asset substitutability implies that investors do not care about the composition of their foreign exchange portfolios. It would not *matter* whether assets are in US dollars, Russian rubles, Japanese yen, or whatever. This is not likely to be true as long as there are separate monetary systems and exchange rates are free to change. Then there will always be a "currency risk" premium.

- In the absence of perfect asset substitutability, neither uncovered interest parity nor real interest parity is likely to hold. In other words, real interest rates will not be the same across different jurisdictions.

- With a "credible" fixed exchange rate system, however, or (obviously) with a common currency, perfect asset substitutability will be restored, and interest rates cannot differ between jurisdictions. This is another way of saying that monetary policy will not "work" under these circumstances.

Problems

1. There is now a single European currency:
   (a) How has this changed the ability of each Euro zone country to conduct independent countercyclical monetary and fiscal policies?
   (b) How has this system impacted the ability of the United Kingdom, which is a member of the EU, but is not currently a member of the single currency and maintains a floating exchange rate, to conduct independent countercyclical monetary and fiscal policies?

2. What is the correct answer? Suppose that under covered interest parity (CIP), foreign interest rates are greater than domestic interest rates. Then (defining exchange rates as we have done above) it must be true that:
   (a) the forward rate and the spot rate are equal
   (b) the forward rate must be greater than the spot rate
   (c) the forward rate must be less than the spot rate

        (d) all foreign assets must be regarded as perfect substitutes

3.   What is the correct answer? In a "credible" fixed exchange rate regime, the domestic interest rate for the small open economy is determined by:
     (a) the monetary policy of the domestic central bank
     (b) the fiscal policy of the domestic government
     (c) demand and supply in the domestic capital market
     (d) the level of foreign or "world" interest rates

4.   What is the correct answer? Suppose that interest rates in London are around 9.5% per annum, compared with rates of 4.5% for comparable securities in New York. Assuming that *uncovered* interest parity (UIP) holds, a reasonable prediction for the behavior of the US dollar against the British pound over the next year would be:
     (a) depreciate by about 5%
     (b) appreciate by about 1.25%
     (c) appreciate by about 5%
     (d) depreciate by about 4.5%

5.   What is purchasing power parity? Why is this concept so important?

14

Economic
Growth and
Competitiveness:
A Macro-Micro
Synthesis

Introduction

In many textbooks macroeconomics and microeconomics are seen as distinct. Micro focuses on market behavior and the efficient allocation of resources. Macro addresses the big picture variables, such as unemployment, inflation, and national income, and looks at the economy "as a whole". However, in reality the two branches of economics are interdependent when we ask the important questions, such as, "How does economic growth and development occur?", and "Why do some countries (or regions) grow faster than others?" Logic tells us that both macro and micro factors must be involved in the process of growth and development.

Economic Growth

The original growth theory was simple. **Say's Law** stated that "supply creates its own demand". At the end of the 18th century in Europe, this proposition might have had some factual basis. Most of the people were peasants; they worked all day and consumed everything they produced. However, in the contemporary global economy of over six billion people, it is reasonable to assume that Say's Law no longer works in quite the same way. There are bound to be mismatches between savers and investors, and between producers and consumers. Adam Smith, writing at about the same period as Jean-Baptiste Say, also began the analysis of economic growth from the microeconomic perspective. He visited a pin factory in Scotland and saw the workers specializing in different tasks and how this **division of labor** led to **economies of scale**. He then attributed economic growth to scale economies, specialization, and trade. Note, however, that this way of looking at things must eventually bring up questions of macroeconomics and aggregate demand also. The degree to which the specialization of production tasks can be pushed depends on **"the extent of the market"**, or demand. These economic ideas later provided the foundation for the assembly line model of production developed by Henry Ford.

Growth Models

The academic literature on economic growth theory falls into three broad categories. The early post-WWII growth models, primarily associated with the work of Evsey Domar and Roy Harrod, emphasized the importance of saving, and capital investment in stimulating economic growth. The basic assumption underlying these models was that the output of the economy depends on the underlying amount of capital investment, and that it is the savings of individuals and firms that make such investment feasible. An economy's output is linked to its stock of capital by the capital-output ratio, which was usually taken to be a technological constant. These early growth models of Domar and Harrod tended to subsume other possible determinants of growth under the rubric of the capital-output ratio.

Partly in response to these limitations, Robert Solow developed what has come to be known as the **neoclassical growth model**. In this model, output grows in response to increases in the inputs of physical capital and labor, as well as the efficiency with which these inputs are used. The model obeys the law of diminishing marginal returns. Each addition of a unit of capital, given a fixed supply of labor, will generate a smaller yield than the one before it, or vice versa.

An important technical feature of the Solow growth model is that in the absence of ongoing technical change the economy will reach a "steady state" in terms of output *per capita* or per head. That is an equilibrium standard of living or level of wealth. This steady state is achieved as follows:

- The levels of savings, investment, and capital depreciation and determine the capital-to-labor ratio (**K/N**).
- From the production function, the capital/labor ratio determines the steady-state value of output per worker (**Y/N**).

Figure 14.1 shows an aggregate production function with output per worker as a function of capital per worker. Output per worker is given by the formula **Y/N = f(K/N)**.

From this we can work out a savings function (per head) as **S/Y = sf(K/N)**, where **s** is the saving ratio. This is then graphed against capital deprecation, **δK**, in Figure 14.2. If δ is 10%, for example, the capital stock is depreciating at a rate of 10% per year. If savings per head is greater than the depreciation of the capital stock, as at point "a" in the diagram, then net investment must be occurring, and the economy is growing. If there is not enough savings per head to cover depreciation, as at point "b", the capital stock must be falling, and **Y/N** declining. The steady state of the economy, giving its permanent "standard of living", is therefore at the point where the savings rate per head just covers capital depreciation. The steady state value of capital per worker is (**K/N**)*, giving a standard of living of (**Y/N**)*.

In order for the standard of living to improve, there would have to be either an increase in the propensity to save that would increase capital accumulation, or a technological innovation that would shift the entire production function outward. Both of these cases may be illustrated by the diagram in Figure 14.3, where the steady-state capital stock increases to (**K/N**)**.

Note that the result here — that an increase in savings improves the growth rate — is the exact opposite to the "Keynesian" logic discussed ear-

Figure 14.1   The Per-Capita Aggregate Production Function

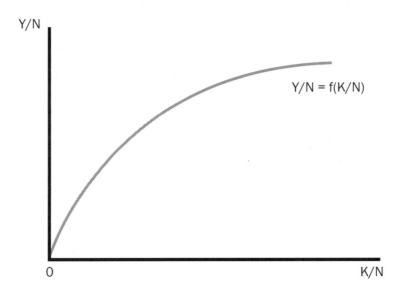

Figure 14.2   Steady State of the Neoclassical Growth Model

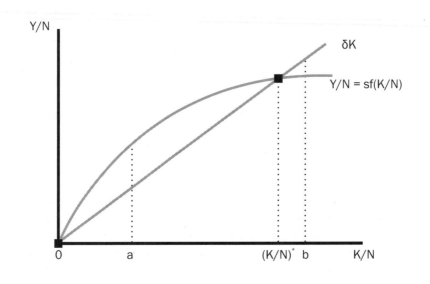

Figure 14.3: Effect of an Increase in Savings or Technical Change

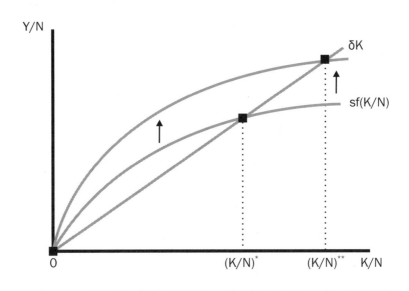

lier, where the argument was that savings takes money *out* of the economy and that spending is the route to prosperity. The reason is that this entire analysis is based on "real" economic values, and there is no discussion of money. Money is considered to be "neutral" in the neoclassical growth and all savings automatically go toward investment.

The neoclassical growth model can also be used for a **growth accounting** exercise to try to identify the main determinants of growth in practice. For this, however, we require a slightly different form of the production function, namely:

$$(14.1) \qquad Y = AF(K, N) = AK^a N^{1-a}$$

K = capital, the stock of physical assets used in the production process (machinery and equipment); N = labor inputs, which is hours worked by members of the work force; and Y = GDP or output. The lower case symbol a is returns to capital, or the share of GDP allocated to capital, normally about 30% for most OECD countries. Therefore, $1 - a$ is labor's share of GDP, about 70% for most OECD countries. As $0 < a < 1$ (i.e., the "a" term is greater than zero and less than one) then, as mentioned, we get decreasing returns to both the factors of production: capital and labor. As we add more machines to a fixed labor force, output increases, but at a decreasing rate. As mentioned earlier, this is called a declining marginal product of capital. We achieve the similar results by increasing the labor force while holding capital assets constant, a declining marginal product of labor. The upper case **A** is defined as **total factor productivity** — the efficiency with which *all* the factors of production are deployed together.

From equation (14.1) we can obtain a **growth accounting** relationship as follows:

$$(14.2) \qquad \Delta Y/Y \;=\; \Delta A/A \;+\; a(\Delta K/K) \;+\; (1-a)(\Delta N/N)$$

In other words, in this framework the rate of growth is explained by the rate of growth of total factor productivity, the rate of growth of the capital stock weighted by the capital share, and the rate of growth of the labor force weighted by the labor share.

Again, it should be noted that this analysis is also based on "real" economic values, and there is no discussion of money. Money is still considered to be "neutral". In general, the message of the Solow model is that the key to long-term growth is technological improvement, or an increase in total factor productivity. In his original work Solow argued that technological change was exogenous, or outside the model. Nonetheless, the model does make clear that ongoing improvements in technology and increases in total factor productivity are critical for long-term economic growth. For this reason, both economists and businesspeople have devoted a great deal of attention to the question of productivity improvement.

One interesting property of the steady-state feature of the Solow model is the prospect it holds for economic **convergence**. If technology is readily available, poorer countries can catch up with the richer countries by saving and investing more and hence growing at a faster rate, until they reach the same standard of living. To some extent, this convergence does occur in the real world, but, as is well-known, convergence has *not* taken place for a large number of developing countries, in particular. Based upon the Solow model, reasons for the lack of convergence could include such things as insufficient national savings and investment, and excessive growth of population relative to the active labor force. Problems may also exist with total factor productivity. There may be issues with respect to access to technology, and developing the necessary social institutions to utilize this technology effectively.

In the mid-1980s, economists such as Robert Lucas and Paul Romer formulated a new model of economic growth that **"endogenizes"** technological progress (i.e., puts it explicitly in the model). The so-called **new growth theory**, as it is commonly labeled, emphasizes the importance of **human capital**, **"learning by doing"**, and **technological spillover effects** in generating economic growth. Also, the new growth theory postulated **increasing returns** to knowledge-based investment. That is, each additional dollar of capital invested specifically in knowledge creation yields *more* than the previous dollar invested. Increasing returns can provide accelerated growth rates over the long term. How might this process of the endogenous growth occur? Basically, we drop the assumption of a decreasing marginal product of capital. With endogenous growth we have no steady state. Therefore, it is possible for richer countries to grow faster than poor countries — quite literally, forever. Unlike the Solow growth model, an increase in savings and investment increases *both* the level of output and the rate of economic growth. To explain these processes would require a broader definition of capital than is usual, to include, for example, both **human capital** and **social capital**. The concept of human capital captures the skills, learning, and educational attainment of the country's labor force. This is not surprising to businesspeople who are always expressing concern about the need for skilled workers and pressures to upgrade the skills of the workforce. Social capital describes how individuals can benefit from memberships in various groups and networks. The basic idea is that all of society can have more "capital", in the broad sense, if the necessary institutions are in place to maximize the value of these social networks. The implications of endogenous growth theory are very powerful, including:

- the possibility that economic growth can be accelerated by supply-side policies designed to increase *all* forms of capital

- the possibility that the gap between rich and poor countries could grow even larger over time

So, the model would purport to explain both the lack of convergence and also suggest ways of improving the situation.

Growth and Business Cycles

The growth theory literature has been almost silent with respect to the relationship between growth and the business cycle. Economic growth and business cycles were assumed to be mainly independent. In the extreme classical-type models, the business cycle should not even exist. Rational economic "agents" would clear efficient markets so quickly that any shocks would be absorbed by the market system. The outcome of this analysis would be that there is no need for active monetary or fiscal policy. However, recall that Schumpeter, whose work was discussed in Chapter 6 in connection with "imperfect competition", disagreed with this characterization of the growth process. He argued that growth occurred through a process of "creative destruction". Businesspeople search for new ideas to (literally) destroy existing competitors while trying at the same time to establish their own position. This approach is very similar to the "disruptive innovation model" developed by Christensen and Raynor.[1] With respect to this model, Christensen argues:

> *[W]hen the challenge is to commercialize a simpler, more convenient product that sells for less money and appeals to a new or unattractive customer set, the entrants are likely to beat the incumbent. This is the phenomenon that so frequently defeats successful companies. It implies, of course, that the best way for upstarts to attack established competitors is to disrupt them.*

Francois and Lloyd-Ellis,[2] meanwhile, have demonstrated how a Schumpeterian process of creative destruction can also cause "herd behavior" by entrepreneurs, fueled by (the similarly anthropomorphic) Keynesian "animal spirits", thus leading to booms and busts in the economy *as well as* providing the underlying stimulus to growth. Also, they suggest:

> *... there is increasing evidence that the strength of cyclical upturns is related to the depth of preceding downturns.*

In other words, business cycles and economic growth are related. This should come as no surprise to most experienced businesspersons.

International Competitiveness

In recent years businesspeople, politicians, and policy commentators have tended to discuss the issues of economic growth and development under the general rubric of **international competitiveness**. Michael Porter[3] defines competitiveness as:

> *... the ability to design, produce and market goods and services, the pricing and non-price characteristics of which form a more attractive package than those of competitors.*

Until relatively recently competitiveness could be viewed primarily from a domestic perspective, since the majority of firms competed only in a domestic marketplace. This is no longer the case. The nature of production

---

[1] C. Christensen and M. Raynor, *The Innovator's Solution* (Boston: Harvard Business School Press, 2003).

[2] P. Francois and Huw Lloyd-Ellis, "Animal spirits through creative destruction", *American Economic Review* (June 2003) 93(3): 530–50.

[3] Michael Porter, *The Competitive Advantage of Nations* (New York: The Free Press, 1990).

Case Study 22

"Returns to Education Underestimated"
World Bank, Washington, DC;
July 4, 2015

For many years, economists, sociologists, and educators have been trying to estimate the value of education. The analysis has usually taken the form of a standard benefit/cost calculation to determine an appropriate rate of return. This analysis was conducted in much the same way a businessperson would undertake an analysis with respect to the purchase of a new machine. However, it is now apparent that a major variable in the analysis was missing: namely, social capital. Labor market efficiencies are more than the simple interaction of supply and demand. As Nobel laureate, Kenneth Arrow, pointed out as early as 2004 labor market efficiency seems to require a networking or relationship function. Businesspersons hire people they know, or those recommended by someone they know and trust. The connection with education is obvious. On average, more time spent in school provides enhanced opportunities to create these networks critical for the proper functioning of a sophisticated labor market.

and distribution in the world economy has changed dramatically in the past 50 years or so. The advent of new technologies (such as microelectronics) and the introduction of new materials (such as plastics) resulted in, for example, the miniaturization of many goods. This has led to the development of manufactured products that are much more easily transported. It is now possible — and indeed, common — to ship significant quantities of automobiles from Japan to North America, an undertaking that would have been unthinkable even 40 years ago. With technological breakthroughs in communications and transportation, there has also been a significant increase in the exchange of **tradable services** in a wide variety of fields, including construction, engineering, architecture, legal and accounting services, and tourism.

As a result of the significant increase in international trade of manufactured goods and services, many economists and business strategists have concluded that competitiveness must now be defined in a broader international context. Competitors are no longer within the same community or nation state. Firms must think of competition as truly global in terms of both gaining export markets and defending against competitors in domestic markets. From a broader societal perspective, however, it is not useful to view global competitiveness as an end in itself. Rather, an internationally competitive economy is a means to an end — the requirement for enhanced social well-being. Wealth creation is necessary in order to fund social services and produce a high and rising standard of living. It also appears to be a necessity for society to ultimately achieve its higher-order goals, including personal freedom, security, and a better quality of life. Therefore, competitiveness must be viewed in a broader societal context that goes beyond materialism. Some definitions of competitiveness are based upon driving down costs to the lowest common denominator: by hollowing out corporations, outsourcing jobs, shifting operations to lower-cost locales, and reducing the wages, benefits, and other entitlements of workers. A more appropriate definition of competitiveness, however, involves the increased productive capacity achieved by innovation, superior technology, continuous skill-enhancing training, and a concern with social equity and environmental preservation. The latter approach can better lead to the creation of a value-increasing society.

The Porter Model

The Porter model attempts to integrate the economic theories of trade and economic development with the corporate strategic theories of creating and sustaining competitive advantage. For Porter, the key question is why some firms in some nations achieve international success while others do not. By assessing the trade and unit cost performance of selected successful nations, he attempts to identify the most influential causes. It is Porter's belief that *nations* do not compete — rather, it is the *firms* within a country that must be competitive.

Porter pays significant attention to the fact that industries tend to be geographically concentrated within their host nations. The USA has

Hollywood and Silicon Valley. In Canada, four of five major banks have their head offices at the intersection of Bay and King streets in Toronto. The fifth is one block south. Porter suggests that in many cases the nation might actually be too large a unit of analysis for assessing competitiveness. However, for political and practical reasons (such as availability of data, etc.), this is the unit used by Porter and most others.

Porter presents a four-factor interactive model of competitiveness that he calls the **"diamond"** (because it can obviously be represented graphically in a four-cornered diagram). The four factors are assessed both quantitatively and qualitatively. It is important to note, however, that this is not a fully determined "model" where the interaction of all the variables has been specified by statistical methods; nor has its predictive validity been determined. Rather, it is derived inductively. It is the outcome of a review of data and qualitative factors used to evaluate an industry's, and therefore a country's, competitive evolution and current position. Porter's diamond is based on the hypothesis that the following four variables are the most significant:

- Factor Conditions

- Demand Conditions

- Related and Supporting Industries

- Firm Strategy, Structure, and Rivalry

Porter also includes two "outside" factors: chance and the impact of government.

Factor Conditions

Porter distinguishes between basic and advanced factors (of production). Basic factors include human and physical capital, generally available knowledge, financial investment capital, and infrastructure. Basic factors are passive: they are undifferentiated base abilities available to most competitors. Advanced factors involve higher levels of knowledge and lend themselves more to building competitive advantage. For example, basic factors are involved in a fishing industry, but advanced factors are required for an industry based on marine biology.

Factors can also be generalized, as opposed to specialized. Porter compares developed economies, which all tend to have generalized factors such as highway systems and public education. Specialized factors involve upgrading personnel to higher-skilled activities — such as training, not just electrical engineers, but electro-optics specialists — and so lend themselves to developing a distinctive competence. Porter maintains that a reliance on general factors makes an economy vulnerable. Economic activity can be easily moved to another jurisdiction where either the cost of these general factors is lower, or advanced factors are being used to create an advantage.

315

Demand Conditions

Market characteristics can be important. Large markets, for example, provide the opportunity to develop economies of scale in production. However, Porter views scale economies as a static advantage, inasmuch as scale, in and of itself, does not necessarily lead to products of greater added value. In his opinion, the "quality" of demand in the domestic market is a more important criterion for success. As nations create wealth, according to Porter, consumers become less price sensitive and are more interested in quality products supported by higher levels of customer service. In marketing terms, higher value-added niches are created, and consumers are less interested in standardized, mass-produced products. As well, Porter believes that a large number of independent buyers leads to more intense pressures within the domestic marketplace and, therefore, to an increased concern for the quality of the goods and services produced. Porter is a firm believer in the importance of intense competition in the domestic market. His public policy recommendations are oriented toward enhancing domestic competitive pressures. This also leads to a synergy with the other factors in the diamond, such as firm rivalry.

Related and Supporting Industries

Because modern industrial economies are complex and highly interrelated, industries require a network of supplier relationships in order to be successful. Porter explicitly recognizes the importance of developing effective supplier relationships as one of the four principal factors in the diamond model. It is important to stress that Porter's concept of related and supporting industries is influenced by Japanese practice in the late 20th century, and represents a substantial change from past North American supplier-purchaser relationships. Porter envisions a working relationship that will help to create both advanced and specialized factor conditions. The net result would be an enhanced competitive base for all of the firms in an interrelated "cluster" of advanced economic activity.

Strategy — Structure — Rivalry

Porter suggests that no one managerial style is best. In Italy, small- and medium-sized family-owned firms have been successful. In Germany, the focus is on technical backgrounds and organizational hierarchies. Differences in managerial approach are dependent upon such factors as the training and orientation of leaders, group versus hierarchical styles, the relative importance a society attributes to individual responsibility and initiative, relationships with customers, and the state of labor-management relations. He also suggests that different firm structures and management styles work best in different industries.

Porter stresses the importance of organizational goals. These goals may differ from country to country, depending upon such factors as ownership structure, motivation of owners, debt structures, and alternative forms of corporate governance. The roles of banks and capital markets may differ as well. Porter argues that the USA has a greater focus on taking risks and on restructuring mature sectors than many other developed countries. For example, the USA has developed capital market mechanisms that have created funding for new ventures and start-ups.

Porter also stresses the importance of domestic rivalry in this component of the diamond to ensure the development of sophisticated and specialized factors of production. As well, domestic competition is based upon a "level playing field" and must normally be construed as a fair test. On the other hand, foreign competition may be considered "unfair" because rules and regulations differ from country to country. Finally, Porter strongly opposes the creation of monopolies, cartels, or national champions as an approach to succeed in international markets. In his opinion, a lack of domestic competition inhibits the development of world-class, internationally competitive firms. Note the major difference here between this point of view and the relatively relaxed attitude to monopoly in the theories of "creative destruction" discussed above.

The Roles of Government and Chance

Porter does *not* believe that government is integral to the diamond. Rather, its role is that of a facilitator, only influencing the factors in the diamond. For example, governments can provide assistance to firms by reducing pressures in the business environment that impede competitiveness. Alternatively, they can slow the process of adapting to competition if they unduly protect industries from domestic and international pressures. Porter acknowledges the role of chance in the development of competitive industrial structures. Wars, technological change, and other factors can lead to the development of new competitive industries. For example, many important synthetic materials, such as nylon, were developed during WWII when natural resources became unavailable or were diverted for military use. Another example is that an antitrust case in the USA led to the creation in Canada of Nortel Networks, which went on to become one of Canada's major innovators at one time.

Stages of National Competitive Development

Porter's analysis suggests that there are four stages through which a national economy evolves. The first three involve growth, and the fourth indicates decline.

The Factor-Driven Stage

In the first, or factor-driven stage, the nation competes on the basis of the basic factors of production, such as raw materials, climate, and a pool of labor. These factors form the basis for a limited range of industries. At this stage of wealth creation, technology is transferred into the nation but is not created domestically. The factor-driven stage is highly sensitive to world business cycles, changes in exchange rates, and changes in international prices. Porter suggests that it is possible to sustain a high standard of living in the factor-driven stage, but that it represents a poor basis for long-term growth.

The Investment-Driven Stage

In the second, investment-driven stage, the emphasis is on acquiring and improving upon foreign technology. This stage features investment in large, modern facilities, the development of a pool of skilled workers, and the development of domestic rivalry and some focus on external markets. The investment-driven stage also focuses on upgrading institutional structures such as education and research institutions. However, competition in this stage is driven primarily by standardized production for a relatively unso-phisticated home demand. While a nation can experience rapid growth in the investment-driven stage, its economy can be vulnerable to increasing costs in the factors of production and to a continuing dependency on foreign technology. At this stage, government can play an important role by focusing on the creation of risk capital and promoting risk-taking and export activities.

The Innovation-Driven Stage

The third, innovation-driven stage represents a significant advancement. Porter suggests that in this stage the nation reaps the benefits of the entire diamond with all of its interactions. For example, increasing consumer sophistication in local demand necessitates increased development in sophis-ticated industrial production. New entrants into the business community increase rivalry, and firms are forced to innovate further. Clusters of related firms and industries both deepen, through the enhancement of supplier and related industries, and widen, through the development of new industrial activity. There is also a focus on innovation, particularly in the export of higher value-added services, such as engineering, law, and advertising. In the innovation-driven phase, government takes on a new role. There is less of a necessity for direct intervention by government, and it can now focus on creating the advanced and specialized factors of production that are required for a sophisticated market economy. As well, government can provide an environment that facilitates new-business start-ups, and increase rivalry in the domestic market.

The Wealth-Driven Stage

The final, wealth-driven stage leads to decline. In this phase there is less rivalry within the domestic market, and labor-management relations become more adversarial as the key players in the economy attempt to preserve their existing positions. Porter suggests that the wealth-driven stage leads to an increase in non-functional business activities, such as mergers, acquisitions, and takeovers by foreign firms. This non-functional activity leads ultimately to a decline in personal income, which erodes quality demand in the home market. At this stage, price becomes an important consideration, and the economy is no longer quality driven. In the wealth-driven stage it is possible to observe a dual economy with pockets of wealth and some highly successful firms, but also with a great deal of unemployment and a general sense of drift. The government may be forced to introduce taxes on wealth to pay for the sophisticated social services that were developed when the economy experienced sustained growth. These taxes further dampen the rewards to successful economic activity.

Using Porter's methodology, IMD, an international school of business in Switzerland and the home to the World Competitiveness Center, has actually created a "World Competitiveness Scoreboard". An examination of the countries identified in this list is sometimes quite interesting. At the time of writing, Finland is the top-ranked nation, and an examination of the top 20 nations contains a number of "surprises" in addition to Finland. The list currently includes such countries as Singapore, Iceland, Israel, Malta, and Estonia. In an attempt to determine the "fates of human societies", Jared Diamond[4] concluded:

> *... the striking differences between the long term histories of peoples of the different continents have been due not to innate differences in the peoples themselves (but) attempts (to deal with) differences in their environments.*

Fundamentals of International Competitiveness

Scholars have long debated why capitalism succeeds in some societies at different times and in different places, but not in others. Why, for example, did the Industrial Revolution start specifically in Britain in the 18th century? It can be argued that many other civilizations at different points in history were as sophisticated, or more sophisticated, as Britain in terms of

---

[4] Jared Diamond, *Guns, Germs and Steel: The Fates of Human Societies* (New York: Norton, 1999).

Case Study 23

"The Importance of Cities has Declined"
Johannesburg; February 21, 2055

Throughout most of human history, cities have been seen as a key engine for economic growth. Cities gained a comparative advantage through agglomeration economies with the provision of infrastructure and social services. This was followed by economies of scale in manufacturing and distribution. Of course, this was aided by proximity to large population centers. Now, however, the forces of decentralization seem overwhelming. Technology allows the provision of information, education, cultural and social services instantly, and over long distances. Suburban and rural areas are no longer disadvantaged in the provision of higher levels of social services, including cultural amenities. One of the main benefits of this decentralization is the ability of a world with a population of over 12 billion people to reduce congestion and pollution levels.

technology as, or had more resources than Britain in the 18th and 19th centuries. The list would include China, India, ancient Egypt, the Roman Empire, the Greeks, and the Incas. So the question is, why did capitalism develop in Britain at that particular time and not at other times and in other places? Obviously, the answer must be attributed to something in the sociopolitical environment in Britain at the time that was not present in other societies at that point. In an interesting study, Jones[5] puts forward one important argument, as follows:

> *Quantitative analysis of (the model) assigns a major role to changes in property rights in explaining growth over the very long term.*

In other words, the legal institutions surrounding property rights were one of the key factors in promoting prosperity and a successful capitalism at the time.

This exact theme is echoed by de Soto[6] in a recent attempt to explain why capitalism has *not* been successfully developed in many parts of the *modern* world:

> *... I intend to demonstrate that the major stumbling block that keeps the rest of the world from benefitting from **capitalism** is its inability to produce **capital**. Capital is the force that raises the productivity of labor and creates the wealth of nations. ... Even in the poorest countries, the poor save. The value of savings among the poor is, in fact, immense — forty times all the foreign aid received throughout the world since 1945. ... But they hold these resources in defective forms: houses built on land whose ownership rights are not adequately recorded, unincorporated businesses with undefined liability, industries located where financiers cannot see them. Because the rights of these possessions [are] not adequately documented, these assets cannot readily be turned into capital, cannot be traded outside of narrow local circles where people know and trust each other, cannot be used as collateral for a loan, and cannot be used as a share against an investment.* (Emphasis added.)

In line with de Soto's argument, a recent study by the World Bank[7] examined government policies with respect to starting a new business. The results are fascinating:

- It takes two days to register a business in Australia, but 203 days in Haiti.

---

[5] Charles Jones, "Was an industrial revolution inevitable? Economic growth over the very long run", National Bureau of Economic Research, 1999.
[6] Hernando de Soto, *The Mystery of Capital* (New York: Basic Books, 2000).
[7] The World Bank, *Doing Business in 2004*.

- You pay nothing to start a business in Denmark, while in Cambodia you pay five times the country's average income and, in Sierra Leone, more than 13 times.

- In many countries, including Singapore and Thailand, there is no minimum on the capital required by someone wanting to start a business. However, in Syria, the minimum is 56 times the average income; and in Yemen, it is 170 times.

- Business can enforce a simple commercial contract in seven days in Tunisia and 39 days in the Netherlands, but it takes almost 1,500 days (over four years) in Guatemala.

- It takes less than six months to go through a bankruptcy proceeding in Ireland and Japan, but the time stretches out to more than a decade in India and Brazil.

The results of this World Bank study seem to reinforce de Soto's conclusion that appropriate policies need to be established in order to support business development. The pro-market Fraser Institute, meanwhile, produces an annual *Economic Freedom of The World Report*, ranking different countries by this criterion. They define economic freedom as:

> ... *personal choice, voluntary exchange, freedom to compete, and protection of person and property. Institutions and policies are consistent with economic freedom when they provide an infrastructure for voluntary exchange, and protect individuals and their property from aggressors seeking to use violence, coercion and fraud to seize things that do not belong to them. Legal and monetary agreements are particularly important: governments promote economic freedom when they provide a legal structure and law enforcement system that protects the property rights of owners and enforces contracts in an even-handed manner ... economic freedom also requires governments to refrain from many activities ... when taxes, government expenditures and regulations are substituted for personal choice, voluntary exchange, and market coordination.*

It is interesting to compare such a ranking of Economic Freedom with the Human Development Index (HDI) created by the United Nations.[8] The HDI ranks countries from the "best" to the "worst" places to live. In fact, there is a high correlation between the economic freedom rankings and the

---

[8] United Nations, *Human Development Report 2004*.

HDI index. Another index, developed by Transparency International,[9] indicates the degree of "corruption" by country. There is also a high correlation among the HDI, the Economic Freedom rankings, and the (inverse) rankings of Transparency International. It is unlikely that this is a result of pure coincidence. The proponents of economic freedom would certainly argue that there is more than a relationship; there is causality — that is, a high rating on the HDI is a *result* of economic freedom and of a more honest society in its business dealings.

On the controversial question of globalization, Lindert and Williamson[10] suggest that while the world has become much more globalized and, of course, overall standards of living have risen, the world economy has become more *unequal* over the past two centuries. Nonetheless, these authors conclude the following:

> *Globalization probably mitigated rising inequality between participating nations. The nations that gained the most from globalization have been those poor ones that changed their policies to exploit it, while the ones that gained the least did not, or were too isolated to do so ... the net impact of globalization has been far too small to explain the long run rise in world inequality since 1800.*

In other words, the argument is that openness to globalization may help the development process in those countries that have been prepared to restructure their economies and societies to participate actively in the global economy. This would be consistent with a framework that argues that countries must compete against the "best" in order to achieve the term **competitiveness**. It might also be remarked that a world that was more equal but in which the average standard of living was similar to that of the 1800s would hardly be a viable alternative to current economic arrangements.

The Main Social Institutions of Capitalism

One feature of the previous discussion in this chapter, and of economic thinking as a whole, as reflected elsewhere in the book, is a tendency of different writers to pick out just *one* characteristic of the social system that

---

[9] Transparency International, *Global Corruption Report 2004*.

[10] P. Lindert and J. Williamson, "Does globalization make the world more unequal?", National Bureau of Economic Research, 2001.

seems to them important in promoting prosperity — the market, entrepreneurship, property rights, effective demand, or whatever — and then focus on that to the exclusion of the others. However, a more compelling argument, we think, is that what is called capitalism is actually a *complex* system based primarily on the following *four* underlying social structures or institutions, namely:

I.   Money
II.   Private property
III. Markets
IV.   Entrepreneurial business

The legal, social, and governance systems must allow these institutions to function effectively and *also* generate sufficient effective demand for the products of capitalist innovation if there is to be economic growth and development.

The word **money** in the above list obviously does not just mean notes and coins, but the entire system of social relations covered by that rubric.[11] These would include the following: first, a money of account; second, a well-identified asset (not necessarily a physical asset), denominated in the unit of account, and serving as the final or ultimate means of settlement; third, a developed banking/financial system that enables secure credit relations. These are the requirements for such things as price lists and rational accounting to come into existence and, ultimately, for the very feasibility of a system of production that entails taking a long position in goods and services and that functions *via* the generation and realization of profits calculated in monetary terms.

Property rights are important for such a society because in a system centered on the profit motive (and for that matter also on the receipt of wages for services rendered) it is important that the recipients of these income streams be able to control their final disbursement. In other words, they are important precisely for incentives. For the incentive system to work, in principle those remunerated should be able to retain their rewards and dispose of them as they see fit — and not be subject to arbitrary confiscation, etc. This statement does not in itself de-legitimize taxation, particularly when conceived of as an act of sovereignty rather than appropriation. On the contrary, it can be argued that the existence of a state "authority" in this sense may itself be a requisite for the establishment of commercial society in the first place. This is the argument of the contemporary neo-chartalist school, for example, that "taxes drive money".[12] That is, that the ability of the state to

---

[11] Geoffrey Ingham, *The Nature of Money* (Cambridge: Polity Press, 2004).

[12] L. Randall Wray, *Understanding Modern Money* (Cheltenham: Edward Elgar, 1998).

levy taxes is, in turn, the foundation of the monetary system. What the concept of private property *does* imply, however, is that there is a definite set of both economic and legal principles that sharply delineate the scope of taxation, if the system is to function.

Note that the idea of markets actually appears only in third place on the above list, and this would no doubt seem strange from the viewpoint of much of the orthodox economic theory discussed earlier in this book. As we have seen, from that perspective, market exchange is seen as co-extensive with economic activity. The market is the mainspring of the whole system, based on a supposed natural "propensity to truck, barter and exchange", as in Adam Smith's original formulation. In this view markets, *as such*, perform all the necessary functions of providing information, coordinating activity, and ensuring productive efficiency. Moreover, money need not really be involved — in principle all that is going on is barter exchange, and the information content, in fact, consists of just these barter exchange ratios, rather than accounting notions of profit. However, in actual social systems things are far more complicated. In particular, each set of social institutions must build on those already existing at a different level, in a process known in philosophy as "iteration".[13] The argument here, therefore, would be, for example, that markets and the notion of market exchange can only be built upon the prior institutions of money and private property — in short, that the ordering set out above is the correct one. Market exchange finally slots into the picture because if we are to have a system in which the incentive for production is profit (and profit that is actually quantifiable in monetary terms — not vague notions of utility or satisfaction), there clearly must exist a number of actual or virtual locations where the output of production can be sold. This is the most simple and obvious function of markets in the system, hence the crucial function of "marketing" or advertising in actual business. If the output cannot be sold there can be no profit. Markets, of course, also *do* serve the regulatory/validating function hinted at in the idea of the "invisible hand", or "optimal resource allocation", and even the old Marxian notion of "socially necessary labor time". If someone, somewhere, is prepared to buy the output of the producer, presumably the effort that went into its production was indeed "socially necessary", at least in the opinion of the purchaser at the time of sale. This is so, even if in a certain percentage of cases the later regrets the decision due to product quality, or for any other reason.

The role of business in the system, finally, is to organize productive activity in the pursuit of profit. The term **business** is used here in a generic sense — including all types of business organization: the individual entrepreneur, partnerships, and all corporate forms. It might, therefore, perhaps

---

[13] John Searle, *The Construction of Social Reality* (New York: The Free Press, 1995).

have been adequate just to use the term **business operations** here. However, the qualifier **entrepreneurial** is employed to recognize the point stressed, for example, by both Schumpeter and Keynes, that, given an accommodative framework provided by the other institutions, the essence of the system is then the incentive for entrepreneurial innovation and dynamic change.

It is interesting to compare the above account with the six-fold schema of the sociologist Max Weber.[14] According to Weber, the structure of capitalism consists of:

1. Rational capital accounting
2. Freedom of markets
3. Rational technology
4. Calculable law
5. Freedom of labor
6. Commercialization of economic life

Weber's category (3), arguably, does not really fit in a list of *prerequisites* or *preconditions* because historically rational technology must surely be seen as the *outcome* or result of capitalism rather than its precondition. It is an important feature of capitalism, but the causality goes from the capitalist social system *to* rapid technological innovation, and not vice versa. Otherwise there seem to be several correspondences between the remaining five Weberian categories and the four mentioned above. For example, point (1) about rational accounting is essentially subsumed in the earlier point (I) about the importance of money, and points (2) and (5) are both covered by (III) on the overall role of the market. Point (4) about calculable law is also implicit in points (I) and (II) about money and private property. Both require a legal system for the protection and enforcement of contracts — money, for example, is intimately involved in the systems of debts and credits — it is in this sort of field that legal considerations apply, rather than legal tender laws per se. Finally, point (6), about the commercialization of economic life, is obviously connected with (and brought about by) entrepreneurial business as in item (IV).

Rostow has also argued that economic development occurs in five stages:

i. Traditional society
ii. Preconditions for take-off
iii. Take-off
iv. Time to maturity

---

[14] Max Weber, *General Economic History* (Mineola, NY: Dover Publications., 2003 [1927]).

v.   Age of high mass consumption.

Stages (ii) and (iii) are consistent with our argument that economic growth occurs as a result of the synergistic combination of a number of social and economic variables.[15]

Some Final Remarks

The Solow, or neoclassical, growth model identifies savings, investment, and technological change as the keys to economic growth. An examination of the data indicates that the model can be a reasonably accurate predictor of economic growth and development in some cases. However, the neoclassical model is silent with respect to the business cycle and demand. In the model, cycles are viewed as a separate phenomenon from the underlying processes of long-term economic growth. Keynes, however, argued that there is a role for government to moderate business cycles on a national and, increasingly, international level by sustaining the level of aggregate demand. The developed world has not experienced a major depression in over 70 years, and this may arguably be the result of more active monetary and fiscal policy even though it has come to be fashionable to deny this. Increasingly, there is also a reliance on international institutions to assist in preventing the booms and busts of international business cycles.

The neoclassical growth model implicitly assumes a trained work force, an existing capital stock, technological development, and that the necessary sociopolitical institutions are already in place. Given these assumptions, the neoclassical model may do a reasonably accurate job of describing economic growth for the developed and for some developing nations. However, it may also be necessary to dig deeper to understand the most important underlying characteristics behind the growth process. Schumpeter's analysis of the process of creative destruction, for example, is consistent with research in the business literature, and is certainly sensible from the point of view of the businessperson. It seems important that governments and societies allow this process of creative destruction to take place, while at the same time providing safeguards for the more vulnerable members of society.

Also, finally, for a society to grow and develop requires more than just the technical factors of "savings, investment, and access to technology". Porter, de Soto, and others suggest that it is important to have the appropriate institutions in place. These would include the rule of law, secure credit relations, economic freedom, and the absence of corruption. These institutions, in conjunction with investment, a manageable rate of

---

[15] W.W. Rostow, *The Stages of Economic Growth*, Cambridge University Press, 1960.

population growth, and access to technology can provide the basis for a high and rising standard of living.

Chapter Summary

- Economic growth and development occur as the result of a complex interaction of macro and micro variables.

- In the Solow, or neoclassical, growth model, savings, investment and the application of technology lead to economic growth.

- In the neoclassical growth model, steady-state equilibrium occurs when (i) additions to the capital stock exactly offset depreciation and the addition of new workers into the labor force, and (ii) technology remains unchanged.

- The model has some interesting properties. Economic growth occurs as a result of technology, and the model exhibits diminishing returns.

- Diminishing returns and the general availability of new technologies may facilitate convergence between richer and poorer countries.

- The neoclassical model is helpful in explaining some of the patterns of development over the past 50 years — for example, the rapid return of Japan and Germany to developed country status after WWII, and the accession of, for example, Singapore, Finland, and South Korea to developed country status.

- Porter argues that the correct macroeconomic policies, while important, are, in themselves, not sufficient to ensure economic development.

- Porter's diamond model articulates the microeconomic foundations for growth. These are factor conditions, demand conditions, firm strategy/ structure/rivalry conditions, and conditions in related and support industries. Government cannot create competitiveness, but it *can* create an appropriate environment within which firms can become internationally competitive.

- To become truly competitive, a nation or region must develop "clusters" of interrelated economic activity.

- Transparent government, property rights, and an absence of corruption appear to be important characteristics associated with economic growth and high standards of living.

Problems

1. Explain the relationships among output, investment, and savings.

2. What conditions would be necessary to cause another world-wide Great Depression like that of the 1930s?

3. How might endogenous growth theory be of benefit to developing nations?

4. Is corruption caused by poverty, or does corruption cause poverty?

5. What are the key characteristics of the Porter model of economic development?

Case Study Questions | # The Comeback of Caterpillar

Competitive Advantage

1. Comparative advantage is based on factor endowments. Competitive advantage is created. How has Caterpillar used its employment involvement and labor relations program to create a competitive advantage?
2. Why are developing nations important for Caterpillar's growth strategy?
3. Discuss the role of capital investment in the Caterpillar strategy.
4. Why is cost-effective access to capital important for the heavy construction equipment industry?

Hint: Comparative advantage is based on initial factor endowments. Caterpillar executed a comprehensive strategy to create a competitive advantage: outsourcing, product line expansion, employee involvement, plant modernization, dealerships, information technology, diversification, and joint ventures.

Case B

The Comeback of Caterpillar

Isaac Cohen
San Jose State University

* This case was presented at the October 2001 Meeting of the North American Case Research Association (NACRA) at Memphis, Tennessee. Copyright by Isaac Cohen and NACRA. Reprinted with permission. All rights reserved.

Introduction

For three consecutive years, 1982, 1983, and 1984, the Caterpillar Company lost one million dollars a day. Caterpillar's major competitor was a formidable Japanese company called Komatsu. Facing a tough global challenge, the collapse of its international markets, and an overvalued dollar, Caterpillar had no choice. It had to reinvent itself, or die.

Caterpillar managed to come back as a high-tech, globally competitive, growth company. Over a period of 15 years, and throughout the tenure of two CEOs — George Schaefer (1985–1990) and Donald Fites (1990–1999) — Caterpillar had transformed itself. George Schaefer introduced cost-cutting measures and employee involvement programs, outsourced machines, parts, and components, and began modernizing Caterpillar's plants. Donald Fites diversified Caterpillar's product line and reorganized the company structurally. He also completed Caterpillar's plant modernization program, revitalized Caterpillar's dealership network, and altered radically Caterpillar's approach to labor relations.

As Donald Fites retired in February 1999, Glen Barton was elected CEO. Barton was in an enviable position. The world's largest manufacturer of construction and mining equipment, and a Fortune 100 company, Caterpillar generated 21 billion dollars in revenues in 1998, the sixth consecutive record year. Leading its industry while competing globally, Caterpillar recorded a $1.5 billion profit in 1998, the second best ever.[1]

How precisely did both Schaefer and Fites manage to turn Caterpillar around?

The Heavy Construction Equipment Industry

The heavy construction equipment industry supplied engineering firms, construction companies, and mine operators. The industry's typical product line included earthmovers (bulldozers, loaders, and excavators), road building machines (pavers, motor graders, and mixers), mining related equipment (off-highway trucks, mining shovels), and large cranes. Most machines were offered in a broad range of sizes, and a few were available with a choice of wheels or crawler tracks. Most were used for the construction of buildings, power plants, manufacturing plants, and infra-structure projects such as roads, airports, bridges, tunnels, dams, sewage systems, and water lines. On a global basis, earthmoving equipment accounted for about half of the industry's total sales in the 1990s (Table B1). Among earthmovers, hydrau-

---

[1] Caterpillar Inc. *1999 Annual Report*, p. 39

Table B1: **Global Demand of Heavy Construction Equipment by Major Categories, 1985–2005**

Item	1985	1994	2000	2005*
Earthmoving Equipment	50%	49%	49%	49%
Off Highway Trucks	8%	7%	7%	7%
Construction Cranes	9%	11%	10%	10%
Mixers, Pavers, and Related Equipment	6%	6%	7%	7%
Parts & Attachments	27%	27%	27%	26%
Total Demand (billions)	**$38**	**$56**	**$72**	**$90**

*Percentages do not add up to 100 because of rounding.
Source: Andrew Gross and David Weiss, "Industry Corner: The Global Demand for Heavy Construction Equipment," *Business Economics*, July 1996, p. 56.

lic excavators accounted for 45% of the sales. Excavators were more productive, more versatile, and easier to use in tight spaces than either bulldozers or loaders. Off-highway trucks that hauled minerals, rocks, and dirt, were another category of fast selling equipment.[2]

Global demand for heavy construction machinery grew at a steady rate of 4.5% in the 1990s. The rate of growth, however, was faster among the developing nations of Asia, Africa, and Latin America than among the developed nations. In the early 2000s, North America and Europe were each expected to account for 25% of the industry's sales, Japan for 20%, and the developing nations for the remaining 30%.[3]

The distinction between original equipment and replacement parts was an essential feature of the industry. Replacement parts and "attachments" (work tools) made up together over a quarter of the total revenues of the heavy construction equipment industry (Table B1), but accounted for a substantially larger share of the industry's earnings for two reasons: first, the sale of replacement parts was more profitable than that of whole machines; and second, the market for replacement parts was less cyclical than that for original equipment.[4] As a rule of thumb, the economic life of a heavy construction machine was 10 to 12 years, but in many cases, especially in developing countries, equipment users kept their machines in service much

---

[2] Andrew Gross and David Weiss, "Industry Corner: The Global Demand for Heavy Construction Equipment," Business Economics, 31:3 (July 1996), pp. 54–55.
[3] Gross and Weiss, "Industry Corner," p. 54.
[4] Gross and Weiss, "Industry Corner," p. 55.

longer, perhaps 20 to 30 years, thus creating an ongoing stream of revenues for parts, components, and related services.[5]

Another characteristic of the industry was the need to achieve economies of scale. According to industry observers, the optimal scale of operation was about 90,000 units annually; in other words, up to a production level of 90,000 units a year, average equipment unit cost declined as output increased, and therefore capturing a large market share was critical for benefitting from economies of scale.[6] The relatively low volume of global sales — 200,000 to 300,000 earthmoving equipment units per year (1996)[7] — further intensified competition over market share among the industry's leading firms.

Successful marketing also played an important role in gaining competitive advantage. A widespread distribution and service network had always been essential for competing in the heavy construction equipment industry because "downtime" resulting from the inability to operate the equipment at a construction site was very costly. Typically, manufacturers used a worldwide network of dealerships to sell machines, provide support, and offer after sales service. Dealerships were independent, company owned, or both, and were normally organized on an exclusive territorial basis. Since heavy construction machines operated in a tough and inhospitable environment, equipment wore out and broke down frequently, parts needed to be rebuilt or replaced often, and therefore manufacturers placed dealers in close proximity to equipment users, building a global service network that spread all over the world.

Manufacturers built alliances as well. Intense competition over market share drove the industry's top firms to form three types of cooperative agreements. The first were full scale joint ventures to share production. Caterpillar's joint venture with Mitsubishi Heavy Industries was a notable case in point. The second were technology sharing agreements between equipment manufacturers and engine makers to ensure access to the latest engine technology. The joint venture between Komatsu and Cummins Engine, on the one hand, and the Case Corporation and Cummins, on the other, provided two examples. The third type of agreements were technology sharing alliances between major global firms and local manufacturers whereby the former gained access to new markets, and in return, supplied the latter with advanced technology. Caterpillar utilized such an arrange-

[5] Donald Fites, "Making Your Dealers Your Partners," *Harvard Business Review*, March–April 1996, p. 85.

[6] U. Srinivasa Rangan, "Caterpillar Tractor Co.," in Christopher Bartlett and Sumantra Ghoshal, Transatlantic Management: Text, Cases, and Readings in Cross Border Management (Homewood IL.: Irwin, 1992), p. 296.

[7] Fites, "Making Your Dealers Your Partners," p. 85.

ment with Shanghai Diesel in China, and Komatsu did so with the BEML company in India.[8]

History of Caterpillar

At the turn of the century, farmers in California faced a serious problem. Using steam tractors to plow the fine delta land of the San Joaquin valley, California farmers fitted their tractors with large drive wheels to provide support on the moist soil; nevertheless, despite their efforts, the steamer's huge wheels — measuring up to 9 feet high — sank deeply into the soil. In 1904, Benjamin Holt, a combine maker from Stockton, California, solved the problem by replacing the wheels with a track, thereby distributing the tractor's weight on a broader surface. Holt, in addition, replaced the heavy steam engine with a gasoline engine, thus improving the tractor's mobility further by reducing its weight (a steam tractor weighed up to 20 tons). He nicknamed the tractor "Caterpillar", acquired the "Caterpillar" trade mark, and applied it to several crawler-type machines that his company manufactured and sold. By 1915 Holt tractors were sold in 20 countries.[9]

Outside agriculture, crawler tractors were first used by the military. In 1915, the British military invented the armor tank, modeling it after Holt's machine, and during World War I, the United States and its allies in Europe utilized Holt's track-type tractors to haul artillery and supply wagons. In 1925, the Holt Company merged with another California firm, the Best Tractor Company, to form Caterpillar (Cat). Shortly thereafter, Caterpillar moved its corporate headquarters and manufacturing plants to Peoria, Illinois. The first company to introduce a diesel engine on a moving vehicle (1931), Caterpillar discontinued its combine manufacturing during the 1930s and focused instead on the production of road-building, construction, logging, and pipelaying equipment. During World War II, Caterpillar served as the primary supplier of bulldozers to the U.S. Army; its sales volume more than tripled between 1941 and 1944 to include motor graders, diesel engines, and electric generators, apart from tractors and wagons.[10]

Demand for Caterpillar products exploded in the early post-war years. Cat's equipment was used to reconstruct Europe, build the U.S. interstate highway system, erect the giant dams of the Third World, and lay out the major airports of the world. The company managed to differentiate itself

---

[8] Gross and Weiss, "Industry Corner," p. 58.

[9] William L. Naumann, *The Story of Caterpillar Tractor Co.* (New York: The Newcomen Society, 1977), pp. 7–9.

[10] "Caterpillar Inc.," Hoover's Handbook of American Business 1999 (Austin: Hoover Business Press, 1999), p. 328; "The Story of Caterpillar." Online. Caterpillar.com. Retrieved March 9, 2000.

from its competitors by producing reliable, durable and high quality equipment, offering a quick after-sales service, and providing a speedy delivery of replacement parts. As a result, during the 1950s and 1960s, Caterpillar had emerged as the uncontested leader of the heavy construction equipment industry, far ahead of any rival. By 1965, Caterpillar had established foreign manufacturing subsidiaries — either wholly owned or joint ventures — in Britain, Canada, Australia, Brazil, France, Mexico, Belgium, India, and Japan. Caterpillar's 50/50 joint venture with Mitsubishi in Japan, established in 1963, had become one of the most successful, stable, and enduring alliances among all American-Japanese joint ventures.[11]

Caterpillar's distribution and dealership network also contributed to the company's worldwide success. From the outset, the company's marketing organization rested on a dense network of independent dealers who sold and serviced Cat equipment. Strategically located throughout the world, these dealers were self sustaining entrepreneurs who invested their own capital in their business, derived close to 100% of their revenues from selling and supporting Cat equipment, and cultivated close relationships with Caterpillar customers. On average, a Caterpillar dealership had remained in the hands of the same family — or company — for over 50 years. Indeed, some dealerships, including several located overseas, predated the 1925 merger that gave birth to Caterpillar.[12] In 1981, on the eve of the impending crisis, the combined net worth of Cat dealers equaled that of the company itself, the total number of employees working for Cat dealers was slightly lower than the company's own workforce.[13]

The Crisis of the Early 1980s

Facing weak competition both at home and abroad, Caterpillar charged premium prices for its high quality products, paid its production workers, union-scale wages, offered its shareholders high rates of return on their equity, and enjoyed superior profits. Then, in 1982, following a record year of sales and profits, Caterpillar suddenly plunged into three successive years of rising losses totaling nearly $1 billion. "Quite frankly, our long years of

---

[11] Michael Yoshino and U. Srinivasa Rangan, *Strategic Alliances: An Entrepreneurial Approach to Globalization* (Boston: Harvard Business School Press, 1995), p. 93; Naumann, "Story of Caterpillar," pp. 12–14; William Haycraft, *Yellow Power: The story of the Earthmoving Equipment Industry* (Urbana Illinois: University of Illinois Press, 2000), pp. 118–122, 159–167, 196–203.

[12] Fites, "Making your Dealers Your Partners," p. 94.

[13] Rangan, "Caterpillar Tractor Co.," p. 304; James Risen, "Caterpillar: A Test of U.S. Trade Policy," *Los Angeles Times*, June 8, 1986. Online. Lexis-Nexis. Academic Universe.

success made us complacent, even arrogant," Pierre Guerindon, an executive vice president at Cat conceded.[14]

The crisis of 1982–84 stemmed from three sources: a global recession, a costly strike, and unfavorable currency exchange rates. First, the steady growth in demand for construction machinery, dating back to 1945, came to an end in 1980, as highway construction in the U.S. slowed down to a halt while declining oil prices depressed the world-wide market for mining, logging, and pipelaying equipment. Second, Caterpillar's efforts to freeze wages and reduce overall labor cost triggered a seven month strike (1982–83) among its U.S. employees. Led by the United Auto Workers (UAW) union, the strike accounted for a sizable portion of the company's three year loss. The third element in Caterpillar's crisis was a steep rise in the value of the dollar (relative to the Yen and other currencies) that made U.S. exports more expensive abroad, and U.S. imports (shipped by Caterpillar's competitors) cheaper at home. "The strong dollar is a prime factor in Caterpillar's reduced sales and earning... [and] is undermining manufacturing industries in the United States," said Cat's annual reports for 1982 and 1984.[15]

Taking advantage of the expensive dollar, Komatsu Limited had emerged as Caterpillar's principal rival. Komatsu ("little pine tree" in Japanese) had initially produced construction machinery for the Japanese and Asian markets, then sought to challenge Caterpillar's dominance in the markets of Latin America and Europe, and eventually penetrated the United States to rival Caterpillar in its domestic market. Attacking Caterpillar head-on, Komatsu issued a battle cry, "Maru C," meaning "encircle Cat." Launching a massive drive to improve quality while reducing costs, Komatsu achieved a 50% labor productivity advantage over Caterpillar, and in turn, underpriced Caterpillar's products by as much a 30%. The outcome was a dramatic change in market share. Between 1979 and 1984 Komatsu global market share more than doubled to 25% while Caterpillar's fell by almost a quarter to 43%.[16]

---

[14] Cited in Kathleen Deveny, "For Caterpillar, the Metamorphosis Isn't Over," *Business Week*, August 31, 1987, p. 72.

[15] Cited in Dexter Hutchins, "Caterpillar's Triple Whammy," *Fortune*, October 27, 1986, p. 91. See also Robert Eckley, "Caterpillar's Ordeal: Foreign Competition in Capital Goods," *Business Horizons*, March–April 1989, pp. 81–83.

[16] James Abegglen and George Stalk, *Kaisha, the Japanese Corporation* (New York: Basic Books, 1985), pp. 62, 117–118; Yoshino and Rangan, Strategic Alliances, pp. 94–95; "Komatsu Ltd.," *Hoover's Handbook of World Business*, 1999, p. 320.

Turnaround: George Schaefer's Caterpillar, 1985–1990

Competition with Komatsu and the crisis of 1982–84 forced Caterpillar to reexamine its past activities. Caterpillar's new CEO (1985), George Schaefer, was a congenial manager who encouraged Cat executives to openly admit the company's past mistakes. "We have experienced a fundamental change in our business — it will never again be what it was," Schaefer said as he became CEO. "We have no choice but to respond, and respond vigorously, to the new world in which we find ourselves."[17] Under Schaefer's direction, Caterpillar devised and implemented a series of strategies that touched upon every important function of the company, including purchasing, manufacturing, marketing, personnel, and labor relations.

Global Outsourcing

Traditionally, Caterpillar functioned as a vertically integrated company that relied heavily on in-house production. To ensure product quality as well as an uninterrupted supply of parts, Cat self-produced two-thirds of its parts and components, and assembled practically all of its finished machines. Under the new policy of "shopping around the world," Caterpillar sought to purchase parts and components from low-cost suppliers who maintained high quality standards. Working closely with its suppliers, Caterpillar moved towards the goal of outsourcing 80% of its parts and components.[18]

An additional goal of the policy was branding, that is, the purchase of final products for resale. Through its branding program, Caterpillar sold outsourced machines under its own brand name, taking advantage of its superior marketing organization, and keeping production costs down. Beginning in the mid 1980s, Cat contracted to buy lift trucks from a Norwegian company, hydraulic excavators from a West German manufacturer, paving machines from an Oklahoma corporation, off-highway trucks from a British firm, and logging equipment from a Canadian company, and resell them all under the Cat nameplate. Ordinarily, Caterpillar outsourced product manufacturing but not product design. By keeping control over the design of many of its outsourced products, Caterpillar managed to retain in-house design capability, and ensure quality control.[19]

---

[17] Quoted in Yoshino and Rangan, *Strategic Alliances*, p. 96.

[18] Yoshino and Rangan, *Strategic Alliances*, p. 97; Eckley, "Caterpillar's Ordeal," p. 84.

[19] Eckley, "Caterpillar's Ordeal," p. 84; Business Week, August 31, 1987, p. 73; Yoshino and Rangan, *Strategic Alliances*, p. 97.

Broader Product Line

For nearly a decade, the DC10 bulldozer had served as Caterpillar's signature item. It stood 15 feet tall, weighed 73 tons, and sold for more than $500,000 (1988). It had no competitors. But as demand for highway construction projects dwindled, Caterpillar needed to reevaluate its product mix because heavy equipment was no longer selling well. Sales of light construction equipment, on the other hand, were fast increasing. Between 1984 and 1987, accordingly, Caterpillar doubled its product line from 150 to 300 models of equipment, introducing many small machines that ranged from farm tractors to backhoe loaders (multi-purpose light bulldozers), and diversified its customer base. Rather than focusing solely on large clients, i.e., multinational engineering and construction firms like the Bechtel corporation — a typical user of heavy bulldozers — Cat began marketing its lightweight machines to a new category of customers: small-scale owner operators and emerging contractors. Still, the shift in Cat's product mix had a clear impact on the company's bottom line. Unlike the heavy equipment market where profit margins were wide, intense competition in the market for light products kept margins slim and pitted Caterpillar against John Deere and the Case corporation, the light equipment market leaders.[20]

Labor Relations

To compete successfully, Caterpillar also needed to repair its relationship with the union. In 1979, following the expiration of its collective bargaining agreement, Caterpillar experienced an 80 days strike, and three years later, in 1982, contract negotiations erupted in a 205 days strike, the longest company-wide work stoppage in the UAW history.[21] Named CEO in 1985, George Schaefer led the next two rounds of contract negotiations.

Schaefer's leadership style was consensual. By contrast to the autocratic style of his predecessors, Schaefer advocated the free flow of ideas between officers, managers, and production workers, and promoted open communication at all levels of the company. A low-key CEO who often answered his own phone, Schaefer possessed exceptional people skills. Asked to evaluate Schaefer's performance, John Stark, editor of *Off Highway Ledger*, a trade journal, said: "Schaefer is probably the best manager the construction machinery industry has ever had."[22]

Schaefer's social skills led to a significant improvement in Cat's relations with the UAW. Not a single strike broke out over contract negotiations during Schaefer's tenure; on the contrary, each cycle of bargaining

---

[20] Ronald Henkoff, "This Cat is Acting like a Tiger," *Fortune*, December 19, 1988, pp. 67, 72, 76; *Business Week*, August 31, 1987, p. 73.

[21] Eckley, "Caterpillar Ordeal," pp. 81, 83.

[22] Quoted in *Fortune*, December 19, 1988, p. 76.

was settled peacefully. Under Schaefer's direction, furthermore, the union agreed to reduce the number of labor grades and job classifications, and to streamline seniority provisions; a move that enhanced management flexibility in job assignment, and facilitated the cross utilization of employees.[23] More important, improved labor relations contributed to the success of two programs that played a critical role in Caterpillar's turnaround strategy, namely, an employee involvement plan based on team work, and a re-engineering effort of plant modernization and automation.

Employee Involvement

An industry-wide union famous for its cooperative labor-management efforts at the Saturn corporation, the NUMMI plant (a GM-Toyota joint-venture in Fremont California), and elsewhere, the UAW lent its support to Caterpillar's employee involvement program. Called the Employee Satisfaction Process (ESP), and launched by Schaefer in 1986, the program was voluntary. ESP members were organized in work teams, met weekly with management, and offered suggestions that pertained to many critical aspects of the manufacturing process, including production management, workplace layout, and quality enhancement. Implemented in a growing number of U.S. plants, the program resulted (1990) in productivity gains, quality improvements, and increased employee satisfaction. At the Cat plant in Aurora Illinois, for example, the local ESP chairman recalled: the ESP program "changed everything: the worker had some say over his job.... [and t]op management was very receptive. We zeroed in on quality, anything to make the customer happy." Management credited the ESP teams at Aurora with a steep fall in the rate of absenteeism, a sharp decline in the number of union grievances filed, and cost savings totaling $10 million.[24] At another ESP plant, a Cat assembly-line worker told a *Fortune* reporter in 1988: "Five years ago the foreman wouldn't even listen to you, never mind the general foreman or plant supervisor .... Now everyone will listen." Caterpillar applied the ESP program to outside suppliers as well. Typically, ESP teams made up of Caterpillar machinists visited suppliers' plants to check and certify equipment quality. The certified vendors received preferential treatment, mostly in the form of reduced inspection, counting, and other controls. Only 0.6% of the parts delivered by certified suppliers were re-

---

[23] Eckley, "Caterpillar Ordeal," p. 84, *Fortune*, December 19, 1988, p. 76; Alex Kotlowitz, "Caterpillar Faces Shutdown with UAW," *Wall Street Journal*, March 5, 1986. Online. ABI data base.

[24] Barry Bearak, "The Inside Strategy: Less Work and More Play at Cat," *Los Angeles Times*, May 16, 1995. Online. Lexis-Nexis. Academic Universe.

jected by Caterpillar compared to a reject rate of 2.8% for non-certified suppliers.[25]

Plant with a Future

Caterpillar's employee involvement plan went hand in hand with a $1.8 billion plant modernization program launched by Schaefer in 1986.[26] Dubbed "Plant with a Future" (PWAF), the modernization program combined just-in-time inventory techniques, a factory automation scheme, a network of computerized machine tools, and a flexible manufacturing system. Several of these innovations were pioneered by Komatsu late in the 1970s. The industry's technological leader, Komatsu had been the first construction equipment manufacturer to introduce both the just-in-time inventory system, and the "quick changeover tooling" technique, a flexible tooling method designed to produce a large variety of equipment models in a single plant.[27]

To challenge Komatsu, top executives at Caterpillar did not seek to merely imitate the Japanese. This was not enough. They studied, instead, the modernization efforts of several manufacturing companies, and arrived at two important conclusions: it was necessary 1) to change the layout of an entire plant, not just selected departments within a plant; and 2) to implement the program company-wide, that is, on a global basis both at home and abroad. Implementing such a comprehensive program took longer than expected, however, lasting seven years: four under Schaefer's direction, and three more under the direction of his successor, Donald Fites.[28]

The traditional manufacturing process at Caterpillar, known as "batch" production, was common among U.S. assembly plants in a number of industries. Under batch production, subassembly lines produced components (radiators, hydraulic tanks, etc.) in small lots. Final assembly lines put together complete models, and the entire production system required large inventories of parts and components owing to the high level of "work in process" (models being built at any one time). Under batch production, furthermore, assembly tasks were highly specialized, work was monotonous and dull, and workers grew lax and made mistakes. Correcting assembly mistakes, it should be noted, took more time than the assembly process itself because workers needed to disassemble components in order to access problem areas. Parts delivery was also problematic. Occasionally, delays in delivery of parts to the assembly areas forced workers to leave the line in

[25] *Fortune*, December 19, 1988, p. 76.

[26] Brian Bremner, "Can Caterpillar Inch its Way Back to Heftier Profits?" *Business Week*, September 25, 1989, p. 75.

[27] Abegglen and Stalk, *Kaisha*, p. 118.

[28] *Fortune*, December 19, 1988, pp. 72, 74; *Business Week*, September 25, 1989, p. 75.

order to locate a missing part. Occasionally, the early arrival of parts before they were needed created its own inefficiencies.[29]

To solve these problems, Caterpillar reconfigured the layout of its manufacturing plants into flexible work "cells." Grouped in cells, workers used computerized machine tools to perform several manufacturing steps in sequence, processing components from start to finish and sending them "just-in-time" to an assembly area, as the following example suggests. To manufacture steel tractor-tread under the batch production layout, Cat workers were required to cut, drill, and heat-treat steel beams on three distinct assembly lines. Under cellular manufacturing, by contrast, all three operations were carried out automatically in single tractor-tread cells linked together by computers.[30]

Caterpillar, in addition, reduced material handling by means of an automated electrified monorail which delivered parts to storage and assembly areas, traveling on a long aluminum track throughout the modernized plant. When parts arrived at the delivery point, a flash light alerted the assembly line workers, semi-automatic gates (operated by infrared remote control) opened, and a lift lowered the components directly onto an assembly. Don Western, a manufacturing manager at Cat Aurora plant, observed: "Materials now [1990] arrive at the assembly point only when required — and in the order required. At most, we hold about a 4 hour supply of large parts and components on the line."[31]

Caterpillar, finally, improved product quality. Formerly, components moved down the assembly line continuously, not intermittently, and therefore workers were unable to respond quickly to quality problems. Managers alone controlled the speed of the line. Under the new assembly plan, on the other hand, components moved automatically between work areas and remained stationary during the actual assembly operation. More important, under the PWAF plan, managers empowered production workers to change the speed of the assembly line at will, granting them the flexibility necessary to resolve quality and safety problems.[32]

The PWAF program resulted in productivity and quality gains across the board in many of Caterpillar plants. At the Aurora plant in Illinois, for instance, factory workers managed to reduce the assembly process time fourfold, building and shipping a customer order in four rather than 16 days, and cutting product defects by one-half in four years (1986–1990).[33]

---

[29] Karen Auguston, "Caterpillar Slashes Lead Times from Weeks to Days," *Modern Materials Handling*, February 1990, p. 49.

[30] Barbara Dutton, "Cat Climbs High with FMS," *Manufacturing Systems*, November 1989, pp. 16–22; *Business Week*, August 31, 1987, p. 73, September 25, 1989, p. 75.

[31] Quoted in Auguston, "Caterpillar Slashes Lead Times," p. 49.

[32] Auguston, "Caterpillar Slashes Lead Times," pp. 50–51.

[33] Auguston, "Caterpillar Slashes Lead Times," pp. 49, 51.

At the Cat plant in Grenoble, France, to mention another case, workers slashed the time it took to assemble machinery parts from 20 to 8 days in three years (1986–1989). Company wide changes were equally impressive: collectively, Caterpillar's 30 worldwide plants cut inventory levels by 50% and manufacturing space by 21% in three years.[34]

Looking back at Schaefer's five-year-long tenure, Caterpillar had reemerged as a globally competitive company, lean, flexible, and technologically advanced. Caterpillar's world market share rebounded from 43% to 50% (1984–1990),[35] revenues increased by 66% (1985–1989), and the company was profitable once again. As Caterpillar prospered, Komatsu was retrenching. In 1989, Caterpillar's sales totaled over $11 billion or nearly twice the sales reported by Komatsu, Caterpillar's profit margins exceeded Komatsu's, and the gap between the two companies — in terms of both market share and income on sales — was growing (Table B2).

The Transformation Continued: Donald Fites' Caterpillar, 1990–1999

Notwithstanding Schaefer's achievements, the transformation of Caterpillar was far from over. For one thing, the company stock lagged far behind its

Table B2: **George Schaefer's Caterpillar Highlights of Financial Data: Caterpillar versus Komatsu**

	CAT		KOMATSU	
	Sales ($ bil.)	Income as % of Sales	Sales ($ bil.)	Income as % of Sales
1985	$6.7	2.9%	–*	1.8%
1986	$7.3	1.0%	–*	2.8%
1987	$8.2	3.9%	$5.1	1.3%
1988	$10.4	5.9%	$6.2	0.4%
1989	$11.1	4.5%	$6.0	2.6%

*Sales are available only in Yen: 1985, 796 billion Yen; 1986, 789 billion Yen.
Source: For Caterpillar, *Hoover's Handbook of American Business*, 1995, p. 329; For Komatsu, *Hoover's Handbook of World Business*, 1995–96, p. 291.

[34] *Business Week*, September 25, 1989, p. 75.
[35] Yoshino and Rangan, *Strategic Alliances*, p. 98

earnings; Cat shares underperformed the S&P 500 index by over 50% for five years (1987–1992).[36] For another, Caterpillar was facing an industry-wide downturn in both its domestic and international markets. Partly as a result of the cyclical nature of the construction equipment industry, and also as a result of an increase in the value of the dollar (a weak dollar in the late 1980s helped Caterpillar's foreign sales), Caterpillar revenues and profits fell. During the two years following Schaefer's retirement, the company actually lost money (Table C5).

Replacing Schaefer in the winter of 1990, Donald Fites viewed Caterpillar's financial troubles as an opportunity to introduce change: " I certainly didn't count on ... [a] recession ... but [the recession] made it easier to accept the fact that we needed to change."[37] "It's hard to change an organization when you're making record profits."[38]

Reorganization

A marketing manager, Fites was convinced that Caterpillar did not pay sufficient attention to customer needs because global pricing decisions were made at the company's headquarters in Peoria with little knowledge of the local market conditions around the world. In 1985, as he took charge of Cat's worldwide marketing organization, Fites delegated district offices the authority to set prices, thereby pushing responsibility down the chain of command to the lowest possible level. Promoted to President in 1989, Fites applied the same principle to Caterpillar's entire structure, developing a company-wide reorganization plan under Schaefer's direction.[39]

Caterpillar's old organizational structure was archaic. It was a functional structure suitable for a small company that operated just a few plants, all located within the United States. A centralized body with only four primary functions — engineering, manufacturing, marketing, and finance — the old structure served Caterpillar well until World War II, but as the company expanded globally in subsequent decades, the limitations of such a structure had become apparent. First, decisions were made at the top of each functional unit, and executives were reluctant to delegate authority to mid-level or low-level managers. Second, each functional unit tended to focus on its own goal rather than the enterprise's objectives (marketing was preoccupied with market share, engineering with product safety, manufacturing with assembly problems, etc.), making it difficult for top management to coordi-

---

[36] Jennifer Reingold, "CEO of the Year," *Financial World*, March 28, 1995, p. 68.

[37] Quoted in "An Interview with Caterpillar Inc. Chairman and CEO Donald V. Fites," *Inter-Business Issues*, December 1992, p. 32.

[38] Quoted in Tracy Benson, "Caterpillar Wakes Up," *Industry Week*, May 20, 1991, p. 36.

[39] *Business Week*, August 10, 1992, p. 57.

nate functional goals.[40] And third, the bureaucratization of the decision making process impaired effective communication. Under the old structure, Fites recalled, the flow of information upwards was "so filtered with various prejudices — particularly functional prejudice[s] — that you didn't know whether you were really looking at the facts or looking at someone's opinion."[41]

To equip Caterpillar with the flexibility, speed, and agility necessary to operate in the global economy, Fites broke the company into 17 semi-autonomous divisions or "profit centers," 13 responsible for products (tractors, engines, etc.), and four for services.[42] He then required each division to post a 15% rate of return on assets, and threatened to penalize any division that fell behind. He stood by his words. When Caterpillar's forklift division failed to improve its return on assets in 1992, Fites transferred it into an 80%–20% joint venture controlled by Mitsubishi.[43]

Caterpillar's new divisional structure facilitated downsizing. Under the new structure, Caterpillar cut 10,000 jobs in three years, 1990–1993 (Table B3). Of the 7,500 employees who lost their jobs between January 1990 and August 1992, 2,000 were salaried managers and 5,500 hourly workers.[44] As Caterpillar's sales grew from $10 billion to $15 billion in the first half

Table B3:   Donald Fites' Caterpillar — Employment and Sales

	Number of Employees	Sales ($bil.)
1990	60,000	11.4
1991	56,000	10.2
1992	52,000	10.2
1993	50,000	11.6
1994	54,000	14.3
1995	54,000	16.1
1996	57,000	16.5
1997	60,000	18.9
1998	64,000	21.0

Source: for 1990–1997, *Hoover's Handbook of American Business*, 1999, p. 329; for 1998, *Caterpillar Inc. 1999 Annual Report*, p. 1.

[40] Quoted in Benson, "Caterpillar Wakes Up," p. 32.
[41] "An Interview with Fites," *Inter Business Issues*, p. 32.
[42] Benson, "Caterpillar Wakes Up," p. 33.
[43] *Business Week*, August 10, 1992, p. 56.
[44] J. P. Donlon, "Heavy Metal," *Chief Executive*, September 1995, p. 50.

of the 1990s, the number of managers employed by the company fell by 20%.[45] In addition, the move from a functional into a divisional structure, coupled with the drive for profit making, brought about a change in the methods of managerial compensation. Traditionally, Cat managers were paid in proportion to the size of the budget they controlled or the number of employees they supervised. Under the new plan, Caterpillar based all its incentive compensation schemes on return on assets.[46] Lastly, Caterpillar decentralized its research and development activities. With each division controlling its own product development programs and funding, R&D activities under the new plan were more customer driven than at any other period in the past.[47]

Marketing and Dealerships

Caterpillar's reorganization plan effected the company's distribution network as well. Under the new structure, dealers seeking assistance could contact any of the 17 product and service profit-centers directly, saving time and money; they no longer needed to call the General Office in their search for assistance within the company.[48] The new structure also facilitated a more frequent interaction between Caterpillar's managers and dealers, a development which resulted in "[v]irtually everyone from the youngest design engineer to the CEO" having "contact with somebody in [a] dealer organization [wrote Fites]." Ordinarily, low level managers at Caterpillar communicated daily with their counterparts at Cat dealerships; senior corporate executives, several times a week.[49]

Caterpillar's network of dealerships was extensive. In 1999, 207 independent dealers served Caterpillar, 63 of whom were stationed in the U.S. and 144 abroad. The number of employees working for Cat dealers exceeded the company's own workforce (67,000) by nearly one third; the combined net worth of Cat dealers surpassed Caterpillar's stockholders' equity ($5.5 billion) by nearly one quarter (Table B4).[50] Many of Caterpillar's dealerships were privately owned, a few were public companies. On average, the annual sales of a Caterpillar dealership amounted to $150 million (1996); several of the large dealerships, however, generated annual revenues of up to $1 billion.

---

[45] Andrew Zadoks, "Managing Technology at Caterpillar," *Research Technology Management*, January 1997, pp. 49–51. Online. Lexis-Nexis. Academic Universe.

[46] *Business Week*, August 10, 1992, p. 56.

[47] Donlon, "Heavy Metal," p. 50.

[48] Benson, "Caterpillar Wakes Up," p. 36.

[49] Fites, "Make Your Dealers Your Partners," p. 93.

[50] Caterpillar Inc. *1999 Annual Report*, p. 34.

Table B4:   Caterpillar Dealerships, 1999

	Inside U.S.	Outside U.S.	Worldwide
Dealers	63	144	207
Branch Stores	382	1,122	1,504
Employees	34,338	54,370	88,708
Service Bays	6,638	5,529	12,167
Estimated Net Worth	$3.22 bil.	$3.54 bil.	$6.77 bil.

Source: Caterpillar Inc. 1999 *Annual Report*, p. 43.

To Caterpillar, the informal relationships between the company and its dealers were far more important than the formal contractual relations. Dealership agreements ran only a few pages, had no expiration date, and allowed each party to terminate the contract at will, following a 90-days notice. Notwithstanding the open ended nature of the contract, turnover among Cat dealerships was extremely low. Caterpillar actively encouraged its dealers to keep the business in their families, running seminars on tax issues and succession plans for dealers, holding regular conferences in Peoria for the sons and daughters of "dealer Principals" (dealership owners), and taking concrete steps to encourage a proper succession from one generation to another.[51]

Caterpillar's worldwide distribution system, according to Fites, was the company's single greatest advantage over its competitors. It was a strategic asset whose importance was expected to grow in the future: "[u]ntil about 2010," Fites predicted, "distribution" — that is, after-sales support, product application, and service information — "will be what separates the winners from the losers in the global economy."[52] Contrasting American and Japanese manufacturing firms, Fites elaborated:

> *Although many Japanese companies had the early advantage in manufacturing excellence, U.S. companies may have the edge this time around .... [T]hey know more about distribution than anyone else.... Quite frankly, distribution traditionally has not been a strength of Japanese companies. Marketing people and salespeople historically have been looked down upon in Japanese society.*[53]

[51] Fites, "Make Your Dealers Your Partners." pp. 89, 91–92, 94.

[52] Quoted in Donlon. "Heavy Metals," p. 50.

[53] Quoted in Fites, "Make Your Dealers You Partners," p. 86.

Information Technology

Fites' Caterpillar invested generously in expanding and upgrading Caterpillar's worldwide computer network — a system linking together factories, distribution centers, dealers, and large customers. By 1996, the network connected 1,000 locations in 160 countries across 23 time zones, providing Caterpillar with the most comprehensive and fastest part delivery system in the industry. Although Caterpillar had long guaranteed a 48-hours delivery of parts anywhere in the world, by 1996, Cat dealers supplied 80% of the parts a customer needed at once; the remaining 20% — not stocked by the dealers — were shipped by the company on the same day the parts were ordered. With 22 distribution centers spread all around the world, Caterpillar serviced a total of 500,000 different parts, keeping over 300,000 in stock, and manufacturing the remainder on demand.[54]

A critical element in Caterpillar's drive for technological leadership was an electronic alert information system the company was developing under Fites. The new system was designed to monitor machines remotely, identify parts which needed to be replaced, and replace them before they failed. Once fully operational in the mid 2000's, the new IT system was expected first, to help dealers repair machines before they broke down, thereby reducing machine downtime, on the one hand, and saving repair costs, on the other; and second, provide Caterpillar and its dealers with the opportunity to slash their inventory costs. In 1995, the value of the combined inventories held by Caterpillar and its dealers amounted to $2 billion worth of parts.[55]

Diversification

Fites' Caterpillar expanded its sales into farm equipment, forest products, and compact construction machines, introducing new lines of products, one at a time. Between 1991 and 1999, Caterpillar entered a total of 38 mergers and joint venture agreements, many of which contributed to the company's efforts to diversify.[56]

The growth in Caterpillar's engine sales was the company's largest. Caterpillar had traditionally produced engines for internal use only, installing them on Cat machines, but beginning in the mid 1980s, as the company was recovering from its most severe crisis, Cat embarked on a strategy of

---

[54] Myron Magnet, "The Productivity Payoff Arrives," *Fortune*, June 27, 1994, pp. 82–83; Benson, "Caterpillar Wakes Up," p. 36; Fites, "Making Your Dealers Your Partners," pp. 88–89.

[55] Quoted in Steven Prokesch, "Making Global Connections in Caterpillar," *Harvard Business Review*, March–April 1996, p. 89, but see also p. 88, and Donlon, "Heavy Metals," p. 50.

[56] "Caterpillar's Growth Strategies," Copyright 1999. Online. www.Caterpillar.com.

producing engines for sale to other companies. In 1999, engine sales accounted for 35% of Cat's revenues, up from 21% in 1990, and Cat engines powered about one-third of the big trucks in the United States. Apart from trucking companies, Caterpillar produced engines for a variety of other customers including petroleum firms, electric utility companies, and shipbuilding concerns (see Table C6 on page 354). Only 10% of the diesel engines manufactured by Caterpillar in 1999 were installed on the company's own equipment.[57]

Two important acquisitions by Caterpillar helped the company compete in the engine market. In 1996, Donald Fites purchased the MaK Company — a German maker of engines for power generation. Partly because governments of developing countries were reluctant to build large power plants, and partly because the utility industry in the United States deregulated and new electrical suppliers entered the market, worldwide demand for generators was fast increasing. The rise in demand helped Caterpillar increase its sales of power generators by 20% annually between 1995 and 1999.[58]

Similarly, in 1998, Fites bought Britain's Perkins Engines, a manufacturer of engines for compact construction machinery, for $1.3 billion. The new acquisition contributed to Caterpillar's efforts to increase its share in the small equipment market which was growing at a rate of 10% a year. Perkins' best selling engine powered the skid steer loader. A compact wheel tractor operated by one person and capable of maneuvering in tight spaces, the skid dug ditches, moved dirt, broke up asphalt, and performed a wide variety of other tasks.[59]

Labor Relations

Perhaps no other areas of management had received more attention than Caterpillar's labor relations under Fites. For nearly seven years, 1991–1998, Fites fought the UAW in what had become the longest U.S. labor dispute in the 1990s. On the one side, a union official described the UAW relationship with Fites as "the single most contentious ... in the history of the union;" on the other, a Wall Street analyst called Fites "the guy who broke the union, pure and simple."[60]

---

[57] *Wall Street Journal*, March 13, 2000; David Barboza, "Aiming for Greener Pastures," *New York Times*, August 4, 1999.

[58] De'Ann Weimer, "A New Cat on the Hot Seat," Business Week, March 9, 1998, p. 61; *Wall Street Journal*, March 13, 2000.

[59] *Business Week*, March 9, 1998; *Wall Street Journal*, March 13, 2000.

[60] The quotations, in order, are from Reingold, "CEO of the Year," p. 72; Carl Quintanilla, "Caterpillar Chairman Fites to Retire," *Wall Street Journal*, October 15, 1998. Online. ABI data base.

In part, Fites' opposition to the UAW was ideological: it "is not so much a battle about economics as it is a battle about who's going to run the company."[61] Yet economics did matter, and Fites was determined to ensure Caterpillar's global competitiveness by cutting the company's labor cost. His principal target was a UAW "pattern" agreement, a collective bargaining contract modeled on agreements signed by the UAW and Caterpillar's domestic competitors, John Deere, the Case Corporation, and others (a pattern agreement tied separate labor contracts together so that changes in one led to similar changes in others within the same industry). Fites rejected pattern bargaining because Caterpillar was heavily dependent on the export of domestically manufactured products, selling over 50% of its American-made equipment in foreign markets, and thus competing head-to-head with foreign-based, global companies like Komatsu. Cat's U.S.-based competitors, by contract, exported a far smaller proportion of their domestically made goods. Because Cat's global competitors paid lower wages overseas than the wages paid by Cat's American-based competitors at home, Fites argued, Caterpillar could not afford paying the UAW pattern of wages.[62]

The first Caterpillar strike erupted in 1991, at a time Caterpillar's 17,000 unionized employees were working under a contract. The contract was set to expire on September 30, and Fites was prepared. He had built up enough inventory to supply customers for six months, giving Cat dealers special incentives to buy and stock parts and equipment in case a strike shut down the company's U.S. plants.

One casualty of the 1991–1992 strike was Caterpillar's Employee Satisfaction Process. The strike effectively put an end to Cat's ESP program which George Schaefer had launched in 1986 and strove so painstakingly to preserve. As the climate of labor relations at Caterpillar deteriorated, the number of unresolved grievances increased. At the Aurora plant at Illinois, the number of grievances at the final stage before arbitration rose from less than 20 prior to the strike to over 300 in the year following the end of the strike. When Cat employees began wearing their own ESP buttons to read "Employee Stop Participating," Caterpillar terminated the program altogether.[63]

The 1994–95 strike broke out in June 1994, lasted 17 months, was bitterly fought by the striking unionists, and came to an abrupt end when the UAW ordered its members to return to work "immediately and uncondi-

---

[61] Quoted in Reingold, "CEO of the Year," p. 72.

[62] "An Interview with Fites," Inter Business Issues, pp. 34–35; "What's Good for Caterpillar," Forbes, December 7, 1992. Online. ABI data base.

[63] Michael Verespej, "Bulldozing Labor Peace at Caterpillar," Industry Week, February 15, 1993, Start p. 19. Online. ABI data base.

tionally" in order to save their jobs.[64] During the strike, Caterpillar supplemented its workforce with 5,000 reassigned white collar employees, 3,700 full-time and part-time new hires, 4,000 union members who crossed the picket line, and skilled workers borrowed from its dealerships. The company, furthermore, shifted work to non-union plants in the South. Additionally, Caterpillar supplied the U.S. market with equipment imported from its plants in Europe, Japan, and Brazil.[65]

Operating effectively all through the strike, Caterpillar avoided massive customer defection, and managed to keep up production, expand sales, increase profits, and drive up the company stock price. In 1995, the company earned record profits for the second year in a row (Table B5).

In February 1998, at long last, Caterpillar and the union reached an agreement. The terms of the 1998 agreement clearly favored Caterpillar. First and most important, the contract allowed Caterpillar to break away from the long-standing practice of pattern bargaining. Second, the contract allowed Caterpillar to introduce a two-tier wage system and pay new employees 70% of the starting union scale. A third clause of the contract provided for a more flexible work schedule, allowing management to keep employees on the job longer than eight hours a day and during weekends (without paying overtime). The contract also granted management the right to hire temporary employees at certain plants without the union's approval, and reduce the number of union jobs below a certain level. Running for six

---

Table B5: **Caterpillar's Financial Results During the Labor Disputes of the 1990s**

	Sales ($ mil.)	Net Income ($ mil.)	Income as % of Sales	Stock Price FY Close
1991	$10,182	$(404)	–	$10.97
1992	10,194	(2,435)	–	13.41
1993	11,615	652	5.6%	22.25
1994	14,328	955	6.7%	27.56
1995	16,072	1,136	7.1%	29.38
1996	16,522	1,361	8.2%	37.63
1997	18,925	1,665	8.8%	48.50

Source: *Hoover's Handbook for American Business*, 1999, p. 329.

---

[64] Cimini, "Caterpillar's Prolonged Dispute Ends," p. 9; Robert Rose, "Caterpillar Contract with UAW May be Tough to Sell to Workers," *Wall Street Journal*, February 17, 1998. Online. ABI data base; Reingold, "CEO of the Year," p. 72.
[65] Cimini, "Caterpillar's Prolonged Dispute Ends," pp. 8–9.

years rather than the typical three years, the contract was expected to secure Caterpillar with a relatively long period of industrial peace.[66]

Several provisions of the contract were favorable to the union. The contract's key economic provisions included an immediate wage increase of 2–4% and future increases of 3% in 1999, 2001, and 2003; cost of living allowances; and substantial gains in pension benefits (the average tenure of the 1994–95 strikers was 24 years). Another provision favorable to the UAW was a moratorium on most plant closings. But perhaps the most significant union gain was simply achieving a contract, as AFL-CIO Secretary Treasurer Rich Trumka observed: "The message to corporate America is this: Here's one of the biggest companies, and they couldn't walk away from the union."[67]

Why, then, was Fites willing to sign a contract? Why did a company which operated profitably year after year without a contract, and operated effectively during strikes, suddenly seek to reach an agreement with the UAW?

Fites' decision was influenced by two developments. First, Caterpillar's record revenues and profits during 1993–97 came to an end in 1998–99, as the industry was sliding into a recession. Revenues and profits were declining as a result of a strong dollar coupled with a weak demand for Cat products. Caterpillar, therefore, needed a flexible wage agreement, stable employment relations, and a more cooperative workforce in order to smooth its ride during the impending downturn. Another reason why Fites sought accommodation with the union was the need to settle some 400 unfair labor practice charges filed by the NLRB against the company during the dispute. These charges were not only costly to adjudicate but could have resulted in huge penalties which the company had to pay in cases where the NLRB ruled in favor of the UAW. One of Caterpillar's principal demands in the 1998 settlement — to which the UAW agreed — was dropping these unfair labor practice charges.[68]

The Future [as of 2001]: Glen Barton's Caterpillar 1999–

In January 2000, Caterpillar's Board of Directors revised the company's corporate governance guidelines to prohibit retired Cat employees from sit-

---

[66] Carl Quintanilla, "Caterpillar Touts Its Gains as UAW Battle Ends," *Wall Street Journal*, March 24, 1998; Dirk Johnson, "Auto Union Backs Tentative Accord with Caterpillar," *New York Times*, February 14, 1998.

[67] Quoted in Philip Dine, "Gulf Remains Wide in Caterpillar's Home," *St. Louis Post Dispatch*, March 29, 1998. Online. Lexis-Nexis. Academic Universe. See also Cimini, "Caterpillar's Prolonged Dispute Ends," P. 11.

[68] "The Caterpillar Strike: Not Over Till Its Over," *Economist*, February 28, 1998.

ting on the board. The move was intended to safeguard the interests of stockholders and prevent the company's inside directors from opposing swift actions proposed by the board's outside members.[69]

Barton faced other difficulties. In 1999, Caterpillar's profits fell 37% to $946 millions, the worst results since 1993, and its North American market, which accounted for half of Cat's sales and nearly 2/3 of its profits, was in a slump.[70]

Barton believed that the downturn in the U.S. construction market could be offset by an upturn in the international market. He thought that Caterpillar could take advantage of its global positioning to cushion the U.S. decline by increasing sales in Asia and Latin America whose economies were rebounding. But being cautious, Barton also realized that he needed to ensure the future of Caterpillar in the long run. He therefore embarked on four growth strategies: the expansion into new markets; diversification; the development of a new distribution channel; and the build up of alliances with global competitors.

New Markets

In 1999, 80% of the world's population lived in developing countries, and Caterpillar's sales to developing nations accounted for only 23% of the total company's sales. Developing countries had limited access to water, electricity, and transportation, and therefore needed to invest in building highways, bridges, dams, and waterways. Under Barton's leadership, increased sales of Caterpillar's equipment to the developing nations of Asia, Latin America, Eastern Europe, and the Commonwealth of Independent States (the former Soviet Union) was a top strategic priority.[71]

Diversification

Just as globalization protected Caterpillar from the cyclical movements of boom and bust, so did diversification. Cat's expansion into the engine business is a case in point. In 1999, Caterpillar's overall sales fell by 6%, yet its engine sales rose by 5%. Cat's engine business itself was further diversified, with truck-engine sales making up just over one-third of all Cat's engine sales in 1999 (Table B6).

Such a diversification, according to Barton, assured the company that any future decline in truck engine sales could be offset, at least in part, by

---

[69] *Business Week*, February 21, 2000, Start p. 148.
[70] *Business Week*, February 21, 2000, Start p. 148.
[71] "Growth Strategies." Caterpillar.com, p. 2.

Table B6:   Cat Engine Sales to End Users, 1999, 2000

	1999	2000
Trucks	34%	27%
Electric Power Generators	26%	33%
Oil Drilling Equipment	20%	19%
Industrial Equipment	11%	13%
Ships and Boats	9%	8%

Source: Caterpillar Inc. *1999 Annual Report*, p. 24; and *2000 Annual Report*.

---

an increase in sales of non-truck engines. By 2010, Caterpillar's total engine sales were expected to double to nearly $14 billion.[72]

Of all Cat engine sales, the growth in sales of electric diesel generators — 20% a year since 1996 — had been the fastest (Table B7). Caterpillar's energy business clearly benefitted from the energy crisis. Large corporations, manufacturing facilities, internet server centers, and utility companies had installed back up diesel generators for standby or emergency use; in the nine months ending May 2001, Cat sales of mobile power modules (trailer equipped with a generator) quadrupled.[73]

The world's largest manufacturer of diesel generators, Caterpillar nevertheless faced a serious challenge in its efforts to transform itself into an ET (energy technology) company: diesel generators produced far more pollution than other sources of power. To address this problem, Barton's Caterpillar accelerated its shift towards cleaner micro power. In 2001, only 10% of Caterpillar's generators were powered by natural gas; in 2011, the corresponding figure was expected to climb to 50%.[74]

To diversify the company in still another way, Barton planned to double its farm equipment sales in five years (1999–2004).[75] In the agricultural equipment market, Caterpillar needed to compete head-to-head with the John Deere Co. and the CNH Corporation (former Case Corp. and New Holland), the leading U.S. manufacturers.

---

[72] *Wall Street Journal*, March 13, 2000.

[73] David Barboza, "Cashing In On the World's Energy Hunger," *New York Times*, May 22, 2001.

[74] *New York Times*, May 22, 2001; "Energy Technology: Beyond the Bubble," *Economist*, April 21, 2001.

[75] Heather Landy, "Putting More Cats Down on the Farm," *Chicago Sun Times*, March 28, 1999. Online. Lexis-Nexis. Academic Universe.

Table B7:   Caterpillar's Sales of Power Generators

	Power Generators Sales ($ bil.)	Power Generators as % of Total Revenues
1996	$1.2	7.3%
1997	1.3	6.9%
1998	1.6	7.6%
2000	1.8	9.1%
2001	2.3	11.4%

Source: David Barboza, "Cashing In On the World's Energy Hunger," *New York Times*, May 22, 2001.

A New Distribution Channel

Under Barton's direction, Caterpillar expanded its rental equipment business, reaching a new category of customers both at home and abroad. Formerly, Caterpillar sold or rented equipment to rental centers, and these centers, in turn, re-rented the equipment to end-users. Rarely did Caterpillar rent directly to customers. Now Barton was making aggressive efforts to help Cat dealers diversify into rentals. Nearly half of all Cat's machines sold in North America in 2000 entered the market through the rental distribution channel, and the fastest growing segment of the business was short-term rentals. Implemented by Barton in 1999–2000, the Cat Rental Store Program was designed to assist dealers in operating a one-stop rental shop that offered a complete line of rental equipment from heavy bulldozers and tractors, to light towers, work platforms, and hydraulic tools.[76]

Joint Ventures

Increasingly, Caterpillar had used joint ventures to expand into new markets and diversify into new products. In November 2000, Barton's Caterpillar announced a plan to form two joint ventures with DaimlerChrysler, the world's leading manufacturer of commercial vehicles. One was for building medium-duty engines, the other was for manufacturing fuel systems. The combined share of the two companies in the medium-duty engine market was only 10%, yet the medium-duty engine market generated world-wide

---

[76] Michael Roth, "Seeing the Light," *Rental Equipment Register*, January 2000. Online. Lexis-Nexis. Academic Universe; Nikki Tait, "Cat Sharpens Claws to Pounce Again," *Financial Times*, November 8, 2000. Online. Lexis-Nexis. Academic Universe.

Table B8:   Caterpillar: Five Year Financial Summary
(Dollars in million except per share data)

	2001	2000	1999	1998	1997
Sales and Revenue	$20,450	$20,175	$19,702	$20,977	$18,925
Profits	$805	$1,053	$946	$1,513	$1,665
As % of Sales & Rev.	3.9%	5.2%	4.8%	7.2%	8.8%
Profits per Share	$2.35	$3.04	$2.66	$4.17	$4.44
Dividends per Share	$1,390	$1,345	$1,275	$1,150	$950
Return on Equity	14.4%	19.0%	17.9%	30.9%	37.9%
R&D Expenses	$898	$854	$814	$838	$700
As % of Sales & Rev.	4.4%	4.2%	4.1%	4.0%	3.7%
Wage, Salaries & Employee Benefits	$4,272	$4,029	$4,044	$4,146	$3,773
Number of Employees	70,678	67,200	66,225	64,441	58,366
December 31					
Total Assets Consolidated	$30,657	$28,464	$26,711	$25,128	$20,756
Machinery & Engines	$17,275	$16,554	$16,158	$15,619	$14,188,
Financial Products	$15,895	$14,618	$12,951	$11,648	$7,806
Long Term Debt Consolidated	$11,291	$11,334	$9,928	$9,404	$6,942
Machinery & Engines	$3,492	$2,854	$3,099	$2,993	$2,367
Financial Products	$7,799	$8,480	$6,829	$6,411	$4,575
Total Debt Consolidated	$16,602	$15,067	$13,802	$12,452	$8,568
Machinery & Engines	$3,784	$3,427	$3,317	$3,102	$2,474
Financial Products	$13,021	$11,957	$10,796	$9,562	$6,338

Source: *Caterpillar Inc. 2000* and *2001 Annual Report* (2000. p. 39, 2001, p. 25).
Note: For additional financial data, as reported in the company's annual reports
and other financial documents, check out Caterpillar's website at
<www.caterpillar.com>.

sales of $10 billion annually. The sales of fuel systems were even more
promising. Fuel systems were designed to increase the efficiency of diesel
engines and thereby reduce diesel emissions. Participating in the two joint
ventures were Cat and DaimlerChrysler plants in four U.S. states (South
Carolina, Georgia, Illinois, and Michigan) and at least five other countries.[77]

---

[77] Joseph Hallinan, "Caterpillar, DaimlerChrysler Team Up," *Wall Street Journal*,
November 23, 2000.

Index

L

J, K

M